T0366129

MIAMI
STRETCH

MIAMI STRETCH

The Life, Times, and True Confessions of a South Beach Chauffeur

AN INTERESTING AUTOBIOGRAPHY AND MEMOIR WRITTEN AND EDITED BY,

NIGEL ANTHONY CONRAD LEADER

ARCHWAY
PUBLISHING

Archway Publishing books may be ordered through booksellers or by contacting:

Archway Publishing
1663 Liberty Drive
Bloomington, IN 47403
www.archwaypublishing.com
1 (888) 242-5904

ISBN: 978-1-4808-2412-6 (sc)
ISBN: 978-1-4808-2413-3 (e)

Library of Congress Control Number: 2015918583

Print information available on the last page.

Archway Publishing rev. date: 1/12/2016

CONTENTS

Dedication vii
Preface ix
Chapter 1   INTRODUCTION 1
             a. Port Of Spain, Trinidad 1
             b. Brooklyn 5
             c. Queens 8
             d. Tulsa, Oklahoma 26
             e. Back To Queens 41
             f. Welcome To Miami 52
             g. Atlanta 58
             h. Welcome Back To Miami 59
Chapter 2   INTERMISSION 65
Chapter 3   THE BIRTH OF A NEW CAREER 93
Chapter 4   THE FUN BEGINS 99
             a. My Early Errors 103
             b. The Family Dinner 104
             c. The Luggage Van 106
             d. The Rap Concert 108
Chapter 5   NOW THE FUN REALLY BEGINS 114
             a. Mrs. Grandma 115
             b. The Bachlorette Party 121
             c. The Prom 124
             d. The Not So Good Doctor 126

Chapter 6   REGULAR AND LONG TERM CLIENTS.................. 137
             a. El Gordo 138
             b. The Rich Crackhead 140
             c. The Cocaine Cowboy 142
             d. The Computer Guy 153
             e. ...Tips.. 156
             f. The Reef.. 173
             g. The Hurricane 181
             h. VIP's and Super VIP's 184
             i. The Country Western Singer................. 186
             j. The VIP Party 190
             k. The Miami Dolphin 197
             l. The Really Big Game 204
Chapter 7   BACK TO AVIATION.................................... 211
Chapter 8   ROUND TWO 221
             a. The Rich Dad 223
             b. The Rich Couple 226
             c. My Co-Worker 229
             d. The Secret Celebrity................................235
             e. Mrs. Carter 240
             f. The Supermodel 243
Chapter 9   THE END OF AN ERA...................................251
Chapter 10   SAN FRANCISCO 267
             a. No Longer Naïve 274
             b. The Bus Ride..280
             c. Ms. Lovely 288
             d. The Afropean..298
             e. ...Paris. France 304
             f. Going Back To Cali................................ 310
             g. The Patents... 315
             h. Cousin Rom 323
Chapter 11   MIAMI – THE FINAL RETURN 330

...THE END OF VOLUME ONE.

DEDICATION

The hard work required in writing this book and all of the effort to recall and document all of the stories within this book is solely dedicated to my four beautiful children Raynece, Xavier, Zoe, Willow and my beautiful baby granddaughter Moriya.

Most loving and caring parents I've known want their children to speak well. Well I don't give two cents about the spoken word. In my own personal life experience, the spoken word has very easily and quite frequently gotten me into deep trouble, while the written word has frequently and also very easily gotten me out of deep trouble.

The mastering of the written word to me, is what I think is best for myself and also for my four children.

So this book is written to show and to prove this theory to them and to also prove my own personal opinion that the written word can take you much farther than the spoken word ever will.

Hopefully with the success of this book, this theory will be proven correct.

However, the irony of this theory is this...

...to all of my loving children; when you turn 18 and are of age to understand this book, please know that I am not at all proud of a lot of the things I have done as a young man in my life so just please remember to continue to do as I say, and certainly not as I have done and have written about here.

– LOVE you always my children, Poppa.

PREFACE

Welcome aboard, this book is mainly written to give the reader of this book a small insight into the world and lifestyle of a professional limousine driver in beautiful and world famous South Miami Beach, or better known as "South Beach", the city of Miami, Florida and all of the surrounding areas of sunny South Florida. This book will offer you the reader more than that though; it is a book also written to give hope and inspiration to all who may need it.

The stories and events that have been written about in this book are all real and have been recalled to the best of my ability and recollection, they were not written in any sort of diary. I have learned in my life that I have a very good memory, and that I can recall certain things going all the way back to my early childhood.

When the different events of this book occurred, they were not done with the intent to one day have a story written about them. This book was more written for the reasoning of my recent divorce and more than two year child custody sharing battle with my ex wife, which has left me as broke as I have ever been in my life and unable to be the father I had fully expected to be to my children. I truly believe that this will be the only way that I can be allowed to afford good justice for me and my children. Sometimes I truly believe that the only power that I have is in the power of the pen, I fully intend on using this power.

I am not writing this book to gain fame, fortune or celebrity, I am however writing this book for the future betterment of my children and grandchildren, hopefully and God willingly their children as well.

This battle that I am involved with in the judicial family court system has clearly shown me the injustices towards fathers that I had always heard so much about before my eventual divorce. Especially with the injustices directed towards relatively poor, but good fathers; and in poor I mean not in the sense of third world poverty poor, but rather in the sense that most hard working middle class fathers could never afford for the fair and equal justice that is required to put up a fair fight in an unjust court and legal system that looks mostly negatively towards poor men and hand over all of the power and control to the women who smartly and purposely get themselves entered into this crooked system. I have found that this fight has been completely unjust towards me, in the fact that my over three year long fight in the judicial court system to get shared custody of my three minor children was solely due to my inability to afford to pay legal and lawyer fees, all while my ex gets the full muscle and power of a state government standing right behind her. Over the course of writing this book I have come to the sad realization that my children's time with me has been taken away and severely limited for the sole reason of my inability to afford a good attorney.

If I were to ever somehow ever get the opportunity to correct this crooked injustice, I will do just that. Good law abiding fathers deserve a fair legal fight in the courtroom and should be allowed the same power and justice behind them that are automatically given to mothers in American family courtrooms.

Good fathers, as such as I think that I am and also try very hard to be, have to give away just about everything they have in an attempt to fight an equal fight in this heavily woman's favored system, or just simply give up on their long hard fight for their beloved children. I choose not to ever give up on mine.

Only through this desperation that I have dealt with, which has certainly bought about the urge for me to somehow lead a better life for all of my children than the life that I have had for myself; this is my only motivation behind me writing this book.

Like the saying goes… necessity is the mother of all invention.

This book has been publicized in an attempt to make up for the all of the lost time I have amounted over the past two or three years with my children and one grandchild and so to better provide for their needs in their futures. Godwilling, this will be the way out of this unfortunate predicament that I find myself currently in with the unjust court system for the battle for my children and also for my so far one and only grand-child, Moriya. This book has also been written for my children to have some sort of historical documentation of the events leading up to the separation and eventual divorce of their biological parents.

Although I've done some writing over the years, and I have always enjoyed writing somewhat, I have never written professionally before this book, and I honestly believe it's because I am inherently lazy and I've never seen writing as a career for me, even though in High School one of my teachers had pushed me towards a career in writing or journalism. I have found over the course of my years that I can best express myself in the written word better than any other form of communication that there currently is.

The stories in this book are my life stories up to and including this point in my life, which I believe has some interest and some value. I, over the years have told some of the stories in this book to various friends and family members, and they have always showed deep interest and enjoyed the stories so much so, that they have always begged me to tell them more. This is the inspiration and the roots behind the writings of this book. I truly have about one thousand stories that I can write about in this book; but I will reserve only the best most interesting stories for this book so that you can carry this book in your purse or computer case, I'll try my best but my story may still end up being too long.

I also have a first cousin Mrs. Cheryl Peltier-Davis who also lives be-tween here in South Florida and Trinidad, our birth place, who also hap-pens to be a twice published author while also being a career librarian.

Over the years she has read some of my personal writings and she has always told me that I had talent in writing and that I should someday write a book. She had always directed me to write about being a father to my children. Although I love each one of my children dearly, I have always felt that writing about the love of my kids would be somewhat boring; as we all love our kids. I soon realized however that I had a great story to tell in my long career as a professional chauffeur and I jumped on that writing opportunity just as soon as I recognized what I had to offer an avid reader.

This book is mainly about my experiences and lifestyle as a South Florida chauffeur; however chauffeuring has not been my only fulltime career. Rather, as a seasonal and part time on and off independent contract chauffeur for several different limousine companies throughout South Florida since the spring of 1992.

Since my high school graduation in the summer of 1988, I have been majorly employed in my lifelong chosen career field as a professional aviator. In those years I have been working primarily as an aviation maintenance technician. I have also been employed as a charter airline pilot flying people and cargo throughout the Bahamas, Haiti and all over the Caribbean, including several cities throughout the island of Cuba. I am also soon hoping to obtain an airline flight dispatch license, just to complete and round out my professional aviation licenses and also just to have it within my possession.

My heart has always been in my chosen career field of aviation and I do have some interesting stories, which a few will be mentioned in this book. But my heart rarely goes out to the people of aviation. The aviation industry is a ballbusting, backstabbing, egotistical and testosterone filled industry. Most men of the aviation industry truly believe that they are God's gift to aviation, and they love to have their ego's filled. What they don't know however, is that I am actually God's gift to aviation. I have more qualifications in this field than most, including a qualification to taxi and drive under its own power, a Boeing 747 for engine maintenance runs and engine operational inspections; not too many I know in this field can say that. You would never know that fact from me though; I try my best to stay humble. Unless of course; I am writing a book. So for that reason, I really do not want to bore you to tears and ultimately into a deep dark depression with the egotistical shenanigans that go in the industry of my own personal choosing. So I will leave that chapter for another day and another book, Miami Sky, someday ...maybe.

I have also hustled up cash as a sailboat day charter captain and sailing instructor on the beautiful turquoise waters of Biscayne Bay in Miami. I currently own and have for the past 13years now, a 23' sailboat the s/v Supersonic, which I lease to a small sailboat charter business and sailing school in Miami.

Sailing is a truly fun and enjoyable pastime for me. I've taken many friends and family sailing, but that's all it has been for me, a pastime. I just do not have enough experience to write and entertain about. However, if this book is successful, my love of sailing will lead me to purchase the largest ocean going sailing vessel that I can afford. Then I will happily share on those seagoing adventures. I will christen this vessel with her name s/v "MI VICE". This name will serve a dual dedication purpose. The first will be for the influence that "Miami Vice" the 1980'sTV series has had on my entire life, right along with Crocket aka Don Johnson; hence the title and the design of this book which is an homage to a television show that has completely influenced my entire life. The second dedication purpose will be towards 'my vices', which actually represents my own personal vices and what I will unashamedly detail in this book, and which has ultimately led to many of the interesting storylines in the telling and writing of this book.

Although these other jobs are fun, I truly have no interesting storylines in theses other fields to offer up to an avid reader at this point in time in my life, simply because I just have not done enough experience or good enough stories to write in a book about at this time.

This book is intended to be a tell all, but not at all any type of celebrity name all. It is my intention to name celebrity names when I respectfully and politely can, but I will not name names if I think it will interfere with people's privacy or if I think it will hurt people's reputations and/or family situations. I just may also change a few names of celebrities and non celebrities alike and change a few places and events and maybe some situations to protect the innocent and to also protect the not so innocent as well.

Lastly but certainly not leastly, to all of my wonderful Christian friends and to all of my family members who know that I truly love the Lord and who may read this book.

This book also has an intent purpose, it is truly a story of faith and is ultimately a story of how God is in full control of our lives if only we allow him to be and is not only a confessional but also a testimony of how God has worked for me in my life and also in my dual careers. This book however has not necessarily been written for everyone, especially my Christian friends who may become extremely judgmental towards me after reading this book and only seeing the true confessions part and not necessarily the true testimony part. This book has been written for those people that need to hear this story for all of its worth and for all of those who have an open enough mind to see the entire story through to the end and learn about God from my own lessons and my personal life experiences.

I am hoping that all the effort I have put into writing this book will be well worth it to help and change the life of at least one person who will read this book, ultimately leading them to having faith in Jesus Christ. Hopefully by following from my own personal examples and experiences in this book, or at the very least be beneficial in the same way to any one of my four children who will also eventually read this book.

The majority of practicing Christians honestly believe that as a Christian; which I can proudly say that I have ultimately become. Your involvement, views and experiences with the secular world should only be limited to witnessing and preaching to the secular world as well as harshly pointing fingers at them and reluctantly judging them. If I were to actually believe this and accept this popular theory I could not have experienced what I have thus far in my life and career as a South Beach chauffeur. Chauffeurs cannot pass judgment on the things that they see and may do as they work in this field, especially Christian chauffeurs; as I have happily become. It is a perfect example of a Christian being in the World but not of the World, I have tried my best to do so, but I have sometimes fallen very short especially in the very beginning of my career. Don't judge me however; I have God up above to do that for me. As Christians I believe we have to get out into the world and shine our light, even as a chauffeur on South Beach. Not just in our local churches or the confines of the comfortable four walls that we all call home. Like the old saying goes were not born to just pay bills and die; we must all have a purpose in life.

Christian chauffeurs may not be able to continue to work very long in this line of work if they are to quickly pass judgment on the clients they serve. You simply cannot preach and give your clients a sermon on your own personal morality and beliefs as you drive them around town to all of their favorite bar hopping spots, wild parties, and maybe even be witness to frequenting sex professionals; both sexes using professional men and women of the night in hetero and homosexual situations for that matter.

Of course this is a free country that we live in here and a Christian chauffeur can choose to preach to his or her clients if they please, but it will only take one single complaint from a client to make you lose your chauffeuring career in that quick of an instant; they will certainly call to request a rescue car and driver.

If I were to be that same judgmental Christian that a lot of Christians expect you to be as a Christian, from the very beginning of my chauffeur career I could not have become the experienced chauffeur in South Beach that I have become and I of course would not have had the many blessings and all of the unique experiences in my very full life with both the good and the bad experiences. I must say that I am very happy to now have all of these wonderful career stories that I have gained over my long career and that I also now have the opportunity to happily share them all with you in the writings of this memoir.

Being an experienced chauffeur in South Beach does not make me any less of a Christian believer than any of the most believing and judgmental Christians out there, as we are all sinners and every single one of us all fall short of the glory of God. But of course some Christian people will think differently about this because of that same judgmental attitude and won't accept this argument as if they themselves wear black robes for a living. They will feel that this line of professional driving, particularly in South Beach is unacceptable for a believing Christian to do; I respectfully disagree with them however and I am living proof of that theory and the miracles I write about in this book should prove that.

I am very real and this book is also very real as well. So if you cannot handle real world real life adult situations and/or are easily offended by what you read about the real world and you may also be quick to pass judgment on others, please do not read this book. This is simply because this book is full of real world, real life situations and is also full of sex, drugs, and rock and roll and maybe a story of a groupie or two.

This book is my life as it actually happened and it is also my personal testimony. Yet it is so real that even though it is ultimately my personal testimony, and I will share with you a few miraculous stories where only God's hands could have been at work, I still feel that I truly cannot take this book to a Christian publisher. This is simply because even though the Bible itself is the realest book ever written with all of its adult content, they, as well as all of the Christian folks in general, will only see the negative sides of the personal confessional parts that I will share with you and not necessarily have an open enough mind to actually see the entire picture of the complete testimony that I will share with you. As Christians we are called to be the salt and light of this Earth. In this book I will intend to share my own personal flavor, or salt, by the end of this book being read. I am hoping that despite all of my confessions that I will spill out to you during the course of your reading, that you will see exactly how God has worked in my life and career, and that my light will still eventually shine upon you the reader, but you must see this book all the way through to see that whole picture.

If faithful Christians do choose to read this book however, despite this forewarning, I will patiently await your judgment. But please remember, your judgment towards me after you have read this book will fall on deaf ears. You may also be deeply offended by what you will read in this book, please know that this book has been written for people who need to hear this story, and this story is certainly not about you, or all of the other Christians out there who like to unjustly pass judgment onto others. As Christians we must remember that when you point at others to judge, you have four fingers pointing right back at you. Only God can use anyone exactly where they are at and exactly as they come, even if you as a faithful Christian can't see it. It is not your job as a Christian to see what God sees, but rather to simply keep the faith and pray on.

This intense judgment by the Christian faith is the main reason why I do not feel it as appropriate for me to approach a Christian publisher to publish this book. A Christian publisher and maybe Christians in general may not have an open enough mind to make it all the way to the end of this story without wanting to burn this book because they may feel that it is some sort of sin to hear someone else's personal sinful story; I personally do not think that this is a sin to hear testimony though, but who am I?

My concern is for the eventual Christian communities judgment and backlash that a Christian publisher may receive for the publishing of this book; however that Christian publisher may also miss out on the blessing that this book may eventually become, simply because of the passing of the same judgment that we as Christians are commanded by God as to not to do.

My life over the years has shown me that God is ultimately in full control of everything and that when I pass judgment on others I tend to lose out on certain blessings that could have been if that judgment had never been passed to begin with. So I have learned not to ever pass judgment on anyone, and as Christians we are commanded by God to not pass judgment on anyone. But judgment from the Christian faith is routinely passed in a stylish and hypocritical fashion that by me simply cannot be ignored. For those us who truly love and believe in the Lord, God sees us all the same and we will all be judged accordingly by him and by him alone; no one else's judgment will ever matter or account for our life in eternity.

This is my book of James (my favorite book of the bible) ch5:v16 confessional.

The majority of the vices that I have written and shared about in this book have mainly occurred in my youth and prior to me giving my life to Christ. There are also a few vices that have occurred even after that fact. However, I know who I am, and I know who has died for me. So I fully trust and believe that my personal Lord and savior still loves me and will continue to do so and I will patiently wait for his judgment and of course his judgment alone. I have fully enjoyed my life thus far and I have lived my life to the fullest extent possible up unto this point in my life and just because I have done so, does not mean that I am any less Christian that any other fully practicing faith filled Christian. I have always had full faith in my Lord Jesus Christ and will continue to do so both before and after all have read this book.

I am very proud to be a loyal and dedicated faithful Christian, and I know all about my fellow Christian folk. I also know exactly who Christians are to be, and I will patiently await their judgment. However, I would ask and appreciate that my Christian friends and Christians generally speaking, save all of that negative energy and keep your judgment to yourself and redirect it to your own personal sins, or direct that judgment to someone else who will soak up all of that negativity in because I certainly will not; again your judgment will always fall on my deaf ears; I love the Lord my God and I also love my life and nothing at all will ever change that.

The stories in this book will hopefully be an example to all who read it of how God can make the most out of any person, career or bad situation that we can find ourselves in, to ultimately glorify his good name.

Now, with all of that being said, I will state to you as I do all of my passengers who have rode with me in the past two decades without whom this book could not be possible, whether driving, sailing or flying....

..."PLEASE SIT BACK, RELAX, AND ENJOY THE RIDE."

My solitude...S/V SuperSonic

VOLUME ONE:
THE BEGINNING

CHAPTER ONE

Introduction

PORT OF SPAIN, TRINIDAD

Let me please introduce myself to you; my name is Nigel Anthony Conrad Leader and I have a very interesting story to share with you.

Up unto this point in my life, I have had a very interesting life and career both as a professional chauffeur and as a professional aviator; it's been so interesting that I am more than happy and willing to share it all with you. So where should I begin? Well…

I was born on the beautiful dual Caribbean Island nation of Trinidad and Tobago in the very industrial and capital city of Port of Spain, Trinidad in February of 1969.

I was born on a carnival night, my parents once told me that my mother's water broke while she was partying and parading in the downtown streets of Port of Spain during the revelry of Carnival; I was born a carnival baby. Carnival is the same celebration celebrated here as Mardi Gras in the great state of Louisiana, USA. Like my father has always said to me, I wanted to come on out and join in the revelry…I was actually born to be partying! He certainly didn't lie to me, as you will soon enough find out.

I was left there with relatives by my parents up until the tender age of three plus some months. I have a great feeling that these actions by my parents have had a major positive influence in my life for I am a very independent spirit, and I have lead a very independent life and lifestyle. I have kept my distance from all of my family and all of their influences for my entire adult life. I believe that this has been a positive influence for me because it has forged me into who I am, and I can truly say that I am who I am because of my independent life experiences without any family influences to shape me whether they were to be either positive or negative.

There are very few things that I can recall in those first few early years in Trinidad, and there are some that I can clearly recall for whatever reason. Some of the few of the things that I can clearly remember are…

If anybody knows the Caribbean, there is a sound to me that is almost unforgettable. That sound is the sound of wrought iron patio furniture scraping against the hardness of Caribbean patio concrete.

Is it just me who knows this unique sound? Probably so.

However, all of my life for whatever reason from time to time, I hear this sound in my head. It is not a bad sound, but a memorable one. This sound will never leave my body, but that's OK, because I think that it is just the sound of the Caribbean calling me to one day come back home.

I can also recall the views, specifically the view from my grandmother's house, on a hill. Not of an ocean or water view, but a city view. It was a view of the surrounding mountains, the hills, and the beautiful blue sky. It was an absolutely stunning view. It is a view that I can still never forget. I can also clearly remember having to climb the brick and concrete stairway up the remainder of the thousand or so feet to the top of my grandmothers hill just to also see the view up there, I would then look over at the other side of the big mountain; it was a grand ole' view of downtown Port of Spain and it's beautiful harbor. These are views that I learned to appreciate as a small child and it is also a view like that that I think maybe also calling me home.

Although Grandma's house had this beautiful view, it was not at all a mansion, more like a humble shack, but a humble shack straight out of heaven. I remember the fresh fruit trees all around her house and in her backyard, fresh mangoes, guavas, soursop, key limes, sour oranges and passion fruit. I remember the fresh jams, juices, jellies and chows that my

Grandmother and cousins made from the fresh fruit that I had helped to pick fresh off of the trees. All made with freshly picked hot peppers and very hot and spicy peppersauce. I am a Trinidadian or as we prefer to be called …Trini and everything we eat is with spicy hot peppersauce, even at the very tender age of three.

I remember my grandmother raising chickens under that house, and we all individually naming those chickens. Then I remember Grandma cooking them and us eating them, and further describing how delicious Charlie chicken tasted today. Why do I remember all of this? I have no idea. I think it's a gift.

There are also a few more distinct memories I have from those early years that will not leave my head.

I remember staring at very big things, things that I didn't quite understand, such as road construction equipment and airplanes in the sky. I truly believe that the fascination that I had staring at big yellow steam rollers used for road construction for hours on end, and watching intently at departing airplanes overhead has had a definite influence on my future life, in the direction of me somehow wanting to know and to control these awesome vehicles. Those memories are burnt into my brain like a hot branding iron. I can still see those visions that I had as a child clearly, even to this day. My most favorite aunt in the world only recently told me that she had wondered why I had looked so inherently serious and commanding as I tried to take control of my father's car while sitting behind the wheel whenever my father placed me in his lap while driving his car around Port of Spain when I was only months old.

Why at this very young age of three was I so intent on trying to stare down and try to figure out these amazing behemoths?

Was it born in me?

I would say so…where else would it come from?

These are only some of the memories I have of my homeland at that so very young of an age.

I have since returned to Trinidad several times, but those have bought about different memories altogether. They have had no influence on my adult life, except for the fact that I have flown there a few times as a flightcrew member, on one of those big jets I used to look up to and admire so much, so very long ago.

It was a very proud moment for me when I first touched down at Piarco International Airport while I worked, stepped down the airstair and walked onto the tarmac for the very first time without my parents being there with me. I once felt like kneeling down and kissing the ground of my original homeland when I first arrived there all alone. I would have done so, if only my co-workers and fellow airport employees would not have thought of me as some type of crazy person.

me and one of my cousins at my grandma's modest hilltop home

BROOKLYN

I do not recall when my parents eventually came back for me to take me to New York, but I do have a vision of a lot of people in Trinidad crying around me at that tender young age. Of course I could not know why they were all sadly crying, I was probably looking at them and laughing hysterically. The vision is still very clear in my head, and of course when you take away a child that you have grown to know and to love for at least the past three years, of course there will be a whole lot of crying going on when it is time to part with that beloved child. I am so glad that I was a child and I didn't understand anything that was going on, because if I was any older I would've cried too, and probably fought the return to my biological parents. Good timing mom and dad, you spared me that stress, Thank You.

I do however remember my arrival in New York City though, specifically Brooklyn. Flatbush Avenue. To this very day, I still remember the exact building. The building still stands. My parents however were not quite setup and independent as yet when I first arrived. So we stayed with my play cousin and his family.

That cousin was the famous Mr. Romany Malco. Yes, Romany Malco of the 1990's rap group "College Boyz", Jay the black guy from the hit movie "The 40 year old virgin", Conrad from the cable series "Weeds", Zeek from the movie series "Think like a man", The Love Guru, "Last Vegas" and most recently "Top Five" with Chris Rock fame, amongst many other movies, television series and credits to his name.

His parents and my parents were close to being best friends while they were all growing up together in Trinidad and they all moved to the United States at approximately the same time. They were all close enough to each other that they all considered their children cousins and my parents were living with them when I had first come over to this country at that early age of three. We did not stay with them for very long though, but stayed with them long enough for me to get to know and love my newly found cuz, Rom.

I will have plenty more to write about on my cousin Rom later on in a chapter dedicated to him in this book.

I also do clearly remember the day care that my parents put me and my newly found sister in. It was right downstairs and outside that apartment building there where we were living. I also clearly remember two things specifically about that school.

I remember getting punched in my mouth by some kid and seeing my own blood for the first time ever.

I remember finding out that the kid didn't like me because of my Caribbean accent. Later in life, my father told me that my accent instantly changed after that incident, and me finding out exactly why I got punched in the mouth.

WOW. Really!? Even at three or four years old? Could I have been really that smart at such an early an age to get rid of my Trini accent to try and fit in? Well one thing I know for sure is that I don't have that accent anymore, and I can't really contest the fact of when I lost it.

I wish he had never had punched me though, because I really and truly want my Caribbean accent back.

The other clear memory I have of this day care center is that of one of my teachers, I do not remember her nationality or ethnicity, but I do remember however she had very fair skin, and she also had a tattoo. I can still see that image of that tattoo to this day. I did not know at that time that it was a tattoo though. The tattoo was that of some sort of a spider, I think it was a tattoo of a black widow spider right on the front of her neck, or, on or around her throat area. I would stare at that spider for hours on end when she was taking care of me. I was fascinated. I didn't know what a tattoo was at that time; I was trying to figure out what was going on with her. So, one day, as an innocent child, I asked her what that was on her neck and what had happened to her. She very politely answered my question. I can still clearly remember her response to me. She told me that she had one day swallowed a spider while she was sleeping with her mouth open, and the spider got stuck in her throat and was still stuck there. She said she couldn't get it out. As any four year old would do, and for a very long time, I actually believed her; maybe she wasn't lying and she really did swallow a spider the way that she had said.

I didn't know any better; I never spoke to anyone about this and no one had ever told me any different.

I figured out that it must have been a tattoo sometime later on in my life, because that image never left my mind. I don't who she is anymore so I must assume that it must have been a tattoo, and I really hope that she truly did not swallow a Black Widow spider.

It seems to me, that as a child when I was fascinated about certain things and I would get deeply involved and interested in whatever it was. I became enthralled, and its affects came later on in my life, in this particular case it was not the spider, but rather the tattoo. Even though I have never gotten a tattoo myself, I think I became fascinated with tattoos and maybe more so, insect tattoos, right there and then, as you will see and understand much later on in this book.

I now understand that when children have a very deep interest in something that they are exposed to at a very early age, whatever that maybe. I now understand that, that particular interest may somewhat be involved in their future life. This has certainly been the case for me, as you will see as you continue to learn about me and get to know me better.

Romany and me along with our siblings in Texas

Romany with my little brother and me next to his little brother

QUEENS

My parents were finally both able to establish themselves with good government jobs with both the city and the state of New York. They were soon able to purchase their first home in Jamaica Queens New York, which they still own to this day. I still can remember the first day we moved into that what seemed to me back then, a huge house. I remember walking through this new house with my parents and they telling me which room was going to be mine, the corner room with the two big picture windows. I was six years old. This room will become the room where I would soon become a man.

The first thing that I quickly realized about this new house was that there were plenty of windows to gaze out of, unlike the little Brooklyn apartment because I do not ever recall gazing outside to the Brooklyn streets when we were staying there. I spent a lot of time gazing out of all of the windows in this house, and I watched and wondered about the world going around just outside the doors to this new house. I noticed the neighborhood kids playing outside. I do not recall ever playing with the neighborhood kids in Brooklyn. I did not know these kids just outside my door, but I knew they were having fun. Riding their bikes, and doing what kids love to do. I soon was right out there with them, I just had to get out there and figure them all out.

As time went on, me and my little sister would eventually get to know them all. People in the neighborhood tended to gravitate more to us simply because they all had to eventually walk by our house, because our house was on a corner intersection, and as folks went on by to and fro they just tended to speak with us and eventually get to know us. It was soon after this time I realized I had a mechanical inclination. I started to fix me and my sister's bicycles and soon after that, all of the neighborhood kids' bicycles were in our backyard as they saw that I had liked fixing bikes and having our neighborhood friends over.

We had a big backyard and a separated one car garage that I was always busy in and it was always full of activities with neighborhood kids. I learned a lot about repairing bikes there, bike parts and the use of hand tools in general; I really enjoyed what I was doing and I enjoyed the attention that it bought me.

Some summers when school was out, I remember gazing out our picture windows watching all the kids playing, me and my sister could not go out and play with them though. Our father, who worked the nightshift then, and was an avid reader, would not let us go outside to play unless we would read some sort of classic novel first. Like the classic writings of Mark Twain, Huck Finn and Tom Sawyer, Moby Dick, Shakespeare and the Daniel Defoe novel...Robison Crusoe etc., the stories were good I had always thought, but I hated doing this and being inside the house with a passion. I just wanted to go outside to play in the streets with my new friends, ride my bike and have fun with all of my newly found friends.

Not only did we have to read these classic novels, but we also had to write a book report on what we read that day as well as to prove that we had been actually reading and not just daydreaming as was usually the case for me. Not until dad was satisfied with our book reports were we allowed to finally go outside to play; I always made sure to write it well enough so that he knew that I had understood what I had read and then

I would be allowed to go outside and play, some days that was not until almost dinnertime. I was so traumatized by these long days of reading and writing, that this is reason that to this very day I have not again read another book, and I sometimes wake up at night in cold sweats panicking about if I had finished reading today's book and writing the long book report and if it was understandable enough for him to accept.

These very much forced and incredibly intense writing sessions eventually led me to actually start to enjoy writing. I would eventually wind up writing and co-writing news stories, editing news articles, as well as doing interesting student interviews for my high school newspaper; The Aviation High School Flyer. This is what eventually led to my own personal writing, which has in turn ultimately led me into the writings of this book.

Dad, thank you so very much.

Even though I didn't appreciate what you did for me back then, I now realize that you have taught me to express myself in writing just by the simple fact that I did not want to upset you by getting my book report wrong or somehow being misunderstood by you. My motivation was to get the book report right the first time simply so that I could finally get to go outside and ride my bike and play with all of my friends; I certainly do appreciate those valuable lessons you have taught me back then, now.

I remember being encouraged by one of the supervising high school teachers for the Flyer newspaper that I had a real talent for writing and editing and that I should be concentrating on pursuing some sort of career in journalism, but I truly did not want to hear that at all. Writing to me is boring and is only for nerds; I certainly ain't no nerd I recall thinking to myself, and besides… I'm going to be a professional aviator; I had passed negative judgment on professional writers and writing careers in general even way back then and I may have missed out on probably a much more lucrative career in that of journalism or writing professionally because of that judgment.

As the years went along in the neighborhood, there was one particular friend who stood out the most amongst the rest. He lived two houses away. His name was Trefor Holden, and he eventually became my best childhood friend. He was like me, although he was about one year younger, but he loved mechanical things and most of all loved to fix them. Just like myself. So we naturally bonded and we were always fixing things.

Trefor, unlike myself did not have a father figure living at home with him. He lived with his mother and two older sisters. His father and older brother lived in Providence, Rhode Island and he always spoke fondly of them to me. I had seen pictures of them inside of his mother's house. He had truly loved them, and he truly wanted to be with them much more frequently than he usually did.

Although Trefor did have a father and an older brother, Trefor was a member in the big brother big sister program of New York City, and he had a big brother mentor. We thought his assigned mentor was so cool, because he drove a Datsun 240Z. He used to take Trefor on long drives throughout the city and state. Only Trefor though. The car was only a two seater. I remember Trefor telling me how much he enjoyed those rides around town in that Datsun Z car.

Trefor was much like me, he loved that car, and just like me he also loved to figure things out. I'm sure Trefor was looking intently at his mentor trying to figure out how to drive this sexy vehicle with a big six cylinder engine, a five speed manual shift, and a manual choke that was used on that big monster of an inline six engine.

Trefor was just fourteen, I was fifteen.

In my adult life I have owned three different Datsun Z cars all at different times, two 240z's, and a 260Z 2+2 that was in absolute mint condition. When I like something, I really like something. I jump right in, head first.

As Trefor got to know and grow with his adopted mentor family. They started to trust him more. They began to leave him alone in their house. No adults, and unsupervised.

Are they really leaving him all alone? With that sexy sports car in the garage and the keys to it right there on the wall?

Are you serious!?

Who told them to do that!?

When he was left alone, Trefor started driving that Z car all by himself right at the tender age of 14, because the keys were clearly left in the house. He began to come to my house and pick me up in that Z car, and I happily went along for the rides. This was exciting to me! My turn for the joyous ride through the city! Trefor gave me my first driving lesson at around 15, but with Trefor being at only the age of fourteen, who gave him his first!?

Trefor soon taught me all there was to know about driving a five speed manual stickshift, and I mastered it in no time flat. Trefor's mentor family had always gone out for family nights on the weekends, leaving him there with the Z keys, just hanging there on the wall; to this very day I can still clearly picture the spot on the wall in the kitchen where the key hung. That was our time to shine not as boys but as young men. Cruising for girls, and showing off. No license required. How in the world did anyone not find out!? WOW! God is truly good.

As time went on, we gradually gained confidence in our driving abilities. We were unstoppable teenagers. This is where I learned of the confidence and ego that driving a car can give you. We were always on cloud nine when we were driving. What a feeling for 14 and 15year olds to have.

Either of our parents never knew we were doing this, not even Trefor's mentor parents who had actually owned the Z car that we had been so happily cruising in.

They should have known better though.

As we got older and even more confident in our abilities, we became even bolder and more brazen with our newly gained driving skills.

One weekend, my parents left me home alone for the weekend. I was now around sixteen. They went on a weekend getaway with my sister and my now little brother. Trefor had told me he needed to see his father and brother in Providence. Something was going on up there with them in Rhode Island. He had asked me if I could somehow get him up there and I soon came up with a plan to get us both there.

My mom's Mercedes Benz sedan was sitting in the garage of my parent's house, she's out of town along with my father, and the keys for the Mercedes are in the house, also hanging on the kitchen wall.

Yes Trefor, I really think we can do this.

We did it, just like the brave little stupid boys that we were.

I drove that Mercedes Benz all the way up to Providence Rhode Island with Trefor riding right there next to me shotgun style. My mom's Benz was an automatic, practically an autopilot driven car for us as the experienced stick shift drivers that we were. It was of course a very easy car to drive compared to the five on the floor manual Datsun Z car. Driving all the way up there was no problem for us, even with no driver's license, of course no insurance, no map, no credit cards, and especially, NO MONEY, we did not even know the mechanical condition of the Mercedes or if there was even any oil in the engine, we didn't care; we were young, restless, and more importantly …indestructible.

We drove straight onto Interstate 95 northbound; nonstop. Trefor directed me, somehow, to his father's residence. We hung out there for a little while, while Trefor tended to whatever family business that he had needed to tend to. I think it was a Saturday. I remember this, because when we left his father's house, we went straight to a local night club in downtown Providence. I still remember parking that Mercedes and walking right into that night club feeling like a million bucks, even though I didn't have a dime in my pocket. My ego was as high as the moon that was shining bright that night. I danced with women, or girls. I can't remember which. I talked with them, they talked with me. I was a 16 year old player, whatever that was, or I at least I felt like one. I think I even had a drink or two, and I don't mean coca-cola. I also remember that joints were being passed around. Trefor did not lead me to it; I helped myself, my very first hits of cannabis right there and then on a Providence Rhode Island weekend night.

Oooh yeah, Oh what an awesome feeling to be feeling for the very first time!

After we had our fill of women, wine and weed, and not necessarily in that order, we were gone, southbound on interstate 95; nonstop. Not only were our ego's flying high that night; we were as well.

I remember getting home and just seeing the sunrise. I think this was the first time ever that I recall seeing the sun come up over the horizon. I parked mom's Mercedes Benz back in the garage just as it was, and went right to bed. I think right here at this very moment, life had actually just only now begun for me.

By the graces and mercies of God, we made it back safely. No one, until now, has ever known any different about that weekend jaunt or the taking of that Mercedes Benz; until now that is.

Sorry mom. Sorry Dad.

Never underestimate the determination of growing teenage boys. It is truly a force to reckon with.

Single mothers; please don't get in the way of your teenage son and his dad, it may be dangerous and you just might soon regret it.

Parents, please learn from this.

You would think that this little adventure would quench our thirst for illegal and inappropriate driving, but it did not, as you will soon see.

Trefor Holden and I loved driving so much that even to this very day, we both have commercial drivers' licenses and he is a professional OTR big rig driver driving semi trucks across the country and obviously you know what I do. To me it's extremely funny that we would both end up driving professionally, but not at all surprising considering the experiences and adventures in driving that we had gained at such a very young age and without any adult supervision.

My parents left me home alone on that one particular weekend but that was not usually the case. I believe that weekend they took a jaunt down to the Bahamas in which they frequently did because my dad was a part time travel agent, and he enjoyed all of the fringe benefits that came with that job.

My parents by this time were well to do, with good government jobs with lots of available overtime as well as that part time travel agency job that my father had, so normally we had all taken vacations together during the long summer and winter breaks in the New York City public school system while me and my sister were not in school.

Usually though, our summer travels were shuffled between just four different places.

First, Trinidad, to stay connected with our family members that we had left behind there.

Secondly, the small suburban town of Baytown which is just outside the city of Houston Texas. This is where cousin Romany Malco had eventually moved to with his dad, and we went there to visit them. Even though I loved my cuz, this was one of my least favorite places to visit. I can still smell the smells in the air of all those oil production fields, and this was the first time me and family ever experienced racial prejudice and name calling. I remember me and my little sister frequently being called the 'N' word amongst other racial slurs by some of the local white kids on the streets of Baytown on occasions when we rode our bicycles through town.

We also frequently traveled to Toronto, Canada. I had another cousin there we would visit; this cousin would also make it big in the entertainment industry. This other cousin that we would visit was 'Gee Wunder' Canadian rapper/music producer, aka Greg Baptiste. I really enjoyed these trips. We sometimes flew, we took the train once, but we mainly drove. I loved those drives. The views, mountains, hills, valleys, picking fresh fruit at upstate NY farms and of course there was Niagara and Horseshoe Falls. Who could ever forget that?

Then there was Florida, we had no family there. We went there because as a family, we simply loved it. It was my absolute favorite place to go. We usually always went to Miami Beach, although one year we drove 3 hours south down to the city of Key West in the Florida Keys, what I now call and consider the American Caribbean.

We always stayed right there on the Atlantic Ocean shores in hotels off of Miami Beach, always with a gorgeous view of the always beautiful turquoise colored Atlantic Ocean.

This is where my personal love of the state of Florida and the love of the tropical ocean came for me.

The views were so absolutely beautiful to me, a definite influence on my very young brain.

Oh my goodness. What is this place?

I don't see these beautiful and brilliant colors in the beaches of New York.

With all of this natural beauty, God must live here somewhere I had always thought to myself even as a very young child.

One could never forget the colors and the hues of the Atlantic Ocean from these elevated views from beachfront hotel balconies.

I always cried when it was time for us to leave sunny South Florida. I did not want to go home to old cold and gray New York City and go back home to shovel snow on our corner street home where I had twice the amount of street to shovel as my friend Trefor who lived in the middle of the block. Even at this very young age, it had never made any sense to me as to why we would have to go back to ice cold New York City with all of its snow and ice, especially when there was so much sunshine to be enjoyed year round here in beautiful Florida. I had always wondered why we couldn't just stay here forever and ever.

This is where my original love of sailboats also came from. I would watch them from the beach or from the hotel balconies and wonder to myself, who are these people out there? Who are these little people on these little boats out there on this big broad ocean? I never wondered this about the ocean liners, or the container ships that I also saw out there sailing by. To me, they were not beautiful. I did not care about them; they were not interesting to me. The sailboats were gorgeous and sexy, even though I had not yet known what sexy was. They were appealing to my eye; eye candy before I knew what that was.

I remember from those early beginnings, thinking that this must somehow become my life, and that I must somehow pursue this tropical lifestyle, and live it, at all costs and no matter what.

Most of the family traveling stopped in and around my sophomore year of attending Aviation High school, right about the same time as the unauthorized Providence road trip. This was because as an older teenager I had started working just shortly after that time right after middle school and right after our last travels together as a family unit. I had first started working in a local grocery store; I was originally hired on as a check out cashier because I had aced the math exam required to get hired on at that grocery store, but after working there for only one half of one day, the store manager informed me that I was just too much of a manly man, even at the tender age of fifteen to be working behind a cash register. I truly believe though, it was more because even at the very tender young age of fifteen and on my very first day of work I would still be seriously flirting with my co worker all female cash register staff who were working there with me, yes, flirting with the opposite sex, even on my very first day at work. They would soon after take me off of the register and put me on the grocery store floor to offload the incoming trucks and stock the grocery store shelves; that was quite OK with me though, I had just wanted a good paying job but I guess they thought that shifting me to the grocery store floor would keep me away from all of those beautiful young ladies working there, but it really couldn't. They were absolutely correct; I was a manly man even at the age of fifteen or sixteen.

That grocery store job and all of the hard work that it entailed would all soon change for me though. That was once I was able to finally obtain my very first legally obtained driver's license right along with my first professional aviation mechanics license that I had earned from my studies at my alma matter Aviation High School.

Getting my first driver's license is an interesting story all in itself though, and it is amazing that I even got a driver's license at all with all of the antics I committed as a rambunctious teenager.

Some months after the Providence adventure, me and Trefor were outside riding our bikes as we normally did together after school or whenever we didn't have a car to drive around town in. We had noticed something very unusual one day, there was a big Cadillac sedan, engine running and abandoned down the street on our block. We noticed this vehicle running there for hours on end. We, as curious kids would do, investigated and we surely got closer and closer to the Cadillac as time slowly went on. As the curious kids that we were, we finally peered into it with our young googly eyes into that quietly running car; one of the very first thing that we noticed was that this Cadillac sedan had a flat blade screwdriver clearly sticking out of the ignition!

JACKPOT! We knew exactly what that meant; that screwdriver meant that this Cadillac was now ours to drive. I still can feel the excitement and adrenaline we felt at that moment. We felt like as if we had hit the lottery! We did not even care that we knew that that car was more than likely already stolen. The door was not locked and we did not once think about the fact that this Cadillac was stolen and it was illegal and just plain wrong for us to drive off in this car. I do not think it ever even crossed our minds to go tell our parents or anyone else for that matter. We just thought about driving away in that car, and driving away is exactly what we did with that brand new and stolen Cadillac sedan; we would make this our ultimate driving challenge experience much more so than our Providence adventure.

We drove that car for something like weeks, or maybe months; I can't recall exactly how long we drove it for.

We parked it at different parking spots around the neighborhood every night in an attempt to hide that Cadillac and we treated it like it was ours. We vacuumed that car, washed and waxed that Cadi. We went out on double dates with some of the neighborhood girls. I also showed it off at my part time grocery store stocking job. It was ours. No one could tell us different. We were kings of the roads, and this Cadillac was our chariot.

I drove that car to Aviation High School every day of the week, of course only after dropping Trefor off at his high school and also after I picked up my best Aviation High School bud, Giovanno Sorio. He knew that Cadi wasn't ours and he didn't care. We were true friends. We did everything together. He enjoyed being chauffeured to school, as compared to taking the E or F train lines, the number seven train and the New York City bus to get to school every day.

I remember when it was time for me to take my first driver's exam road test. I failed. All this driving experience I had already amassed and I failed. The reason I failed was because instead of making 90 degree left hand turns, I would make 45 degree left hand turns. I remember the female examiner asking my father why did he teach me to rush and take shortcuts in my driving? If she only knew that my father had not actually taught me how to drive, rather I showed my father that I knew how to drive solely based on the many experiences he unknowingly knew that I had.

After my father drove us both back home from the failed exam, and it was time to go back to high school. I recall telling my father goodbye, and walking away as if I were going to take the city bus to school as I usually did and he would expect me to do. However, in actuality I was walking to that Cadillac parked two blocks away. I remember clearly getting into that Cadillac turning the screwdriver key and saying to myself …"who needs a damn drivers license!", as I started that Cadillac and I drove right off, headed to school that morning. I remember that same day that I was really mad at myself because I had failed the road test; how could I have failed that road test with all of the large amounts of cross country driving that I had previously been doing!?

I also remember that very same morning pulling up next to a police patrol car at a red light on my way to school after my failed driving exam that day. I looked out my window, gazed over at the two officers sitting in that patrol car and I smiled a big old grin to those two police officers, and I asked them how they were doing that day. The officer in the passenger side told me he was good. Great, I replied. He would then ask me how I was doing; I of course said that I was also doing wonderful. Have a nice day I said to him as I drove off and made my way on to school that day.

I truly think that that was somehow the confirmation that I needed to prove to myself that you truly don't need a driver's license to drive in New York City; surely they should've known I was an unlicensed teenager driving through these big city streets, they just didn't mind that I do, that's all I had thought.

Of course though, nothing good ever last for long.

One morning as the three of us were all driving to school in that big brand new Cadillac; I was behind the wheel as usual. For some unknown and forgotten reason, I was driving in reverse down a one way street in the wrong direction, we were all looking behind us as I maneuvered in reverse. At the very same time that I had finished the reversing maneuver, we all turned our heads forward. Lo and behold, police, lights and sirens flashing at us.

Where in heck did they come from!?

Each one of our hearts had literally dropped into our stomachs. My heart was pounding so hard that you could see it right through my shirt. The officer called his partner over to show him my fastly beating heart clearly visible inside of my shirt. I was terrified!

This was it, finally the end of our long Cadillac driving legacy.

We all went to jail that Friday morning. I can still remember that it was a Friday because I had final exams to take on that day and me and my sister had rehearsal for our Sunday confirmation ceremony in our church that same night. I told this to the arresting officers, but of course, it didn't matter. We were busted red handed in someone else's brand new and stolen Cadillac.

We did not get out of jail until late that Friday night or very early that next Saturday morning. Our parents all came to pick us up together. Surprisingly, none of them were very upset. I don't even remember getting yelled at.

Some weeks after our release, I do remember Giovanno's father was given the opportunity to have the charges for Gio dropped before trial, if he would only testify against me and Trefor. His father would have nothing to do with that and would not let that happen. He told Giovanno to suffer right along with the both us, with whatever may happen; we would all be in it together, just like we were in that Cadillac. You did not sell out pops what a special dad you are, making your young boy a young man, thank you sir.

When trial time came around, the owner's of the Cadillac were sitting there in the courtroom, they agreed with the city and dropped the charges against the three of us as first time youthful offenders if we behaved ourselves until the legal age of eighteen. If they all had only known what we had really been doing since we started driving almost one year earlier; we should have been locked up with the key thrown away. Play time was finally now over though. We would now forever have criminal records unless we of course behaved ourselves so that the records could possibly be expunged at the age of eighteen with good behavior and no more law breaking crime sprees amongst us. We had all gotten off extremely light, especially me and Trefor considering all of the previous driving we had illegally done in other cars like my mom's Benz and Trefor's mentor Z car prior to joyriding in the stolen Cadillac. I could have also easily been deported back to Trinidad because I was not as yet an American citizen; I did not realize the break I got until I was a full fledged adult and would learn the laws of this land.

With playtime now being over for me, it was now time for me to become an adult and a young responsible man.

Soon after I retook my driver's exam and eventually passed the road portion of the driving test. I finally learned to not take shortcuts and make the proper 90 degree left turns. Finally after more than a year of illegal driving, I was legally licensed to be behind the wheel. The year was 1986.

Shortly after I received my driver's license, I soon left my after school grocery store stocking job. It was boring to me. No driving involved and I had also just received my first federal license to repair aircraft which helped me to get my first job in aviation as an after school part time baggage loader at JFK airport. I was able to drive baggage tugs, belt loaders, and those big pallet loaders that loaded the baggage cans onto the airplanes. I loved it. These were the big powerful vehicles which I had already dreamed of so many years earlier. When I started, I was already a seasoned driver so they were very easy for me to learn how to handle all of this heavy equipment.

Soon after though, maybe several months, I also got bored doing this and I put in a request for a promotion to a position of an aircraft refueler. I aced the math exam that was required for the promotion, and I was soon after driving fuel tankers at Kennedy International Airport. I would start driving 3000gallon tankers, 5000gallon tankers, and hydrant trucks which pumped fuel out of underground fuel lines. Now this was really fun I thought.

I took a lot of pride in the fact that I routinely fueled both the Concorde's for both British Airways as well as for Air France at such a very young age. This was at a time when only the most elite of people flew on these supersonic Concorde's and travelling on them was the way to be seen as well as being the only way for anybody who was anybody would travel overseas to the European continent.

I would always enjoy when I had to go onboard the aircraft to get the final fuel authorization and fuel delivery signature from the Captain and cockpit crew. I always made sure to take a peek into the Concorde's passenger cabin to see if I could see any easily recognizable celebrity faces; I never really did though, although I have been a near lifelong chauffeur, I've never been good with recognizing celebrity faces unless their faces are more than obvious.

I also fueled Boeing 747's and DC-10's. The best part of this was also when I was able to go onboard the aircraft during pre-departure procedures and converse with the flightcrew for the fuel load acceptance; it made me feel really important, in which I probably was. I was just 17 years old and practically in heaven. I had truly loved this job, but there was one thing that I loved even more, that was…my most favorite hour on television, still even to this day; the 1980's television detective series… Miami Vice.

I worked at JFK airport every day after school from 4:30pm to about 9:00pm. This was the international departure rush time at JFK airport. Very busy, and the time simply flew by, It simply was not work to me.

But on that one day however, when Miami Vice was on, I refused to work late into the night; that would be on Friday Night's. I had to be home every Friday exactly at 9:00pm to watch my favorite television show, Miami Vice; I did not miss an episode. The colors, the music and soundtrack, the photography, the energy and the neon lighting of this television show greatly attracted me, the scenery of the pretty beaches and the gorgeous women; the style and the dress of the colorful characters were extremely outstanding to me. I was hooked on this show like no show had ever hooked me; I had never before been hooked like that before or ever since.

You would think that I would have looked up to detective Ricardo "Rico" Tubbs, him being a handsome brother and all, smooth, suave and sophisticated, yet still as tough as nails. He was not my idol however, my idol was that of the character of Detective Crocket; Mr. Don Johnson himself. He drove fast sexy cars, who could ever forget that style of his, the linen pants and the blazer jackets and his silken T-shirts, the dark Wayfarer sunglasses; I still to this day have my own original pair from way back then that are still very fashionable even to this very day. Sonny was the only Anglo American man that I knew of with a beautiful sexy style that was all his own and in which no one else can claim, no one else has come close to his fashion trending style since. Sonny Crockett had such a trail blazing sense of style for an Anglo American straight middle aged man and he never even wore a belt or socks! This must certainly be against the fashion savvy of most men with fashion sense and I'm sure he broke somebody's golden rule but I can't even imagine what he would be like with him ever wearing them. Sonny also lived on his private sailing yacht, a big beautiful liveaboard sailboat in the waters off of Biscayne Bay in what would now be my favorite city and with a backdrop of the sexy Miami skyline always in broad view; this is where I got my love of Miami and sailboats from.

As a straight man, I am not at all afraid to say this, but this Dynamic Duo of sexy men teamed up together to fight the evils in the city of Miami were better and hotter than any other crime fighting Super hero team that had ever been put together, either before or since them. Batman and Robin, or Starsky and Hutch had absolutely nothing on them; this is just in my humble opinion. To me, these guys were very much real and that's why this TV series has affected my entire life.

This television show was the epitome of all that I had admired and desired for my future life. The movie remake had tried to copy the original episode's artistry and energy, it was good but to me it didn't even come close.

Even in just my teenage years, I knew that this television show was me and all that I wanted to be and I knew that I had to somehow embody it! This was the lifestyle I was describing and imagining to myself on those Miami Beach balconies while vacationing in Florida with my parents as a much younger child!

I had already gained a deep admiration for the beauty of sailboats as I watched and dreamt of them from afar on the beaches of Miami but now I was watching these same beautiful sailboats on this great television show as I watched my favorite character Crockett live the life on them right along with his collection of beautiful women, cars, jewelry and clothes.

This show will be my life guide for now and forever more, I recall saying to myself during a few of the exciting episodes. This television show was more than a television show to me, it was a life to aspire for me and it greatly excited me, it actually created me and all who I will soon be to become!

I think I shed tears when the series finally got cancelled. I remember the critics saying it was too violent for TV. What the heck do you mean!? Too violent!? What do you know? Whoever, "they" were. That show was beautiful and there hadn't been a show like either before or since!

I'm still mad; I haven't watched another Television series since and probably won't ever again or anytime soon for that matter.

I was now in my senior year at Aviation High School. I had to figure out what to do next in my life. I knew that I was not going to go to college. Too expensive, too boring, I could not even pay attention in High school, and I liked my Aviation High School. I took the military ASVAB exam. I got a near perfect, if not perfect score, I was told. I do not recall hearing about an exact score; I do not think that they tell you these things. Soon all branches of the military were knocking on my parent's door and ringing the home phone. I remember severely leaning on becoming a warrant officer in the U.S. Army. I would have been an attack helicopter pilot, but man.. I'm not disciplined enough I remember thinking, I know myself. By this time in my life, I had already known that I was a partier, just like my father had told me. I couldn't do it; there would be no U.S. Army for me. Sorry Uncle Sam.

I was going to be graduating Aviation High School soon, with two federal licenses to repair all manners of aircraft. I can use this. I can build a life for myself, by myself. I also knew that I wanted to become a pilot. So I thought, how can I best combine these two interests to make it all come together and work for me? The answer for me I thought was Tulsa, Oklahoma. I had a recruiter from an aviation technical school there visit me and my parents about their flying curriculum. My parents knew I wanted to fly airplanes. I told him that I would be graduating High School with my aircraft mechanic's license and I knew that American Airlines' big maintenance facility was there, so I asked him if it was possible if they could somehow get me a job there. He told me American Airlines only hired their alumni students and graduates. That's all I needed to hear, I made my decision right there and then. At that exact moment, I signed up for their flying school. I would get a job with American Airlines with my brand new federally issued aircraft mechanic's license and go to flight school all at the same time. I was now extremely excited about this new plan.

This would be a plan for the ages. I was just 18 years old.

My dreams of Miami would have to wait for now.

Cowboy country, here I come.

The Queens corner home

Me at Aviation High School circa 1986

A 1974 Datsun 240Z

TULSA, OKLAHOMA

My parents had agreed with this awesome plan that I had. I did not have to sell it too much to them. They had seen and also felt my excitement and determination with this awesome plan that I thought up.

I enjoyed my final summer in Queens, and it was soon time for me to leave. 9 years in Queens, in my parents' home, finally time to say goodbye.

My father and my little brother had escorted me to my new city. When we had stepped out of the Tulsa airport terminal, it had just finished raining. I remember this as if it were just yesterday; my father was looking up right at a bright beautiful rainbow in the sky pointing it out to me and saying ..."This must be your pot of gold". I had no response, very unusual for me. I did not know what to say, because I did not know what I was doing here. Was I crazy? I remember thinking to myself and that was the end of that.

My father checked me into school, got me an off campus apartment, a bank account, and most importantly a car. A pre owned Volkswagen Scirocco 2 door sports coupe. 5 speed on the floor. It was a sexy, fast sports car, almost like Crocket's or so I thought. It was in really good condition. This was my first official vehicle. It was completely paid for with my dad's cash. All mine.

Dad also helped me find a new job. I got the same job I had left back in JFK as an aircraft refueler, driving 5000 gallon refueling tankers to refuel the big commercial airliners that flew into Tulsa International airport as well as also fueling all of the little private jet aircraft that also flew in to Tulsa, right along with all of the private aviation customer service to the wealthy private aircraft owners that went right along with that new job.

This new company that had just hired me were very impressed with the experience that I had fueling at JFK international airport. This job for me could only be temporary though; it could not possibly fit into my well thought out career plans for flying.

My father also fully furnished my apartment, and he took me to Wal-Mart for the very first time ever. I remember being so shocked at seeing this superstore, we did not have any Wal-Mart's in the NY area at that time. My father got me all of the little knick knacks there to complete my new home. Dad had left me setup as good as any parent could do for their sprouting child. Surely I can't mess this up. I was set up, ready to begin life, ready to become a man. And become a man, I most definitely did.

Dad, and my lil' brother had finally left; back to the big apple they went.

With Dad now gone, it was finally time for me to get this party started right.

Although I was studying at flight school and working a full time fueling job. It did not take me long before I started mingling with the local ladies. They had liked me. They liked the fact I was from New York City, They liked the fact that I was working a good paying job, and was completely independent. The economy was real bad there at that time. The women were easy for me. I was once told that it was very normal for girls right out of high school to become married shortly after graduation. They were all looking for husbands. I wasn't looking for any wife though, but I certainly wouldn't tell them that. I racked them up, one at a time. I had my own car, a fully furnished apartment. Not many of the local guys there had that. I felt that for most of the young ladies, my apartment was an escape from their own communities. I didn't mind and I wouldn't have it any other way. I lived on the far south side of town, far away from my beautiful sistahs and the hood they were raised in. It was practically the suburbs where I lived and I didn't mind at all sharing what little I had at that time, just as long as they would kindly share with me whatever it was that they had to offer; if you know what I mean.

This is where I learned a little bit about myself, and how I learned about how I deal with women. I learned that I loved beautiful women, and that I was not afraid to approach them. Most men I've known are somewhat intimidated to approach beautiful women; not me however. I learned here in Tulsa that my adrenaline goes into hyperdrive when I see a beautiful woman, and I must soon approach that beautiful woman to communicate with her otherwise my adrenaline will never subside; I need to approach her… "For me". This is so that at the very least I can at least calm down and begin to relax, whether there is going to be any rejection or not. This does not have to happen if the woman is less than absolutely gorgeous in my eyes. It did not matter and I didn't care about rejection for that reason; it's better for my heart and for my blood pressure to just simply speak, say hello and let all that increased energy somehow subside. Once I spoke, I would then be able to judge and know which direction I would take with her. I have always felt that approaching an average or not so average woman was not actually worth the risk of rejection and all that comes with it, however with an absolutely beautiful above average woman I had always wanted to take the risk for the potentially greater reward of being with her in more ways than one .

Tulsa is where I also learned about a certain type of sexual charm that I might have. I say "might", because I can't really say, I have never experienced it for myself, but when my adrenaline hits and I am in this hyperdrive state, something comes over me and I become extremely charming and if I find out that I like the direction that this introduction is heading to, I then feel as if I am some sort of wild animal on a hunt. I would pounce on a beautiful female as if I were a hungry and starved cheetah with delicious meaty prey of a meal directly in front of me.

Very few women have seldom escaped me when I get into this hyper mode. I do not know why I have it, but I do know that I do. The ironic part is that if I never enter this hyperdrive state, for whatever reason, you will never see this side of me. I will be the sweetest guy next door type of guy you will ever know. Beautiful gorgeous and sexy women usually turn that key to this sexual prowess. I practiced this a lot in Tulsa, not always with the results I had hoped for back then, but at least I could calm back down. I would quite often go on to speak to a gorgeous woman and not really be impressed with her after just 5 minutes of conversation, it's like seeing an externally beautiful car for sale, then finding out the interior is tore up. Nobody wants that, nobody wants to invest in a major makeover, even if it's just the interior. However, I never let that stop me and I was still always on the hunt. I was free to be me; who could stop me? Life was good for me when it came to women.

Sometimes in life though, I often feel some kind of guilt about this Mr. Hyde side of me, because I feel people that are close to me should know about this, like my parents, or my ex-wife. I do not think they have ever known about this particular side of me, or maybe my ex does, I don't know for sure. I did however attract her at one point in our lives after all. Well anyway, now they know. I don't think I will ever feel that guilty feeling about this anymore.

As a young relatively inexperienced independent teenager, I did not realize the toll that women, work, and school would have on me. I started coming in to work late and I always had an excuse for it. I was fairly warned about it, but of course that was not enough to stop me from my partying ways.

Then one day, while cruising through the neighborhood with my good friend Alberto Barnett; he was just one of the three of the Dynamic Trio of my two buddies who had come all the way to Tulsa with me from Aviation High School, me, AL, and Lawrence J. Parris. On this particular day an elderly woman ran her car right through a stop sign and T-boned my beautiful Volkswagen Scirocco. I was fine, Al was fine, but the Scirocco was totaled. I had just put an expensive alpine stereo system and alpine surround sound speakers in that Scirocco, just so I could attract even more girls. The stereo was still booming when the tow truck towed it away. My beloved Scirocco was gone; my heart was broken and Al and I walked all the way home from the accident scene.

By this time, my job would not have any more excuses for any sort of tardiness or absences from me. The city bus would not be conducive for me to use, I worked the afternoon shift and the transit system there was not designed like New York City's. I lived far away from work, and I got off late at night. No bus service at that time. They tolerated me for a few more days, and then they finally fired me.

Well, technically not fired, rather they simply told me that I did not pass the probation period and that was the actual terminology that they had used to technically get rid of me. What!? Probation!?

Didn't I just finish that in NYC? I didn't know that jobs had probation also! It was OK to me though…this job wasn't in my well thought out plans anyway.

This job was where I also found out the true nature of the aviation industry. This is when and where one of my immediate fueling line service supervisors who was training me at the time actually confronted me one day and told me that he thinks that I smile way too much, and that I was just too much of a happy person to be working in my beloved chosen career field of aviation. I was a very naïve nineteen year old teen at this particular time.

I was not and have never been the type of person to attempt to not be myself just to try and impress someone else even a supervisor. I am who I am, and I will always be as such, and very proudly I will add.

He would then also continue to tell me right there and then at the very start of my aviation career that I would never be successful in aviation because I was just not serious enough, now after twenty five years in the aviation industry, and being somewhat successful in the industry, I have come to learn that there are some truths to those statements that were made to me that day so very long ago.

I have only more recently come to realization and conclusion that he may have been correct in his thinking and that my bubbly personality and my aviation career somehow do not mix. Although I consider my career in aviation to be somewhat successful, starting out as a baggage handler, then on to an aircraft refueler, to an aircraft mechanic and inspector, passenger service and aviation ground security coordinator, and then eventually on to an airline pilot first flying cargo and then flying passengers throughout South Florida and the Caribbean, I have never felt like I actually fit into the mold of a serious professional aviator. I am however, truly of Caribbean decent with the Caribbean attitude to match, and I truly enjoy a more laid back type of attitude and workplace, I have lived all of my life with the 'NO Problems Mon' type of attitude that is so prevalent in the Caribbean. Anyone who has spent any time in the Caribbean will know what this means. In twenty five years in the aviation industry I have never been given or accepted a leadership role, and I certainly don't regret or despise that. I have never been the type of person and may never be the type to sit inside an airline office, in a big chair, behind some silly desk acting like some big shot. This is what the majority of the 10th grade educated aviators in this industry like to often do. I think I might one day end up doing that though, but only if this book sells at least about a million copies and I start my own airline.

I do not know remember who that supervisor was that day or where he is now, but I truly wish I did. Now that I am somewhat experienced in aviation and not quite as naïve as I was on that day I sure do wish that we could have one hell of an interesting conversation regarding those statements he had made to me back then. I would ask him why, of his opinion that day he spoke to me, and I would offer him up a lot of my own personal experiences in life and also as well as in the aviation profession.

I had soon after received a check from the insurance company for that beloved Volkswagen Scirocco, for actually the exact same price dad had paid for it. However I had purchased that car very inexpensively and it was in excellent condition. I tried very hard to purchase another car in the same condition as the one that was just wrecked, but it was near impossible. I did finally find the same car, and a little bit cheaper. It proved to be very unreliable, and it was soon abandoned in my driveway. As my car went, so did the female attention. I could not go get them, and they couldn't come to me. That was also OK for me; they weren't really in my plans either. I needed to concentrate on my original plans, flight school, flying, and getting on with American Airlines. Stupid and silly me.... that's what I should have been doing all along!

I started hitching rides to the main campus of the school, with the intention of having the school fulfill their promise of getting me on with American Airlines, Why wasn't I doing this before the accident?

After several visits of nagging the school administration intensely, they finally gave me a date in which American Airlines were giving interviews for their most recent graduates. The school told me they could not get me an official interview because I was not a graduate of their school, but they would allow me in to introduce myself. Good I thought, I could work with that. On the date of the interviews, I suited up. I was in my Sunday best, even though it might have been a Tuesday. I wish I hadn't though. This would turn out to be, my very first but certainly not last, aviation industry let down.

I arrived at the office where the interviews would be given. There he was, the man who would hold the key to my future in his hand, the regional maintenance manager who was in charge of maintaining those big jets and who was also in charge of hiring the mechanics who maintain them. I was impressed and I was ready with both federal licenses in hand; the airframe and the powerplant mechanics licenses.

This was exactly the moment that I had long been waiting for ever since I had made that decision to move out here to Tulsa with my master plan and this was what it was all about for me coming here.

I remember waiting a very long time to speak with him. I think they did all of the already scheduled interviews before they even thought about talking with me. I was patient; good things come to those who wait I thought to myself, my very future was at hand.

Eventually, they did allow me in to speak with him. Here he was, the man that held the key to my immediate dreams, future, and plans. He was the reason I had decided to come to Tulsa and he was now right in front of me. I introduced myself, and gave him my story. He was a very polite man, very tall, very Anglo. After giving him my long speal and me giving him my very best professional impression, he kindly said to me…"we really can't hire you because you did not graduate from this particular school." Excuse me!? My federally issued licenses are just as good as anyone else's who graduates from this school, I remember thinking to myself. Are you serious? I remember asking him. Yes, he politely said, I'm very serious…is there anything else that I can help you with at this time?

Do you really mean that your company is currently hiring for the position that I am applying for, and I am fully qualified for this position and also here for an interview for that same position but I cannot get a chance at being hired by this airline for this very specific and professional position!? All of these little thoughts flashed through my head in what seemed like a split second but was actually probably more like a full minute as I stood there saying nothing with my mouth wide open in complete and utter shock.

I had no other choice except to quietly and subtly walk out of his office, no hand shake needed or given.

What I think he was telling me, in much nicer words of course, was that… your licenses are no good here in Tulsa at this here American Airlines maintenance facility; my very first negative airline experience.

Welcome to the wonderful world of aviation. I have finally arrived. My plans are now sitting in the toilet.

No car, no job, no woman. What could be worst?

All of these events happened within the first three months of my stay in Oklahoma, I had not told my parents of any of this, and it was not in my intention to tell them. I must make it here on my own, I will stick it out no matter what, I would say to myself. So, what's next here? I must move on and now.

Since I had never been the type of person to just sit around and allow things to happen to me without attempting to do something about it, I had to do something and I had to do something quickly.

I decided to take whatever job I could find that was within walking distance from my apartment. There were a whole bunch of fast food joints all around, so I took the first available job…flipping burgers.

I enjoyed working in fast food, I was good at it and I enjoyed the lots of free food, it helped with expenses, but the pay was not what I was accustomed too. I worked a lot of overtime to make up the difference, but I was tired from working 16 hours a day and walking to work. School was almost nonexistent at this point; I could no longer afford the flying lessons. I had to do something. This was definitely not in my brilliant plans that I had thought up three long months ago.

I thought I could fix it, as industrious as I am; I kept on looking for bigger and better jobs. I found one. It was for a kitchen prep chef for a local popular four star restaurant. This job would pay twice as much, so I wouldn't have to work twice as long, and all that free food was still there! I enjoyed that job even more, I learned to prep and cook all kinds of good food there, which I still appreciate to this day. I also enjoyed the waitresses and hostesses; I got really friendly with a few of them in my time there. Life was coming back, however so slowly but surely. I worked hard and grew in the kitchen from prep cook to line cook, right next to the two master chefs. I also learned a lot from the sous chef. He was really cool. I still remember his name to this day, even though it's been almost 30 years. I was learning the business. This was getting good. I'd be back flying again in no time at all, or so I thought.

Until….

One late lonely night, I was sitting at home relaxing after working in the restaurant. There was suddenly a loud and aggressive knock on the door. Who could this be? I remember asking myself. I was not expecting anyone, especially at this time. I answered the door; surprise. It was one of the many lady friends that I had gotten familiar with in my apartment a couple of months earlier, and she was not here for a social call. She immediately began to inform me that she was very much pregnant and that the child was mine. OK, I recall saying, so what are you going to do about it? I remember asking her calmly.

I still remember her immediate and very unique yet typical response that you can only get from a true sistah with the upbringings of an inner city urban setting. Hands on the hip, rolling of the eyes, and her voice going up an octave or two while telling me… "I'm certainly not having it" she said with arms waving and fingers snapping right inside of my doorway because I hadn't yet let her back in my tiny apartment. She had blurted that out to me with the same intensity as a mad sista in some type of Tyler Perry movie; I call that BLACKITTUDE. As in… "Don't give me none of your Blackittude baby, I ain't got no time for that." because I have only seen this sort of response and somewhat negative type of attitude in only that of my beautiful black women and not necessarily in any other race of people except for maybe a beautiful Latina or two.

"I don't know you"… she would then also continue to tell me with the same type of Blackittude. I had completely agreed with her though and she was surely correct; we did not know each other at all. We had had nothing more than a one night stand. Supposedly, it was supposed to have been an anonymous one time encounter I thought. But how can an encounter be anonymous if the encounter is at your very own residence, I had now finally realized this inside of my thick skull. I suddenly thought about all of the other supposedly anonymous encounters that I had at my little one bedroom apartment, and how many other women out there may be carrying a child of mine. For some unknown reason, I had never thought about that before this very moment. Reality had finally hit home for me.

We both came to the harsh but simple conclusion that we would not have this child. We did not know anything at all about each other, how could we possibly raise a child; we were in full agreement in regards to that fact. The state of Oklahoma's right to choose laws only allowed termination until the end of the first trimester, so the time to plan this termination was extremely short. We had to act fast to get this done legally in Oklahoma, so we did act fast and pressed on with our mutually agreed upon decision.

We went to the nearest parental planning office to schedule everything that needed to be done. Everything would soon be set, with the procedure dates and also confirmation of the pregnancy.

How am I supposed to pay for her college education; I can't even pay for mine, I remember thinking to myself. This was for surely going to be the best for both of us I had easily convinced myself to believe.

We were now scheduled for the absolute very last day possible for a legal termination in the great state of Oklahoma. I remember the day before the procedure were to be done, we had to visit the office together like if we were a genuine family or something to learn about the upcoming procedure, and also to watch a video explaining and showing the procedure that would be accomplished the very next morning. I also paid for the procedure, and signed all necessary documents. The procedure was now scheduled for an early 10am appointment the very next morning. As a somewhat responsible young man, I made sure to tie all loose ends that I needed to cover, such as making sure that I had the day off from work already approved, and that I borrowed my friend's car to drive us to and from the clinic, because she did not have a vehicle and neither did I at this point. Everything was now set for the next morning; I set the alarm clock that my father had bought me months earlier for 8am. I said a special prayer because I knew what I was about to do was wrong, and I peacefully went to bed earlier than I normally do that evening.

The alarm went off just as it was supposed to at 8am. I laid around in bed daydreaming as I so often do before I get out of bed. This day was different however. I kept hearing a voice in my head, saying three simple little words over and over. "Stay in Bed", "stay in bed", "stay in bed", I heard these words just as clearly as you are reading this sentence. I kept hearing those three words three times consecutively, over and over again. This has never happened to me before, and has never happened since. I had to listen to that voice; it was just too loud and just so finely clear. So, I did just that, I stayed in bed and went back to sleep. I would wind up sleeping well past noon; this I had probably never done before, I have always been an early riser. She did not come to see me to find out what happened, neither did she call me because I did not own a phone at that time, and she also did not drive. The day's appointment had come and gone without the procedure being done on the last day possible. To this day, I have never told her why I didn't show up for the scheduled appointment as she has never asked. We were now seriously pregnant with her first child, and also my first child…. that I know of.

I did not know what I was getting myself into with this decision, so

I did what I know best. I offered up a prayer to God for this yet unborn child and I told God that I would not worry about anything with this child and this child's future like college or career; I would leave everything up to God himself and I would go about my life and the business of living as however he saw fit for me. Although I would now have a lot of complaints thrown in my direction from my so called friends and co workers as to how I could possibly have a child with a woman that I did not know or ever previously cared for; I always replied that I had no concern over it. I just took the laughing and the jeering that I was receiving from my friends for having a child with an absolute stranger as hatred and jealousy towards me, simply because I was probably the first of my group of peers from my high school class to be knowingly becoming a father.

People all over this country and maybe the world tend to pass judgment on having children out of wedlock, especially potentially having kids with complete strangers. This was certainly the case here for me, but I simply could not ignore or reject the very strong voice telling me so very specifically what to do in this matter.

Although this decision was somewhat confidently made by me, I was still scared about going through this but I was also excited about the unknown future ahead for me and this yet unborn child who was now to soon come.

As the months went on by, I continued to work in the restaurant and I also started to do a little more flying. I had decided on my own that I would accept this child for whoever it was going to be and that I would get to know the baby's mother a lot better, so I decided to have her come over from time to time and I would practice my cherished kitchen skills on her. I also started to pay her and her family visits and just generally get to know her, after all it was my fault in more ways than one that she was pregnant. I did not do this for me; I also did this for the sake of the child. It was the very least that I could do.

It seems to me that in my life, that just as soon as things get going for the good, from somewhere, a wrench must be thrown into my gears of life. The job at the restaurant was very enjoyable to me.

However, the powers that be eventually did not appreciate my friendly personality, especially with the ladies of another skin tone who worked in the front dining room. They started to try and make things difficult for me and attempted to start to make me feel like I didn't give a shit anymore. It is what I call "idontgiveashititis". I started to get the symptoms from the "idontgiveashititis" bug that was constantly being thrown right in my face from all directions from the management and from the employees of another race in the back of this restaurant.

You see, I started as a prep cook, getting all of the foods ready for the deep fryer, grille and broiler, prepping salads, and helping the baker. Then I went to the line as a line cook, working the deep fryer and helping at both of the grilles under the command of a certified chef. When my friendliness with the beautiful ladies of the front got noticed, I started to feel the pressures of a jealous work force in the kitchen. It didn't matter to me, because I can't stop being who I am just for the sake of a job that I never had in my plans anyway.

Management would soon after start to have me working as a dish-washer when the dishwasher wasn't there. I didn't mind in the beginning, but when I started to wash dishes when the designated guy was there, I realized what was going on. When they saw that this did not bother me, and I was still very friendly with the girls up front, they began to give me even more, and they took me away from the cooking line altogether. It was now my job right along with dishwashing, to clean the stainless steel ceilings and exhaust ducts every night before I went home, with powerful industrial strength grease cutters that constantly burned my already chocolate skin. I still didn't care. I did it all. I was about to have a baby, and I needed that job, dishwashing or not.

I remember the night that the baby was born; I was at work in the restaurant. My baby's mother had decided to have the baby right across the street from my job, at the Oral Robert's University hospital in South Tulsa. Her water had broke and she was about to deliver. Member's of her clan came over to the restaurant and informed me she was about to give birth. I asked permission from management to watch my baby come into the world, they finally gave it to me reluctantly, but of course I had to come back to the restaurant to finish my nightly scrubbing. OK, I agreed and went off to meet my daughter soon to be introduced to the world.

I did not actually go right into the delivery room to witness the actual child birth, but I stood just right outside the delivery room door. I did not feel as I deserved to be in there with baby momma, she was not my wife and I had interest in many other women. I was satisfied with just waiting outside to soon be finally introduced, as I did. Patience is a virtue, I again thought to myself. When my daughter finally came out and was introduced to me, I thought she was beautiful, she looked just like me, and I was a very proud poppa, the first of many more proud moments with her to come.

The one thing that I immediately noticed about this baby and will not ever forget was that her eyes were wide open, so wide open I decided to look right into her eyes, deeply. This baby looked right back at me very intensely; we had a sort of like stare down competition for what seemed like a very long time. She would not blink, and I'm not trying to either. Who would win this competition I asked myself. I can't have this ten minute old baby girl beat me at a stare down. I finally blinked, she won, I don't know when she blinked again. It did not matter. Who is the little 10 minute old baby who beats her daddy at a stare down? She must be something special…something special she indeed will turn out to be. Her mother named her Raynece. Raynece Lashaun Leader, some of you reading this book may know that name, for those who don't, you will soon find out the person she would eventually become. I said my good-byes at the hospital and I returned back to work for my much anticipated cleanup session. WooHoo!

I will tell you more on my beautiful darling daughter Raynece a little bit later in the coming stories.

I had wanted to, and I tried very hard to visit my new born baby girl as often as I could, but my situation did not frequently allow me too. I had to work, and I still had my flying to do. To me, flying was still my priority. That is what I had came here for, besides my plans of getting onboard with American Airlines, which was now long gone.

Months after I began my flight training, I finally completed my first solo flight in an airplane, and it was now time to start the real flight training. Long cross country flights to nearby cities completely by myself.

One day, I had a practice training flight of about two hundred miles away. I would usually fly in the morning and try to back before my 4pm afternoon start of my shift. This particular day was not what I had planned. I left on time early in the morning and safely made it to my destination, however the return trip to Tulsa was going to be the problem.

When I left in the morning, the weather was brilliant, but when I checked the forecast for my return trip, the weather was not going to be conducive for my qualifications for the return flight. There would be thunderstorms over Tulsa, me and my little airplane were not equipped for any type of thunderstorms. I made a telephone call to the restaurant. I told them about my predicament, yet they were not at all impressed. They told me to make sure that I saw the boss as soon as I returned. No problem, I recall saying as I hung up the pay telephone. I had to spend the night there in that small town because I was not as yet night flight qualified for a return trip at night after the storm over Tulsa had finally subsided.

The next morning, the weather was as we say in the industry "severe clear". I got in the airplane and took off heading straight for the tower at ORU that I could clearly see up at 10,000 feet, some 200 miles away. As the flight continued on, the tower got larger and larger until I could no longer track it, because I was vectored by air traffic control for my final approach into Tulsa riverside airport. It was still very early in the morning when I arrived into Tulsa, so I went to my apartment and got ready for that looming meeting with the boss that I certainly was not looking forward to having.

When I got to work the next day, I started working just as I normally would until they called me in. I was certainly not going to remind them of yesterday's phone conversation, maybe it would all just disappear I had hoped. But it didn't, they did remember and eventually did finally call me into the office with someone who I assumed must have been maybe the owner of the restaurant whom I had never met.

I was seated with the restaurant manager who was my direct supervisor, and that same someone whom I did not recognize. I had thought that it must have been the owner of the restaurant, who obviously had the ultimate say in firings. We all shook hands and we let the conversation begin. They then proceeded to ask me what had happened the previous day, and I explained it to them just as I had over the phone the day before. I got stuck in the bad weather we had here yesterday, you guys know that I am in flight school...right? They knew, and they didn't care. They gave me an option. Give up flight school or give up my job. Here we go again…are you serious? I am only a dishwasher now, and that was the very first and only time that I have ever missed a day of work and I've never even been late, I remember telling them. They didn't care, and finally, neither did I. I had finally succumbed to their constant bombardment over the past several months of their idontgiveashititis flu bug that they were always contaminating me with. I finally caught that stupid virus right along with all of its symptoms; I certainly now didn't give a shit anymore. I would not give up my dreams of flying for this crappy dishwashing job, maybe if I was still working on the line as a cook I may have considered it. I kinda learned a lot there and I had actually enjoyed being there, but there was no chance in hell that I would quit flying to wash dirty dishes. I didn't care. Job or no job, especially about some lousy dishwashing job; maybe I smiled too much for them as well. I happily walked out of the rear kitchen door that same day, and never returned; not even to collect my last paycheck. Now with this relief I thought I could finally concentrate on all that I needed to do for my real career, even though I didn't know how I was going to do it especially with no job and no vehicle.

I truly was not expecting this to happen so fast at this restaurant, even though they were throwing the 'itis' at me for so long. I was not prepared, so I did what I had done some months earlier. I pounded the pavements knocking on nearby restaurant doors inquiring about kitchen help. I found one really quickly, however it was not a four star machine as the restaurant I had just walked out of. It was more like a small café, not quite as busy as the previous, and the pay was not as much, so I could no longer afford flight lessons. This was not in any of my well thought out plans I had had almost one year earlier. I again had to something, and quickly. This time though I didn't know what to do. I was tired of all the bull. What am I going to do now?

I did something that I had not done previously in all of my previous mishaps. I called my parents. I told them about all that had happened in the previous months. They did not like what they were hearing. So for that reason I did not proceed in telling them that I had a brand new baby girl as well. I did not want to upset them anymore than they already were. They gave me the option to come back home and start all over again. I reluctantly agreed. I made sure to say goodbye to all of my friends, coworkers, and now…family? I packed up the few belongings I had, gave away what I couldn't bring and said goodbye to Tulsa. I had been there for 13 long and tiring months. I left Tulsa with less than what I came with. I can still clearly remember thinking to myself as that airplane rolled off that Tulsa runway…Some pot of gold Dad.

BACK TO QUEENS

Once I had returned to my parent's home in Queens; more specifically my old corner bedroom. I found it to be extremely small and claustrophobic, especially since I had to share it with my now ten year old brother. I accepted the fact that I had no other options at this point. But, that would have to soon change because with all of the life experience I had received, I now felt like the man I was supposed to be. So, I got out there and I did what I learned I do best… go out there and pounded the pavement to find a new job. It did not take me long. Within one month of my arrival back to New York, I found a good paying job with Pan American World Airways as an aircraft maintenance technician, finally utilizing my hard earned federal licenses. This is the way it was supposed to be I thought; unlike the awful debacle in Oklahoma with American Airlines.

While I was back at my parents, and my working schedule being nine to five with the weekends off, I made sure to behave myself unlike I was doing in Tulsa. I thought it was so boring to be back at home, but of course it was necessary. That all changed though, when my 90 day probation period was over and my worldwide free flight benefits began. I somehow started to do what I had been doing in Tulsa, but now on a much more international scale.

On my very last day of probation, I sent my entire family to Trinidad for carnival celebrations. I would travel there the next day. I had truly enjoyed myself at my very first carnival as an adult, although I had fully behaved myself but not by my choice. I had only stayed there for a couple of days, me and my father returned to New York because we both had to work.

On the return trip from Trinidad we could not get a direct flight to

New York due to overbooking, so we had to connect through Miami. During our stopover, we had found out that the weather in New York was bad and that the flight was going to be delayed until the next morning. We decided that we were going to spend the night at the airport because the flight was going to leave very early in the morning. We found our spots to relax right there at the airport terminal and settled in for the long night ahead.

Sitting just across from where we had settled in, I noticed a very beautiful young lady, we were about the same age. She had a gorgeous choc au lait complexion and a very nice figure. I also noticed that she had a very visible and large hue colored love bite or hickie on her neck. I thought it was sexy and a complete turn on for me knowing that this beautiful young lady more than likely had …"messed around"; I acted accordingly.

I am who I am; I know what I like, I found it to be extremely sexy and quite exciting. Don't judge me.

I was fascinated by this strange young woman and I could not stop staring at her, she would eventually notice the intensity of my hard stare. I approached her, introduced myself to her and we started to talk. The cheetah hyperdrive mode kicked in for me right away and I was now a hungry animal ready to devour something juicy and sweet; she was the unsuspecting prey. While living with my parents again, it had been quite some time since I had had some delicious meaty prey. I liked her, and I think she liked me. She was from Belize I can still clearly remember her telling me. She was also delayed on the same New York bound flight. She was also with her family. I would soon enough start to slowly and gently coax her away from her family though, as I convinced her for us to go for a walk together, I couldn't believe it but she agreed. We were gone for a few hours and when I returned to my father, he had asked me where I had been. I replied to him that I went to pay a visit to the city that I had loved while I was on a long slow walk through the vicinity of the Miami International airport terminal; this was only partly true, I did go on a long walk however, amongst other things.

My father gladly accepted the story that I gave him but what I did not tell him was that I was with that young Belizean girl slowly walking through the airport terminal as well as the fact that we had also been enjoying each other's company on the hood of someone's parked car somewhere in the dolphin parking garage at the Miami International Airport. After I gave him that brief only partly true explanation for my long absence, in which he had no other choice but to accept, we continued to go about our business of trying to get on that Pan Am flight headed back to New York City. Sorry Dad; a young man has got to do what a young man's got to do whether or not you're in the vicinity.

I would never again see this beautiful and exotic Caribbean Belizean beauty, but I somehow took this little adventure in as my adult greeting and welcoming to the city of my boyhood dreams, this also solidified my love for the city of Miami and this was the beginning of my now truly anonymous relationships with women.

After that adventure was over, we all got on the delayed flight and returned safely to New York City. I must return to this beautiful city and I must do it soon, I remember feeling as I departed that airplane at the JFK international airport in the cold February weather, gloomingly headed back there to shovel ice and snow and lay down salt crystals on the corner streets of our Queens home; what could be worst!?

During my time that I was employed with Pan American World Airways, I had greatly enjoyed the time and experiences that I had gained there, working and playing literally all over the World. It was my time to sprout as a young man and sow my wild oats. I would greatly take advantage of my worldwide free travel benefits, and I would also take advantage of the opportunities it gave me to introduce myself to all of the different nationalities and all of the beautiful women out there in the world.

Me and my newly found coworkers and friends would travel just about every single weekend to a different location in the world after careful thought and lengthy discussions in our work week as to where we should go next. With our work schedule, we would usually leave Friday evenings after work was over, and usually be back on a JFK bound flight leaving Sunday night, to be back at work Monday morning. Sometimes that plan worked out fine, sometimes it did not.

On one particular trip to London, England, I had gone there with a coworker to visit his family there. On the usual Sunday night return trip, my coworker was allowed to board the flight because his company seniority got him a seat on the flight back to JFK; however my seniority did not allow me to board. He left and continued on without me, I was stuck all alone in London; not for very long though. As I was figuring out a way to reroute my trip to get me back home so that I could return to work the next morning. I befriended a coworker, a beautiful coworker. She was in the same situation that I was in; she was stuck in England due to her low company seniority. She told me she was a flight attendant who was also visiting family in London. She also told me that she was Brazilian. We quickly came to the conclusion that it was going to better for us to be stuck together rather to be stuck alone as individuals. She was cool, smart, and sexy. In a very short time we were laughing together, sharing jokes and generally just enjoying each other's company. We made a bad situation better with the company we shared, and we soon quickly forgot our troubles. We were determined to make lemonade out of the lemons we were handed.

We still both had to get home and back to work the very next day though.

After getting much needed help from the London ticket agents researching our options, we were rerouted to JFK through a flight departing from Frankfurt, Germany which was leaving the next morning. The flight out of Frankfurt was wide open for standby travelers, so we would not have a problem getting on that flight as free traveling employees. We got on another Pan Am flight out of London, which took us to Frankfurt's airport for our flight to JFK in the morning. We sat together on the flight over to Frankfurt as if we were a long married couple, laughing and joking around as we continued to enjoy each other's company.

On the flight over to Frankfurt, we decided that we would spend the night at the airport terminal because the flight over to JFK was leaving so very early in the morning; the layover was only going to be several hours. When we arrived at Frankfurt, we realized that there was train service to the city center right at the airport, we had a few hours to kill, so we now decided that we would journey into the city and see a few sights of Frankfurt. We walked around the city, had a bite to eat at a brew house, and enjoyed some good German beer. All the while talking, laughing, and having a truly wonderful time together. We were genuinely enjoying each other's company.

When our time was nearly up for our brief tour of Frankfurt, we headed back to the train station for the train which would take us back to the airport terminal. By this time it was very early in the morning and the train station was completely deserted that very early in the morning. We were all alone in this German train station, I think this was the first time we were actually alone together since we had first met. We both looked at each other straight in the eyes, and it was if we both had the same exact thought at the exact same moment. Fireworks flew, at least for me anyway, and we took our newly found friendly relations to the very next level right there in that Frankfurt train station. This gorgeous young lady straddled me right there on an empty train station bench as I sat on there in complete shock wondering how this happened in this train station and on this empty station bench. Don't judge me, I truly did not mean for this to happen. Even though we had only just met several hours ago, I truly saw her as a coworker, and I never actually went into cheetah mode like I normally would before a particular conquest. I think it was just the culmination of two consenting adults consummating a great day together.

It was real I thought, as real as you can get with someone. I also thought it was wonderful, and not in an egotistical type of way even if my ego was on cloud nine; it was pure unadulterated animalistic passion.

On the flight over to JFK we sat next to each other, and we mostly slept on the long flight over the Atlantic Ocean because we were very tired from our very long previous day and our adult activities in Frankfurt. Over the course of the rest of my life, I had always somewhat regretted that fact that we had only slept on the flight back because I have never been a member of the mile high club and that may have been my one and only opportunity to have joined that exclusive club but life of course goes on.

Once we passed through customs and immigration together at our final arrival at JFK, we hugged each other tightly, said our goodbyes, and we forever parted ways and I made my way on to work, albeit a little bit late, well worth the adventure. I would never see her again, not even on any of my many flights with Pan Am throughout the next few years. I always looked for her on all of those flights, to no avail and I don't even think we knew each other's names. I've since that time always asked myself, why I did not ask this gorgeous young lady for her phone number or for any of her contact information?

I've come to the hard thought out conclusion that; at that particular time in my life I must have been an inherently shy person. Yes, Mr. Cheetah himself. That particular time of my life I think I didn't mind sharing an evening of passion with a beautiful woman, but please; please don't ask me to share my one and only life. Then again, maybe I was just afraid of being rejected and trying to avoid the embarrassing... don't call me I'll call you moment of rejection. I truly don't know; it really didn't matter. This weekend trip however, it finally hit me square in the head and confirmed to me who I truly was, as if I didn't already know.

I was a lover of women. I was a lover of women of all races, colors, and nationalities. I think that they all made me very happy and I also think they all loved me right back; I could somehow get used to this I thought.

Over the next several months while still living with my parents, I did a lot of worldwide travel. Sometimes alone, but mostly with my co-workers. I visited the Caribbean including Antigua, The Virgin Islands, Barbados, The Dominican Republic, Argentina, Bahamas, Bermuda, Mexico, Brazil, Canada as well as also all over the United States.

After all of this global travel in such a short period of time, my parents did not appreciate the fact that I did not have a savings account. With all of the money that I was making, they insisted that I get one and I maintain it for my future use. I would argue with them that this was a free life experience and that the worldwide exposure was better for my future than a boring old bank account ever would. I literally had the World at my doorstep, I would argue to them, but of course they didn't see it that way and they would not buy that argument from me. Even though they themselves knew the benefits of travel, my dad was a travel agent after all and shoot...I learned about the value of travel solely through them. However, they still requested of me that every Friday I should hand over to them my hard earned weekly paycheck. They would then give me a weekly allowance out of my own paycheck that they deemed would be enough for me to survive on until the next paycheck would come the following Friday.

Would that measly allowance give me an opportunity to invest in the entire world as I saw it? NO, I certainly don't think so! With me being the person who I am, I was certainly not willing to have something I don't agree with happen to me even if it's against my very own parents, what in this world should I do now?

I was enjoying the benefits of all of my hard work and I loved meeting new people and seeing new places that I would never have had the opportunity to see if I had not been employed by Pan Am and taking full advantage of my many employee benefits.

I was not willing to have that stop, not for anyone. Not even for my loving, caring and kind parents. Their intentions were well, but their good intentions for me just simply weren't my intentions for me, and not my idea of living my life. This was also about the same time that my parents found out about the little bundle of joy that I had left behind in Tulsa, and they would also encourage me to do more than I was doing for her; I still refused. I was so stubborn and selfish.

I also did not care if I ever had money in the bank or not. So I reluctantly decided that I would move out and get my own place because I could not agree with my parents plans that they had for me and some bland old bank account that did absolutely nothing for my heart, mind and soul.

It did not take long after my parents let me know of their intentions before it was time for me to move out. I would eventually find a basement apartment in the Rochdale section of Queens all to myself.

The day that I moved out was a day that I will not soon ever forget. After I removed all of my belongings, I said my goodbyes and did the hugging thing with my mom, she then asked me for my key to the house. It was the same key that I'd had since about six or seven years old when we first moved into that house. It was the same key that went to Tulsa with me. It was also the same key that traveled around the world with me. My mother wanted it back. Although I had another key for an apartment to go to, for the first time in my life, I truly felt homeless. How could my mom do this to me I thought, her very own son. Looking back on that fact, I believe that it had turned out to be the greatest thing my mom ever did for me, because that day I swore to heaven and Earth that I would never return to live in that house again. This one little key that I cherished so much, actually being taken away from me, and this one little action by my mom, even though it hurt deeply, and I was still very young… it made me a man. I now had no one else to depend on, but myself, and of course God, but at that time I hadn't yet known that. I truly did not appreciate it back then, but now I can look back and again say, Thank you Mom. You have made me who I am today, in more ways than one. It was the final release that I may have long been looking for. It was finally freedom, true freedom, freedom that only a young man can understand and appreciate.

Finally moving out on my own was great, and I loved the independence. However, it was very expensive. The weekend trips came to a sudden and instant halt. After paying security deposits and utility payments, I barely had enough money to eat with and this would go on continuously with the rent payment. In New York City the bills would never go away that I had now acquired, that I now had to make up for in pay and pay out every single month. I had to figure something out to make things more interesting. I soon did.

I soon figured out that there was a flight leaving JFK to Miami every evening when I got off of work and I would be able to return to JFK the very next morning just in time for me to make it back to work. This had multiple benefits for me; I could eat at least two full meals, dinner and breakfast and sometimes a first class meal or two. All of the airlines fed their passengers full meals even on short flights during those days. More importantly, I could get intimate with the city that I had come to love solely from watching episodes of Miami Vice. I frequently did this because it was all absolutely free, the flight and the meals and sometimes the adult beverages; sometimes I did this two or three time a week and on some weekends. It was financially beneficial for me because I did not have to pay for the meals or for the travel while getting the experience that I had truly needed in the city that I loved. The only concern I had was that I needed a place to rest my head at night while there, or then again maybe not, it's Miami and the beaches after all.

I became a professional beach bum while I was in Miami. In the Miami airport I would take off my travel clothes and put on shorts, sandals or flip flops and T-shirts and put my belongings in a locker at the airport; those were the days when airports had rental storage lockers available for anyone with just a few coins. I would then wander this brand new city for me like a true local would. I learned to use the metro bus system; the bus system did exactly what I had wanted it to do; it took me straight to beautiful Miami Beach. I would sleep right there on the beach, or right on the boardwalk benches along Collins Avenue or directly on the sands of North Beach, it truly didn't matter to me, I was in Miami, the home of my favorite television series Miami Vice. The bus took me anywhere I wanted to go on the beach. I was truly homeless in this big city, but that was OK…I loved every minute of the time that I was here.

Are you truly homeless if you love where you lay your head at night? I guess you still are, but it certainly didn't feel that way to me. I was truly right at home on Miami Beach, bed or no bed, roof or no roof.

I would usually get about two or three hours of sleep on the beach and then start making my way back to the airport, sometimes I got to the airport several hours early, with time to kill still. This is when I started frequenting the Pink Pussycat, a now defunct local adult night club about a mile outside of Miami International Airport. The scenery there had easily reminded me some sort of seedy scene from an episode of Miami Vice with the glowing neon lights, the smoky atmosphere and all of the shady characters doing only God knows what lurking about the dark corners of the stripclub.

The city bus drove right past it on the short trip to the airport. If I had enough time to kill I would get off the bus two stops prior to the airport stop and go and say hello to all of the lovely Miami ladies of the evening. I would stay at the Pink Pussycat until they closed their door at 5am, sometimes at closing I would walk back to the airport just so I could get a little more intimate with the City. The only problem with me hanging out until 5am was that I did not have any money to make the ladies stay interested in me. I would usually have enough to purchase one or two drinks and I would suckle on those drinks for as long as I possibly could. The lovely ladies soon caught wind of my shenanigans though, and I eventually got tossed out by some of the 'ASSet' protection managers, as I call them, or bouncers, when I got a little too overly flirtatious with one of the lovely ladies working that night. That was the last time that I ever entered Pink Pussycat again. I think I visited the pussycat half a dozen times before I finally got bounced. I didn't mind though, it was just a place for me to kill some time and I didn't think the ladies there were all that attractive anyway. I just would no longer get off of the bus two or three stops early anymore. C'est la vie. No love lost. Life does go on.

When my long night in Miami and the beaches would be over, I would make my way back to the airport, wash up as best I could in an airport bathroom, put back on my travel clothes and get on the flight back to JFK. I would eat a good breakfast on the flight; usually I would request two if there were extra, get some sleep and be back to work by 9am. Not bad hah, I could get used to this; I remember frequently thinking to myself. I did this exact same routine for months. But, I wouldn't have to get accustomed to this lifestyle for much longer, because things were quickly about to change and change for the better.

It was only a matter of a few months after I moved out of my parent's house that I got the opportunity I had been long dreaming of. Due to the recent purchase of National Airlines by Pan Am, Pan Am was now in need of aircraft technicians in... wait... guess where...that's right, Miami, Florida!

I put in my transfer request in with the powers that be without an ounce of hesitation just as soon as I found out about the job openings down there. I certainly would not let this great opportunity pass me by. Less than one year back from Tulsa, and also less than a year with Pan Am and I was headed to my most favorite city in the world. I never imagined that it would happen so quickly, but it did and I was extremely motivated and incredibly happy.

I took out a small personal loan from the Pan Am employee federal credit union to help me get established in Miami. I completely packed up my little white Hyundai Excel that I purchased months earlier, said my goodbyes, did my hugs again as I had did when I moved out of Mom and Dad's and I jetted on down Interstate 95 southbound direct to Miami. I couldn't believe it but here I was, still very young, but I was now finally chasing the dream that I had always had since being a very young boy on vacation with my family on Miami Beach; Sonny Crockett here I come.

I was so excited about getting to my new home in Miami that I received several speeding tickets, all from different states on my drive down to Miami. I think I had received tickets in New Jersey, Virginia, and one of the Carolina's, I can't remember which. I didn't care at all about receiving those tickets; I just wanted to get to Miami as quickly as possible. I was so excited, I couldn't contain myself. Those speeding tickets though, I would soon come to deeply regret, as you will soon find out as you continue to read.

Club Pink Pussycat where I got bounced

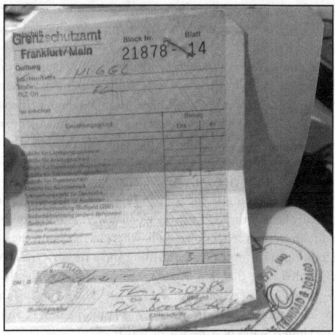
Paperwork I received while in Germany

WELCOME TO MIAMI

When I first arrived in Miami, I had nowhere to live as yet. I stayed in a hotel room right on the beach for the first couple of weeks, I then stayed with one of my travelling coworker friends from New York, who had already moved down to Miami, and who was also already setup with his own one bedroom apartment. I stayed with him at his apartment and slept on his couch until I decided exactly what neighborhood that I wanted to live in; I knew exactly what I had wanted when it came to living, but I didn't as yet know exactly where it was at that I was supposed to be.

After a few weeks, I finally figured out where my new home location would be. It was a beautiful little Island village right in the middle of Biscayne Bay. I got a lovely one bedroom apartment there, on the top floor of the building, they called it a penthouse; it had a stunning view of the bay and the local marina. It was the view that all of my dreams were made of not too long ago when I travelled down here with my parents. I had finally arrived to my new home in Miami, I was extremely happy, and I was now completely on my own to do whatever I wanted and whenever I pleased.

I would now have a very good paying job with full benefits, my very own vehicle and my own gorgeous waterfront apartment. I found out very early on that this was not at all like Tulsa, Oklahoma. The women here were not as easy to get to know as they were in Tulsa. The women were beautiful here, but I found it was extremely difficult to attract and sway women here. They would talk to me in the venues that I frequented, like Strawberries night club (of two live crew fame), but they were not as friendly or as outgoing as the women in Tulsa; in my own personal opinion I truly believe that in Tulsa the woman were looking for a simple and good man to soon settle down with, where as in Miami the women were all looking more for the flash and bling and a certain type of Miami lifestyle. I didn't have that and I didn't have any other of the things of what they might have been looking for; I had felt like a complete foreigner in a completely foreign land, in which I was in a type of way. But I was still in the United States of America, or was I?

I soon got tired of all of the rejection that I was receiving and my self esteem began to suffer for a little while during this time. I truly began to really think that I might be a little bit ugly for this beautiful city of Miami and maybe I didn't really fit in to this really HOT Miami scene; and I ain't talking about just the heat of the South Florida weather. It seemed like the women here would look at me eerily out of the corner of their eyes, like as if they had thought that I were up to something sinister. I always felt as if they were trying to figure out exactly what it was that I was up to or something. I really wasn't up to anything sinister, I just wanted some of what they may have had to offer and some of what was clearly on display for all to see. I was in near desperate need of some of what they had, that's all. It had probably been months already since I had last had some when I first arrived to Miami. There's nothing sinister about that, right? It's just simply human nature to want some of what's flaunted right in front of your face, especially when it is flaunted in front of you like a brightly lit candy shop flashed in front of a sugar addict. Although all of this negativity was happening to me when it came to women, and I was feeling this lonely type of way, it has or had never been in my nature to give up on my love of women. I would just have to keep working at it and it would simply just take a little while.

I recall driving home one rainy Friday night, after partying with a few coworkers at a hotel nightclub and bar near the Miami International airport; I think I might have been driving a little bit tipsy. This night, I got into my one and only auto accident that was completely my fault. I rear ended a woman who was driving home with her two small children, no major damage was done to her car, and the only damage was to the front end of my Hyundai. I got a ticket from the City of Miami for... failure to drive with due care. I didn't know it at the time, but after residing in Miami for months without female companionship, this small little fender bender would wind up being the life changer that was needed for me at that particular time.

While we were waiting in the heavy rain for the police to arrive for the documentation of the accident, we were waiting under the awning at the East side Mario's pizzeria; a popular local pizzeria that stills stands to this day although under another name. We became very friendly and we spoke openly towards each other immediately. We hit it off from the start.

She had just moved here from New York City, and she had also just recently arrived in Miami, so that gave us a lot of things in common and a huge basis on which to communicate on, and communicate we did. I knew her entire life within about the first 30 minutes that I had met her.

She also told me that she was originally from the country of Colombia, and that she was recently divorced. She also told me that her ex husband had also went to my former alma matte Aviation High School. We had a lot in common right from the start. Needless to say, after the police documented the accident and finally released us, she took her two young sons to her mother's house just a few miles away from my apartment, and she came right back to me at mine. We spent the very first night that we had met, together alone in my apartment; we had enjoyed each other's adult companionship. She was several years older than I was, and she was also a mom, but she was also still very shapely, beautiful and sexy to me. She became my very first girlfriend in Miami; no…she would be my very first official girlfriend …period.

We soon were spending many nights alone together at my apartment. We were together as a couple for several months, we partied and danced together in different night clubs, we drank and ate together at fancy restaurants on South Beach, and we took several road trips all throughout Florida and the Florida Keys over the course of the months that we lovingly spent together.

I had always cared for her and enjoyed her company. I could never forget her Colombian American high pitched yet very cute accent that she had, and the way that she would call out my name. With her lovely Colombian dialect, she could never properly pronounce my name as I know it to be called. She would always call me Ny-trel and I loved every single time that she tried to call out my name. To this very day I still have all of the photos that we took together on our many road trips throughout Florida.

I cannot remember and I do not know why we eventually fell apart, I do not remember ever arguing or fighting with her, however I do know that I did deeply care for her and I had appreciated her very much, she helped me regain my own personal confidence back, and made me not lose hope in all of the women of Miami. I also cannot remember her name or her occupation, but I think of her and her two sons often.

During my Pan Am days in Miami, I only had two long term girl-friends, one being the Colombian, and the other was a young Jamaican girl whom I also met in Miami. She was four years my junior, and I also cared for her deeply, and I still do. I am still to this day in touch with her, and I am very happy for her marital and family situation. I have always wished her nothing but the best for her and her family.

The reason why I still have lots of love for these women that I once deeply cared for, is because I truly have the belief that if you at one point in your life if you truly have loved another person and had a genuine heart for them, that love will always have a little spot in your heart for them. The only difference is that you will no longer be able to invest your heart in that little bit of love and to be able to watch that love grow. In my opinion that love will stay in that spot and stagnate until it either completely disappears for whatever reason, or that love gets the chance to bloom once again. This may or may not be true, but thru my personal life experiences, it has just simply become my humble opinion.

During my Pan Am days in Miami, I did not manage to travel as much as I had when I was living with my parents in New York, due to obvious financial constraints. I did however; get to go a few places every now and again. I frequented Rio de Janeiro, Brazil with my same ole' travel buddy from New York who moved down here with me, we always got the most bang for our buck in Rio back then. I remember having gourmet five course meals for around 10 bucks US, with wine. I also managed to travel and spend a long weekend in Antigua, a co-worker in Miami had gone there to visit family and friends and he invited me to tag along. I always took advantage of free room and board on a trip. This particular time was also when I discovered Philly cheese steaks, and I frequently travelled to Philadelphia just to have a few of them before a return flight back to Miami. I went there just to eat; no hotel room required. I also frequented Boston just to dine on that cities delicious Chinese food. I can still clearly remember that in my opinion, Chinatown in Boston still has the best selection of authentic Chinese restaurants and food there, even better than the Chinese restaurants in the China town streets of San Francisco.

The years of Pan Am I enjoyed in Miami did not last for very long however. It lasted just a little over two years for me. I stayed with Pan

Am until the very last day of business, the first weekend in December of 1991. The Friday morning that Pan Am shut the doors, I was getting ready for a weekend trip up to New York City. I had called the automatic Pan Am reservations system to confirm my flight up there and I got that voice message… "as of December 4th, 1991 Pan Am World Airways has ceased operations", I will probably never forget that morning and the female voice I heard on the phone. After hearing that recorded message that Friday morning I took off my first class travel suit, climbed back into bed and I slept that entire weekend. I did not speak to anyone that weekend, and I didn't get out of bed until the next Monday. I was numb because I did not know what to do next without my beloved Pan Am job. When I finally got out of my bed next Monday morning, I had to quickly figure out what was next for me in my life.

The very first thing that I had done was call all of my friends and co-workers to find out what their game plan was going to be next. The word that was getting around was that the Federal government was going to pay for retraining and college educations due to the massive lay off. I thought a college education at this time would be very good for me, and actually looked forward to doing so; I jumped on this band wagon. I thought that I had done enough partying for the moment and that a college education would be the right thing for me. I got together all of the information that I needed to take advantage of this wonderful opportunity in front of me, and I headed off to my local community college.

After taking all of the basic entrance exams and getting my High School transcripts, it was time for me to take a career assessment test that was required by the college prior to enrollment. This assessment test came back that I was an extreme extrovert, this I had probably already known, because I have always been a people person and I always loved people, and meeting and being with new people had always kept me interested in going out in the world. What I did not know though, was that my career assessment recommendation based on this test was for me to become a….get ready for this…a funeral director. WHAT!? That's right a FUNERAL DIRECTOR.

Uuhhmmm…I really don't think so.

I was not at all willing to ever become a funeral director, whether the government was willing to pay for the training or not. I did not care if

God himself was paying for the training. I really did not think that was God's intentions for me and my future life. I simply loved life too much, and I was not at all willing to even think about spending a chunk of my life hanging around with a bunch of boring dead people. I have always known that I genuinely like people, but I certainly knew that I did not like dead people. So, once again I had to quickly figure out what I had to do next. I attended a few basic 101 college classes, I enjoyed them only because of the people aspect, especially when one of my older women professors started flirting with me, I flirted with her right back just for the fun of it, and to kill the boredom of a college classroom and some time. However, I still quickly loss interest. I was still simply just too bored. I knew from years ago earlier that this college type of lifestyle was not going to be the lifestyle for me, even if I could very easily get an A grade from an overly flirtatious college professor.

My twenty year old PanAm ID card

ATLANTA

It was now early in the year of 1992, my younger sister had just graduated from Howard University in Washington DC, and she had just received a great paying job with a major Hotel chain in Atlanta. I had heard that Atlanta was an up and coming city for northern transplants of urban origin, so I thought to myself that Atlanta might be a good place for me to reinvent myself, so I figured that I should check it out. I gave up my beautiful bayside apartment, got a small efficiency apartment just in case I needed to come back and I loaded up my little white Hyundai Excel and took off right up Interstate 75, northbound to Atlanta, Georgia.

After an uneventful drive up to Atlanta, I needed further assistance in getting to my sister's new apartment complex. I pulled into a gas station directly across from Turner Field in Atlanta to use a payphone so that I could call my sister to get more specific instructions to get to her place. After receiving her instructions, I left the gas station and I was immediately pulled over by an Atlanta Police department squad car. The officer asked me for my license and registration. I gave him my driver's license, but my New York state registration had long ago been expired, for I had never changed my registration from New York to Florida. He then later informed me that my driver's license had been suspended, I never knew. I was certain that it was due to all of those speeding tickets I had received on my drive down from New York to Florida a few years earlier. I never took care of them, I literally just ignored them. The officer also told me that he had pulled me over due to the fact he knew that New York State license plates had to have matching registration stickers in the front windshield and they simply were not there. Well, Mr. Officer, sir…I had recently had the windshield replaced from damage it had received from the recent auto accident in which I met Mrs. Colombia; this is what I had thought to myself. I had not yet been in Atlanta for five minutes, and I was already in handcuffs, and the car I just recently paid off was now headed to an Atlanta impound yard. This was not at all what I had planned for visiting this so called up and coming city.

I spent my first night ever in Atlanta, Georgia…in jail, locked up. I had no money or cash to get myself out of jail, but I did have a checkbook, it did not have any funds in there however. I still wrote a check to whatever government entity that I needed to so that I could get the heck on out of that jailcell, but that check bounced so hard that it's still probably halfway out of our solar system still hurtling far and deep into outer space, at this point I did not care. I had to get out of this jail, and get out of this city, right now and at all cost. This problem would never have happened in Miami I remember thinking to myself.

As soon as I was able to I called my mother, who was in town helping to set up my sister in her new town just as my father had done for me some years earlier in Tulsa. I explained to her what had happened as I had gone missing for a night. I told my mother and sister that I immediately knew that Atlanta was not going to be the city for me and that I would be headed back to Miami just as soon as I got my car out of city impound and had a good night's rest. My mother got my car out of impound for me and I got my good night's sleep, the very next morning I was southbound on I-75 no license, still no registration and all, and was headed back to my city. I was more than happy that I decided to not give up on Miami and I had leased that efficiency apartment, my instincts was correct once again for me. I had absolutely no idea what I would do when I got back home to Miami though, but I hurried back to my beloved Miami anyway to blindly find a new chapter in my life to pursue.

WELCOME BACK TO MIAMI

When I got back to Miami, I started doing what I learned to do best in Tulsa, I started pounding the pavements and looking through help wanted ads for any available positions. With South Florida being a major tourist destination, there were a lot of restaurant kitchen positions available, but I consciously avoided the restaurant positions because although I had enjoyed working in the kitchen prepping and cooking food for folks to enjoy, as well as the fact that I love the sounds of fine dining with forks and knives clanking against fine dinnerware, amongst the chitter chatter of diners, I did not want to go back in that industry. The egos of adult men had, no pun intended, put a bad taste in my mouth for returning to the kitchen and restaurant industry in general.

I did not have a valid driver's license so airport and aviation positions would be out of the question for now. I took the only job that I was available to accept immediately, a sales job. I was selling books, children's books, holiday books, cookbooks, whatever books were in season at the time. They were all cold sales; no appointment given, and from door to door, businesses, residences and shoppes, wherever I chose to start my sales run. I made decent money with my people skills and I made sure to make enough money so that I at least ate well every day, but it put too much wear and tear on my already beaten up car. I knew from very early on that this job would not last for me. I kept on doing it though because it paid cash on a daily basis, it paid the small amount of bills I had, and It allowed me to eat every day. I was somewhat content, I have never been greedy. Although I made a decent living while selling books, I never focused on the positivity of the sales that I made, rather I would always focus on the negativity of the rejected sales attempts, and that always led me to feel depressed. I knew from an early start that I could not stay in sales, for sake of my own mental health.

All the while, while I was selling my books door to door, I never stopped looking through help wanted ads for better positions. Eventually, I thought I found one. I was excited about this one. American Airlines were now hiring baggage loaders and handlers for Miami International airport; they were expanding their operations in Miami to fill in the void that Pan Am had left when they closed their operation. They were initially taking ex Pan Am employees primarily. This was going to be the job for me I thought to myself. I already had the experience on all of the loading equipment and if I can get on as a baggage handler then I could eventually make my way back into aircraft maintenance, possibly circumventing that certain Mr. Anglo, way back at the Tulsa maintenance base who so coldly rejected me for a maintenance position there.

The only problem with that plan was that my interview with American Airlines was now set and I did not yet have a valid driver's license. I rushed to a lawyer's office to find out how quickly I could get my driver's license back. He did not have any good news for me. He reminded me that I had tickets in Oklahoma, New Jersey, Pennsylvania, Georgia, and one of the Carolina's. They all had to be taken care of before I would be able to get my license back. This was not what I needed to hear right now. I had an official interview with American Airlines fast approaching and I needed a valid driver's license to get on with them. It would cost me thousands of dollars to get my license back. The problem now was that I did not have thousands of dollars to hand over to a lawyer, and I also could not travel to all of those individual cities to take care of all of these outstanding traffic tickets, so what the heck was I going to do now!?

I did the best thing I thought I could do with what very little I had. I got an official state of Florida ID card. Who knows, the ID card looks the same as a driver's license I thought to myself, maybe they won't recognize that it's not a driver's license. I was not going to blow this interview over some license to drive; I went to the interview anyway. I went through the entire interview process, gave them my ID card, they even photocopied it. I thought I was all the way in with American Airlines towards the end of the interview process. I left the interview with my head held high and feeling proud. I was happy that they never mentioned the fact that it was an ID card that I had handed over to them.

Why would they not mention that to me? Maybe they didn't notice that little detail I thought.

Did they miss that small simple detail on the ID card?

I guess they did not miss that fact, because I never received a job offer from them. Not having a driver's license was of course a legitimate reason for not getting a job on the ramp at American Airlines and I could never complain about not getting hired for that reason, unlike what had happened in Tulsa when I simply did not graduate from their preferred technical school.

Oh well, like I've always liked to say to myself...life does go on, whether you want me working for you or not.

So much for that dream; I would soon be back to my regular grind and selling those books door to door.

When it came to selling books however, it did not take me long at all to figure out that when it comes to a sales position for me, I learned about myself really quick and the fact that I do not like to sell. I could not even sell this book idea as an investment idea to my two most very rich, best and oldest friends before I simply gave up on pitching the investment idea to them or anyone else. This is because I have learned that the slightest amount of negativity aimed at me affects my entire being; mind, body and soul. Selling anything at all would not be my strength or a possible career for me in the near or far future.

Even though I went back to selling books door to door against my heartfelt feelings, I knew that I still needed to fix my driver's license because my career in aviation absolutely depended on it; chauffeuring was not yet in the picture. I didn't know how that was going to happen though; I still did not have any money to fix all of the tickets that were laying around all over the country with my name on them. I did not let that stop me from doing what needed to be done in my life however, like eating well, and chasing the opposite sex all over the city. What would life be without all of these wonderful hobbies?

I had already been driving around Miami for what seemed like months on end without a license, registration, or insurance trying desperately to make a career out of a car trunk full of books all the while trying desperately to avoid the police. Until one day I received very something special in the mail. It was a certified check; a check from my good ole' Pan Am ex-employer. I was not expecting that check. It was a check for a grand total of about $2,600.00. I couldn't be more surprised and happier. I truly felt like partying all of the money away, but I had to show a little bit of constraint and a bit of responsibility. I knew that I did not have a driver's license, and it was bound to soon catch up with me eventually. I had to do it, I had to get my license fixed, I went right to the lawyer's office that I had visited some weeks earlier and I handed him over the $2,000 he had originally requested from me earlier to resolve all of the outstanding tickets that I had accumulated over the years and all over the states. He did just that, and in no time at all I was soon once again legal to drive the streets of Miami. The remainder of the check most certainly went to wine, women and weed, and not necessarily in that exact order. At least my driver's license was now good again, and I could once again now pursue a real career in aviation again. It was life anew for me; it was almost like a grown man being born again and I don't mean in the Christian sense.

Months earlier just after the second of what I had felt was another round of rejection from American Airlines. I had completely stopped looking in the classified ads for aviation jobs because American Airlines had proved to me that I truly was wasting my time in my aviation job hunts without having a valid driver's license, however I quickly resumed those job hunts in the newspapers ads again once I received my driving privileges.

On one particular day, while perusing the classified ads, for no reason at all I noticed an advert in the miscellaneous section of the help wanted ads. That ad was for limousine drivers, no experience required it said, all that was required was a telephone number, and a valid Florida driver's license with a chauffeur's endorsement. I immediately and strongly felt that I could do this job, I felt almost called to do it, I was now extremely excited about the thought of chauffeuring although I had never dreamt of doing this type of work before. There were a couple of small problems though, I had only one of those three requirements, and that was the valid Florida's driver's license. I did not have a telephone or a telephone number, and neither a chauffeur's endorsement. Those could be easily got, I thought. I didn't have the money to get a phone line in my little efficiency apartment; so once again I had to soon figure it all out, I did the very best thing I could do with what little I had.

I was absolutely determined not to have this opportunity pass me by.

Cellphones were not as yet as popular as they are today and I probably couldn't afford one anyway, so I purchased a beeper with a voicemail attachment. They would just have to call my new pager number and leave me a voice message if they wanted me to start work, I made sure to check my voicemail box on an almost hourly and on a most certainly, daily basis.

I also went to the Florida DMV and studied for and passed the chauffeur's endorsement to attach to my now new and valid Florida driver license. Eventually soon after I had received all of their requirements, I did get a phone call and voice message from the limousine company that I had responded to from the newspaper advertisement. I quickly set up an interview date, on that day I put on one of my best first class travel suit that I had purchased for my world wide travels with Pan Am. As I entered that office for my scheduled interview, I held my head high as I walked into that office and showed them all of my best smile and I also put on my very best personality. My sales experience helped a lot I believe, because I sold myself to this employer. I had felt like I had arrived to some sort of final destination, even on this very first day I thought this job was a calling for me I truly felt. I passed the interview with flying colors and I was soon hired on as a brand new limousine chauffeur; I remember feeling as if I was now right at home. So much so that it was also noticed by at least one of my future clients; much later on in my career and more recently to the time of this writing, I had one very lovely lady client tell me that my name along with my look and my position had all seemed to go together. She would also go on to politely tell me that I was probably born to do this; I wasn't at all shocked when she had said this to me. She was probably more than correct in her thinking and her judgment on me. As young as I was, I can still remember my feeling that day, that a brand new and very unexpected career was now born for me.

CHAPTER TWO
Intermission

I have purposely written this long introduction leading up to my experiences as a chauffeur and the sharing of those early stories, for the sole purpose that several of the chauffeuring stories I will write about in this book may be somewhat unbelievable. Everything that I have written about in the long introduction I believe is relative to the whole story that I will be sharing with you. It is also in my opinion though, that having a reader know exactly who I am along with my personality traits and mannerisms will make the stories and the experiences I share more understandable, acceptable and believable if seen closely from my point of view. With this introduction, I had the task of setting up the reader into getting to know my personality and my love of all people and in generally speaking, life itself. This intro I believe will make the stories I tell be a little more acceptable; if only if these stories can be clearly seen through my eyes. This is the reason why I would want a reader to feel and know exactly who I am before I share all of these chauffeuring stories, by me writing about myself as much as possible from my early childhood to this modern day. I also wanted you the reader to know exactly how I had finally come into driving professionally because I never in my early life had an intention of ever doing so; it was only from my desperation in finding some steady income and a steady job that only led me to chauffeuring.

I would first like to write a little bit about the private client who charters out a stretched limousine or a standard luxury sedan for whatever reason they may feel that they need to. Chartering a limousine is an expensive endeavor and there are of course many cheaper options out there. There is usually a very specific reason why someone would spend their hard earned money to get a ride somewhere and then there are also very specific personalities who require this type of service. South Florida does not have a lot of award shows or entertainment events like there is in New York or Los Angeles yet still the South Florida limousine industry has been very lucrative throughout the previous decades.

A lot of clients visit South Florida for business and there limousine charter is on a corporate account to get them professionally driven to exactly where they need to be for the sake of the company that they work for. However these are not the folks that I'm talking about although I have very much appreciated their business over the years. I rather speak of the folks that spend their own hard earned money for an experience of a lifetime. Being professionally chauffeured is a definite luxury that should be experienced by all if the opportunity ever arises. To have a well dressed, well groomed individual show up at your door, take all of your luggage from your door and load it into the car, in the case of an airport transfer, and personally wait on you while you enjoy your dinner party or an evening out on the town and to actually have a permanent designated driver as you get your drink and buzz on, is something that I myself have never experienced but I have been told that it is a very special feeling to experience; maybe one day I will have the opportunity to do so. It is not just about the long car that everyone gawks at as you drive by or pull up to your destination, rather it is about the service; the luxury of being driven and not having to look at a meter and the full chauffeur experience that should be appreciated, as long as you always request a senior chauffeur. An inexperienced chauffeur may not be such an excellent service experience as was the case for me as a very rookie chauffeur, as you will soon be reading about.

People who routinely charter chauffeurs and limos in South Florida are not necessarily doing it for show as what you may see in the entertainment cities such as Las Vegas, or Los Angeles. I can honestly believe that they do so because they know how to enjoy their lives and enjoy the luxury of limousine services and generally just want the best for their lives, their families lives and their friends, it is also a whole lot cheaper to charter a limousine for an evening out than to potentially get a DUI and have to pay for the ultimate consequences of getting busted or getting into a wreck. With a chauffeur there for you have no additional worries to worry about and your cost are all accounted for and no attorney is ever required.

This book will allow the reader to get a small glimpse into who these people are inside of the big shiny stretched cars that are the envy of most who watch them pull up to their destination in style and luxury. After over two decades of chauffeuring I have a story for each group of people who charter limos, whether that be families, individuals, athletes or celebrities and how they all let the luxury of being chauffeured affect them in their own private setting behind the partition and being private while still out in public. People will always tend to be themselves with no holding back when in a limousine while out enjoying themselves in a very rare or probable once in a lifetime event and I am sure you will enjoy the stories that I will share with you. A good example of people being who they really are in a limo is that all people love Hip-Hop music. I had always wondered why the hip hop music industry made so many billions of dollars all the while people have always complained about the content and lyrics of rap music and the artist' who perform them. This however is not the case inside of a limousine; all people have rap music on their ipads, Iphones and music playlists. All people have some sort of rap channel on their Pandora station choices, and it does not matter the age or the ethnicity of the client, white, black, Asian, Latino, male, or female, grandmas or corporate executives; rap music is truly All American music although many of my foreign clients all usually have rap music from their own country and language.

It is also a very awkward situation when you have the whitest of the whitest clients on board who are out partying in the limo and a particular rap song comes on blasting the uncensored lyrics of that rap song and then the "N" word ends up being blared throughout the limos high end sound system. These clients usually get very silent very quickly and immediately go to the next track trying to appease me by not blasting the "N" word throughout the limo; the space behind the driver's seat inside a limo is the client's personal space just as in their home, blast what you like, do as you please, don't limit yourself.

What these clients don't know however is that the "N" word has never bothered me being used by any group of people, the "N" word has been thrown in front of my name ever since my early days in elementary school, usually with the adjective "My" in front of the "N" word and then my name to follow. I have gone a very long time getting very accustomed to this term, as some would describe as a derogatory word. This word has never bothered me ever since way back then many decades ago, anyone can say whatever they like in this world and it will not bother me at all, unless of course those words that they use will affect my paycheck and my ability to feed my family, then I will have a problem with the things that are said; until then, speak on and jam on as you ride in style. I have even had a group of about ten pre teen anglo boys with their three chaperons who were all playing the "bad word alphabet game" while driving in my limo. One of the young boys had the nerve to ask me to please not get offended when they chose a bad word for the letter N; whatever young buck, just as long as pops is paying the bill

So who are these people who have really been complaining about rap music lyrics and the hip hop lifestyle and where are they because they certainly don't ride in limousines; nobody wants to listen to Barry Manilow when they're inside of a limo, believe me I've tried to play him as well as others. Limousines have a separate stereo system from the driver up front, that is in the rear passenger compartment and at the full control of the client and I do not think I have ever seen anyone be back there and NOT blast some sort of Hip Hop music and simply love it while they jam to the urban beats. This is the real that people display when they are out on the town cruising around in a stretched limousine or even in just a luxury sedan.

I would also at this particular time like to write about and share with you a little bit about the actual professional chauffeur, him or herself, as well as the South Florida limousine industry as a whole.

Spending the better part of the last 22 years as a chauffeur and working closely with other chauffeurs, both male and female, I have gained a lot of knowledge into who a chauffeur is and what is required of that same professional chauffeur to be somewhat successful in this high demanding industry.

A chauffeur in my humble opinion is very much an independent spirit; he or she is not necessarily a conformer as you would think of someone in a corporate world or of a corporate structure. Chauffeurs are usually dropouts from this type of corporate organization because of their strong sense of personal independence; unfortunately I think this is a very good example of myself in the aviation industry.

Once a new chauffeur gets accustomed to the lifestyle and the actual freedom that being self employed as a professional chauffeur in South Florida brings, it will then be extremely difficult for them to go back to a normal, regular and mundane nine to five work schedule, four to twelve schedule, or eleven to seven night job schedule or any other type of corporate structure and routine. I have also never liked working in the same place all the time and I enjoy getting out to different locations and settings on a daily basis without some dumb, never ending and boring routine. In a regular nine to five job, you will be limited to an eight hour work shift and whatever little bit of "throwing you a bone" overtime may be thrown your way, as an independent chauffeur you are no longer limited to the hours that are given to you by someone who thinks of you as inferior or limited to a monetary dollar amount of hourly pay. On the other hand chauffeuring in South Florida especially during the winter season is only limited to how much sleep you will need to have. I truly don't need much sleep and the income in chauffeuring for me has been greatly rewarding to me; because of the situation I found myself in towards the latter days of my chauffeuring career I worked full time and I also just about literally worked non-stop.

Working and driving as a completely independent contractor and running your own small business in my opinion is the ultimate in freedom and independence, it is your own individual democracy and it is to me absolutely pure freedom. I would highly recommend chauffeuring to anyone who may be contemplating getting out of their mundane corporate structure or to just simply branch out for their own brand new independent experiences as a chauffeur and as an independent business owner.

Instead of working very mundane hours, dictated to you and having someone who you may or may not like telling you your worth for your daily work. Chauffeuring in South Florida allows you to work as much or as little as you want, just as you yourself pleases to and to create your very own worth based upon that amount of work that you choose to put into it. This, no one can take away from you just as long as you properly maintain your professional credentials and driving record.

I have always appreciated a person who is an independent spirit in all forms of work and life, because it takes a lot of individual courage to think and act outside the box and away from a normal and routine way of doing business or living life, as an independent spirit often must do to separate themselves from the crowd of the normal in which fitting in an independent spirit may very well may be severe torture.

A chauffeur may or may not be a people person, and a chauffeur may or may not be friendly, as they truly don't need to be. The only mandatory requirement of a chauffeur is to be punctual and to pay his or her own taxes; as I have definitely learned this tax fact the hard way. This is because we are all usually independent contractors running our own small personal business, and we sell our services and skills to limousine companies. I have personally met many a chauffeur who are literally quite mean, but they always show up on time to their assigned jobs and are usually good drivers. Having a warm friendly personality is quite a plus however when it comes to receiving cash gratuities, but nowadays gratuities are mostly billed to some sort of corporate account and the majority of frequent limousine passenger's know this fact and they don't usually like to hand out their hard earned cash to their driver especially if they know the chauffeur will be receiving a handsome gratuity in their next paycheck two weeks later.

I have always enjoyed chauffeuring simply because of the fact that I enjoy being around people and I enjoy people watching whether I am in the South of Fifth district of South Beach or the at the famous Breakers Hotel on well to do Palm Beach, and I also enjoy learning and growing from those experiences that I share with different people of all different walks of life, the rich and the not so rich. Chauffeuring fills my daily need for new interpersonal interaction and personal growth that my career in aviation just cannot fulfill for me; every single day is a different day from the other when chauffeuring here in South Florida especially when it comes to meeting and greeting new faces, places and events.

Not ever having the same dollar amount on your paycheck can also attest to this fact; as a chauffeur, your paycheck will never be the same amount of money here in South Florida. A chauffeur's paycheck is completely based on an as worked type basis, where the chauffeur only gets paid for jobs completed for that particular pay period and the pay for that individual job is based on what type of job was completed whether it was a one way transfer or time spent with the client better known as an As Directed. There is no definition of the amount of money that a chauffeur can make during the busy winter season in South Florida, anywhere from fifty dollars up to five hundred dollars; it all depends on how much work that a chauffeur wants to put in for the day. I've heard about chauffeurs who have made five thousand dollars in a day or even given expensive jewelry while they were driving Arab Royalty, there is some truth to this because I myself have made close to around five thousand dollars during the long four day Superbowl weekend of 2007, which I will write about later on, but never in a single day. I have heard a few stories about this though however but those jobs are usually reserved for much more dedicated chauffeurs who have long been committed to their one sole career as professional chauffeurs and they are hardly ever dispatched to chauffeurs who are only part time and are not committed to the trade fulltime.

I have been fired or walked off of many an aviation job, and it has never been due to performance issues or any sort of mishap, rather due to personality conflicts and the contrasting egos of certain men, in which I will share some of these ego filled stories of my aviation firings later on in the chapters of this book but professional chauffeuring has consistently had my back and has never let me down thus far.

My negative experiences in aviation have mostly been with men in management, usually in lower or middle management who do not like or appreciate my friendly, outgoing and personable attitude (like the line fueling supervisor that had said to me that I smile too much) and who tend to use their own brown nosing skills to somehow influence upper management to slowly but surely come against me due to their own personal "for whatever reason" dislike towards me; I've never let that get to me though.

I myself do not brown nose though, as my nose is already brown enough. I am and have always been, throughout both of my careers, way too much of a hard working and legal hustler to ever become some type of a professional brown noser such as the many professional brown noser' s that I've come across throughout my many years in this life; I have always been afraid I will end up kissing the wrong persons' ass. I am here to testify that there are other ways to make it in this World besides becoming a professional brown noser, stepping on the backs of fellow employees to try and attempt to make your way to the top, but you have to know how to do it. The hardest part of that and the most important part of that is by acknowledging God in your life and your career and also having God lead the way for you. If you are a true believer, God will never lead you to step on the backs of anyone for your own personal career advancement just because you may think it is required to do so and just to get ahead in your beloved career. God will not permit a true believer to rise up on the back of someone else just to increase your own self no matter how much you think that you may have or need to do so; God cares about and wants to bless everyone in the workplace, even the slackers.

There is a certain workplace however where I have personally witnessed professional brownnosing and where I do believe that that brown nosing is absolutely required and necessary; that is in the job of a professional hotel concierge. I have personally worked directly with quite a few of them at high end luxury hotels throughout my many years of my chauffeuring career.

I have witnessed this job of the hotel concierge throughout the years fill the needs and request of the very rich and high demanding hotel guests as well as the big dollar clientele the hotel may have.

Whether it is taking out super rich hotel guests out on personal limousine city tours of Miami and Miami Beach as well as out on fine dining tours to the city's newest and finest dining establishments as well as to the best hotspots bars and lounges. All the while the concierge is professionally living it up, drinking right along with the guest all of the expensive bottles of wines and champagne and eating gourmet foods in the top rated gourmet restaurants and these professional people are more than likely probably getting handsomely cash tipped at the end of the night from their very rich clientele.

These concierge's are of course allowed and are expected to get completely intoxicated with the client, if that's what the client wants, all while working on the clock as well as all on the dime of the hotel guests or on the hotel's budget for the wooing of the potential multimillion dollar client contract that the hotel maybe going after, such as international airline flight crew contracts and professional sports teams amongst other corporate and commercial businesses routinely in need of overnight hotel stays.

If the concierge wants to continue this line of work he or she must keep that guest happy, smiling and laughing the whole time they are with the client or guest, just as if they were long time best friends. If you didn't know it, you would swear this was a gathering of people who grew up together; I was in utter shock when I first realized that this type of job existed. This is a job that demands brown nosing on a very high professional level and more importantly professional brown nosing skills and I truly look up to and respect these very professional men and women who take their job very seriously, unlike the low skilled brown nosers with some job simply turning wrenches trying to get another dollar per hour in their pay or forty dollars extra a week in their paycheck. Free cash, free booze, free gourmet food, if ever there were a reason to be a professional brown noser that would be it.

I have however brown nosed in the past though, but only when absolutely necessary and only to law enforcement officers when I get pulled over for speeding or some other bulltype driving infraction; which has actually happened quite often in my career. I make my professional living with my commercial driver's license and I refuse to have it threatened in any type of way, even if I am in the wrong. So I will do whatever it takes to protect my money maker. If anybody ever tells me that I have to brown nose for any other reason besides protecting my professional licenses; I will kindly and politely tell them to kiss MY butt. This is probably the sole reason why I have not seen full success in the aviation industry; I have always believed that with the blessings of God I can always find other work to do if I find out ass kissing is required at any particular job. I do not care however, because I tend to always and will always live my life with no regrets. One of my main problems with brown nosing is that I would have to put faith in the men that I would have to brown nose to; and people tend to brown nose the wrong individual and they usually have to depend on that one individual for any type of success, I will never have this problem in my life. I have never in my life put faith in any man here on this Earth. The only man that I have put all my faith into is not of this Earth, and he would not even allow me to kiss his butt even if he were here.

I cannot and I also refuse to put all of my faith in any one man. I do not even put any of my faith in any of my dispatchers to awaken me with wake up calls for early morning pickups; with both of my careers being time sensitive, to me day is like night and night is like day and I have never been late for an early morning pickup; I actually prefer early morning pickups because of the lack of traffic and I have always wished that all the other drivers on the road would stay in bed. Sleep does not matter much to me and I would much rather lose out on sleep that night than to take a chance at having the dispatcher fall asleep at their desk and not call and awaken me for an early morning pickup. If that were to happen, I would then become way too stressed over being late for that early morning assignment, and then I may get charged by the company for the lost income when the passenger winds up taking a cab to their final destination that morning, all due to me putting my faith in some human. Being also a professional commercial pilot has entwined in me to always be on time and preferably always thirty minutes early; you cannot tell a plane load of passengers that they're going to be late, just because you're late because you overslept and that they'll be missing their connecting flight because you didn't get a timely wakeup call from a sleeping dispatcher. I can only put my faith in God first and then and only maybe myself.

Me and keeping my faith exactly where I have always kept it and where I feel that it is supposed to be has always kept me exactly where I need to be. I would have probably been out of a career and a couple of chauffeuring jobs if I had to depend on the carefree dispatchers that I've worked with over the past years for wake up calls. If you can even just simply imagine yourself being late for any pickup in the limo industry, do not even think about starting to work in this business; punctuality is everything here. It is very stressful as a chauffeur to be late for a client pickup especially knowing that you are being watched by all…clients, dispatchers and especially limousine business owners, who will of course be asking you to fill out incident reports as to why you were late. It is so much less stressful to just simply prepare yourself ahead of time and arrive early for a client pickup; this will make your day much easier.

Although I have been a chauffeur for the good majority of my life, except for the very beginning of me actually learning how to drive; I actually hate driving, but I do actually enjoy chauffeuring if that makes any sense at all. However after all these years and experience in chauffeuring, I must admit to myself that I am truly good at it, in both the driving sense of chauffeuring and in the people part of chauffeuring also. Even though I truly don't want to admit that I'm good at chauffeuring, I must do so. The reason why I really don't want to admit this fact is simply because I've always somewhat looked down on driving as a professional career for myself, for whatever unknown reason that I may or may not have injected into my brain and train of thought. I have passed judgment on chauffeurs and professional drivers although I am one myself and I have come to the realization that I may have missed out on the blessings that a chauffeur can accumulate in a full time South Florida career over the amount of time that I have invested in it, if I had been a fulltime chauffeur as compared to only part time and seasonal.

The reason that I hate driving; especially in Miami is because there are so many bad drivers on the road. From lost tourists, to foreign drivers with their own bad driving habits from their country and also locals who are always on the prowl for an insurance or cash on hand scams like slamming their car brakes immediately in front of you hoping for you to rear end them, and if you do, then asking you for lots of cash that you can hand over to them as to not get the insurance company involved. Or if you don't hand over your cash at hand that the driver who you just rear ended is requesting to avoid the insurance companies, the perpetrator will just get a police report and the next day go see their "doctor" and then go to the insurance company to file a medical claim and eventually collect an insurance check.

I have personally known people who have done this kind of act prior to me becoming a professional driver and I have also been driven as a passenger with someone who was actually attempting to do this act; when it was done I just sat at in the passenger seat and said and did nothing. So I know from actual firsthand experience of what this potential act looks like from afar and I also know how to avoid them when I see them. If you drive under the assumption that all of the drivers around you are possibly scamming for a fraud, you too will probably be accident free in all your years of driving as I have been because this knowledge and experience came to me prior to becoming a professional chauffeur.

Knowing this fact this has helped me out a lot in my professional driving career. I've also learned that just knowing that these people are out there and are actually after your hard earned cash; and also keeping an open eye out for them can actually reduce a lot of rear end accidents and also reduce the stress that driving behind them brings because you are always one step ahead of them. I have always only expected nothing else except the worst from all and any of city of Miami driver's due to this fact and I am almost certain that this is the main reason that I have remained accident free for all of these years that I have been driving professionally here in Miami.

Miami and South Florida is a huge party place, so much so that visiting professional NBA teams routinely avoid staying here during their long stayovers during NBA playoff games and fly back to their home cities for the long layovers inbetween playoff games, so as to focus on their task at hand and to not get caught up in all of the partying atmosphere that is so prevalent here; what other professional NBA city can say that happens also? None. With this type of intense party atmosphere so very prevalent, there are so many of those drunk drivers out there, what you normally see on a weekend night is not at all what you would typically see on a weeknight, all due to the massive amounts of drunk drivers on the road. I've come to the conclusion that there is no way to get rid of them and I have had my many shares of run-ins with them; I have reported a bunch of them to the police whenever I noticed the police close to something I've seen, which over the years have been several. I don't care; they can very easily kill me.

People do not realize that it's much cheaper to have hired a chauffeur and a car for an intoxicating night out on the town than it is to get caught with a DUI charge; I will always encourage people to do this when they want a fun night out and to also attempt keep my industry alive and well and my pockets full.

Then there are so many naturally bad drivers out there, I can always tell when I've arrived in South Florida not by the sights that I see, but rather by the amount of awareness and care that I must exercise when I have arrived here from somewhere else. Miami is the only city in this country where I have seen this type of what I call accident prone driving; this beautiful city just has a lot of driver's that look like they're just driving around trying to just eventually get into some type of an accident. These people driving around like this do not realize how much of a traffic hazard that they are, I will always have much more confidence in a driver whizzing by me at 100MPH, than the driver holding up traffic at 45MPH in a 65MPH speed zone; to me the faster driver has much more control over their destiny than the slower, I don't care about the people held up behind me type of driver and at least the speeder is out of my way in a split second and not holding me or anyone else up with their non chalant driving style.

Miami also has a lot of fulltime everyday Sunday drivers who drive extremely leisurely as if they're going to or coming from Sunday afternoon Church services no matter what day of the week it is or what time of the day it is, these drivers are extremely annoying and are just as prone to get into some sort of traffic accident just as much as those people out there looking to slam on their brakes.

I also won't mention the fact that I've probably lost at least one cumulative year of my life in all of my years of driving, stopped behind red traffic lights; and now at these same red traffic lights they want to take your hard earned cash just because you try to retrieve some of that lost time back and you try to minimize that amount of lost time that you accumulate over time. One red light camera ticket can easily take away a full day's pay if you're not careful and if you get enough of those, the city government will actually end up on your company's payroll. I've already seen an actual chauffeur with over fifteen hundred dollars in payroll deductions for his share of red light camera tickets that he had accumulated.

The only way to try and attempt to eliminate all of that lost time is to try and avoid those traffic lights altogether, but that seems to be getting more and more impossible as the years go along. All of that lost time can greatly diminish the quality of life of a professional chauffeur. When I am planning a certain route, I do not plan for the shortest distance in-between or the least amount of vehicle traffic, rather I try to plan my routes for the least amount of roadblocks that are traffic lights. I have learned throughout my career that just like a blocked artery can stop a beating heart, traffic lights can also completely stop city traffic in South Florida and they actually cause more traffic jams than the actual heavy traffic does down here and I do my best to try and avoid them altogether. Even if I have to drive myself and my clients through the worst neighborhoods in Miami, I would do so simply to just try and avoid those traffic lights and the heavy traffic that Miami brings. This is because the majority of drivers in Miami do not like to drive through Miami's tough seedy neighborhoods and therefore traffic is very much diminished in those areas in the directions of rush hour traffic in these certain sections of Miami. When I plan my routings like this, it always seems to get me to my final destination a whole lot quicker than just simply trodding through the very heavy and accumulated traffic of Miami streets always caused by the numerous amounts of long and exhaustive traffic lights scattered very closely by, throughout the entire metropolitan area and surrounding areas of Miami and the beaches.

Of course traffic lights are meant for safety of everyone on the roads, but they are extremely time consuming. Not necessarily for the twice daily work commuter, but rather the professional driver who spends his days on the roads utilizing those traffic signals all day long. Over time such as years and decades these traffic lights can very easily become excessively stressing as well as frustrating.

Traveling throughout the world in which I have driven or have at least been driven through in the many stops and foreign cities that I have visited, has given me a great appreciation for traffic roundabouts which dominate the rest of the world outside of the United States, as they do not attempt to rob you blindly of the precious time in your life and roundabouts do not attempt to take your picture as you drive through them like a busted criminal in a police mugshot. I've also never heard of T-bone or rear end accidents in a traffic roundabout. If you could just imagine an American metropolitan city the size of Miami having roundabouts in place of the current major intersecting intersections, with all the traffic light systems that go with it. The benefits could be substantial in regards to the energy savings in annual oil consumption for vehicles not waiting on long red lights, the savings on the electrical grid no longer needing to supply the power to the traffic control systems, and the time savings and stress reducing benefits for all of the residents of that city. This could be a quality of life issue that would be certain to reduce the stress of the entire cities inhabitants, possibly bettering the lives of many and probably reducing our American stress related issues that seem to plague us Americans, especially in the big cities such as Miami. Replacing busy intersections with traffic roundabouts, yet somewhat difficult, would still be an easy way for an entire committed city to commit to an attempt at going green. They would also no longer have to worry over the concerns that led to the creation of the red light camera ticket in the first place, a further all around benefit to its taxpaying citizens; that's what I've always called a plus plus, nothing but positives. This is just something that I have been thinking about as I drive through Miami in everyday traffic. If there's anyone reading this right now that's planning on building a new city, please design that city around multiple traffic roundabouts rather than the standard American perpendicular intersections, thanks.

Instead of decreasing accidents as they were originally intended, red light cameras have been proven to actually cause significantly more rear end accidents as people slam on their brakes in an attempt at avoiding getting one of those tickets. This is what I call government sponsored wrecks; I see them all the time. These rear end accidents usually occur when drivers in front try and avoid running through a yellow light and rapidly slam on their brakes while the person behind them are actually trying to get through the yellow light on time. As a chauffeur it is not possible to rapidly stomp on the limousine's brakes to try and avoid running a yellow and potentially red light, simply because you may have clients in the back enjoying champagne and cocktails and you don't want your clients wearing their mojito's and mimosas on their expensive designer clothes; I would much prefer to potentially get a red light ticket than to upset my high end clients, even if I have to pay for it.

I have also previously received red light camera tickets from of all things, a drawbridge red light camera on Miami Beach. With this very expensive ticket that I had received, I had no other choice but to ask myself if these red light cameras are truly about public safety or more about filling the government pockets as a tax to the commuters on the roads, because when I got this ticket, there were no cross traffic accidents that were even possible because it was not at an intersection with opposing traffic and the drawbridge wasn't anywhere near about to be opened. I was certainly not in any kind of danger of potentially falling into Biscayne Bay below, so why is this high priced ticket then a safety based infraction I had to ask myself. The answer is that these red light cameras are not truly based on public safety, but rather to fill the government coffers as a very well disguised tax on drivers; having a drawbridge red light camera that is NOT placed at an intersection where there is opposing or perpendicular traffic that can potentially cause as accident with another vehicle, clearly proves this theory to me.

Most people would fight such a red light camera ticket as this one in court but this is not the case for a chauffeur. That's because chauffeurs usually drive a vehicle that the license tag is not registered to their name and is rather always ticketed directly to the limousine company, which in turn takes the amount of the ticket directly out of the next paycheck of the chauffeur who was assigned to the vehicle at the time that the picture was taken. This completely eliminates the opportunity for us to fight any camera ticket because usually by the time we are notified of the pay deduction it's already too late to fight it in court.

I have also noticed in my years of driving professionally here in South Florida that all of these red lights also enhance and maybe even cause traffic jams and actually make rush hour traffic worst, somewhat like what happens during rubbernecking on freeway accidents. If there is heavy traffic during rush hour traffic red lights contribute greatly to that added traffic congestion during rush hour time instead of letting the traffic flow freely through the city at its busiest and most crowded time; San Francisco has the best example of this type of excellent high traffic management system that I have seen thus far.

To my very surprise on one particular day, my car has already been towed away from on street parking once while parked legally on the curb on a San Francisco street. This happened because of the parking ban on streets during the times of rush hour in San Francisco, eventually my car started to block the streets during the rush hour exodus from downtown San Francisco once the rush hour no parking ban started somewhere around four pm in the afternoon; I hadn't known about this parking ban at the time it happened. I hated the fact that they would actually tow away my once legally parked car at first, but I now realize and appreciate the relative importance and benefits that this traffic management system can bring to a very busy city. San Francisco actually has the best drivers and the least amount of traffic that I have ever seen in this country and I don't recall ever having traffic jams actually being a real issue in San Francisco unlike South Florida and Miami specifically. Big kudos to that city for all of their efforts to keep the traffic free flowing during the busiest times during the cities busy rush hour traffic and to also having enough common sense to know exactly how NOT to inhibit the free flow of vehicle traffic at the most critical times and to also have consideration for its citizens time and well being by not having them sit in unnecessary and prolonged traffic jams. Please keep up the good work and continue to be an example for big cities like Miami to one day look up to and maybe one day follow your cities lead by introducing variable and adjustable traffic light timing to always favor the exodus out of or into the city so that the balance of traffic can be somewhat equalized in the ebbs and flows of big city traffic.

Along with Miami and it's traffic inducing traffic light systems, Atlanta and Los Angeles are amongst the worst places where I have seen great examples of the stressful, non courteous and just plain old bad drivers and heavy slow moving traffic; these were among some of the main reasons that I chose not to ever again live in those particular metropolitan areas.

The cumulative lost time spent behind red traffic lights is completely non-productive time and that time can never again be retrieved, or that lost time made back up, it's a complete loss of life's precious moments. The natural urge is for me to bust right through all of those red lights, especially when you're running late, but of course you can't do that and you must fight those urges and temptations if you want to stay employed as a chauffeur and if you want to hold on to your valid driver's license. I have seemed to also realize that red light times have seemed to have gotten a lot longer over the years, coinciding with the introduction of the red light cameras. This to me is a provocation to temptation to produce more red light runners thusly generating greater financial income to the city and its bankrolls; this is just the opinion that I have gained as I watched these red light cameras gain in popularity over the years.

Since the original writing of this chapter, the Florida laws have been changed to outlaw the use of red light camera tickets in the state of Florida. This was done when the Florida Supreme court ruled that city or county government municipalities did not have the right to do the job of issuing traffic tickets of its citizens by replacing the traditional job of a sworn police officer enforcing driving and road rules. I wish someone had thought of that logic before spending millions of citizen's tax dollars on very expensive high tech spy equipment and issuing even still more millions in mail issued traffic tickets. To me this was simply legal…highway robbery, pun intended, and I know that I will never see the four tickets totaling hundreds of dollars that I have paid out already to my Miami-Dade county and it's very wealthy coffers.

I highly encourage other citizens of other states that you too should also contest the use of red light camera tickets issued by government offices instead of a sworn police officer, it makes perfect sense to me. This still does not help the fact that there are way too many traffic lights in Miami and Miami Beach though.

Cities like Miami and especially Miami Beach have way too many traffic lights to begin with and have far too many automobiles utilizing those same traffic lights to be as effective and as efficient as maybe they once were. These traffic control devices were probably designed for traffic of the Art Deco era when the traffic and the traffic speeds were a whole lot different from those of today where the speeds and the amount of vehicles have probably quadrupled from the original traffic light designs thusly adding to the stress and the temptation to try and gain some time by speeding through a quickly changing yellow light.

Driving in a large metropolitan area like Miami and South Florida can be extremely stressing, especially if you do not properly prepare yourself for the jobs ahead of you. That excessive stress can very easily be transferred to your passengers, and ultimately affect your performance and of course your cash gratuity.

In the beginning of my driving career, I really did not like or want to drive very much because of all those stresses that I was just learning about; It seemed like I was stressed out all the time due to driving clients professionally, but over the years I have learned to reduce and manage those stresses by planning and giving myself more time ahead of a job. This practice greatly eliminates the majority of stresses, but practicing time management can also be stressful in itself, but time management must be mastered by a chauffeur if they want to make a career in chauffeuring with a minimum amount of stress.

South Florida is also a major market for the limousine industry as a whole, but unbelievably only in the winter months, unlike a market such as Los Angeles or New York City where the limousine market is all year round. The South Florida winter months is when people with real expendable cash come to South Florida to get away from the northern winter weather, these same people also leave South Florida when the sun, heat and humidity become unbearable in the hot summer months down here in South Florida. I think a lot of that winter cash gets thrown around because all of the rich snowbirds are just so happy and excited to be away from the cold frigid tundra of the northern latitudes and they're probably just so darn happy to be out of their winter time blues and it's probably worth every nickel and dime that they will eventually spend down here.

South Florida is not a known place to make a lot of executive money such as New York or Chicago. South Florida is primarily tourist based, but it is a place where these same people from these money earning cities come to enjoy our beautiful South Florida winters and to spend all of that hard earned money that they have earned throughout the year right here in sunny South Florida; finally getting away from their long, cold winter months up north. This is also when snowbird season actually begins when all of the Canadians come down to happily utilize their three month tourist visas. There used to be a time that the Canadians were the bulk of the visiting snowbirds, but now that title would go to the new snowbirds, the Russians. They now flock here from the Arctic Circle to spend all of their newly found wealth.

The winter months is also when and where large corporations come down to do their winter and spring conferences, and have their annual conventions for their best employees and biggest earners and top team players as a reward for their hard work throughout the rest of the year.

These corporations also like to spend all of this cash before the close of the business tax years and in what I believe is to take advantage of the corporate tax structures and benefits that the tax deduction system brings to a major corporation. You always know when the slow season is just about over because some of the corporations, usually right after Labor Day, start their convention season when the school year is back in session. Right after the long summer school break in which their employees spend time with their kids and families and those companies start flying their executives down here to get them psyched up and ready for another year of business and all of the hard work ahead that that entails.

When the summer season comes here in South Florida for a chauffeur it is just like being a school teacher on summer break, the chauffeur had better have saved up their winter nuts because the summer season is a very lean season when it comes to a chauffeurs income in South Florida and the market shrinks down to a market size as somewhere such as a city like West Bubbleton, Floriho, in other words...like this city doesn't actually exist, so is it also for the limousine industry in the very high heat of summertime South Florida, the limousine industry also does not exist. If a chauffeur has not saved some of their lucrative winter earnings to help get them through the long summer, they had better have complete faith that God will get them through the very long and slow summer season as a South Florida chauffeur because the less money that a chauffeur will earn over the summer will actually make the short summer season seem even longer than what it actually is.

Actually, the limo market shrinks down to the size of some small southern city where limousine service is mainly used for weddings, funerals, proms and airport transfers. I call this cycle reverse hibernation, and a South Florida chauffeur has got to get accustomed to this very deep income cycle. A South Florida chauffeur has to set himself or herself up to make it through the summer months; this is the only way to make it as chauffeur in South Florida, a really good and busy South Florida chauffeur can make all of his or her income in all of the winter months down here and save up enough cash to have a six month vacation somewhere else in the world just as many foreign chauffeurs do here in South Florida.

Professional chauffeurs from South Florida usually can also travel to other cities like Los Angeles, Las Vegas or New York where they can still hustle up some cash chauffeuring in those cities during the summer months as many of them do, but they always make sure that they are back in Miami by the latest, mid November for the start of the new season and start the winter cycle to get their nonstop hustle going on until the end of May, because the market and the potential income from driving down here during the height of the season is that huge in South Florida during the long winter months.

South Florida is the only warm place in the continental US with beach weather during the American winter season and everybody who can wants to flock here then. The very busy South Florida Winter limo season unofficially begins in the month of October with the start of the NBA season and the reopening of Joe's stone crabs on South Beach when a steady stream of limousine reservations begins to slowly work its way at first then eventually turning into a fever pitch. The sheer volume of limousine reservations are astronomical all the way through the remainder of the winter season and since the inception of the now huge Miami and Miami beach's art festival known as Art Basel, this very popular and busy art fair in the early days of December has since been the official start of the very long and very busy winter season for the South Florida limousine industry and is now the largest worldwide tourist attraction event in all of South Florida.

December is actually the beginning of very busy work season for limo companies and chauffeurs all over South Florida and the work does not stop until the end of spring next May just right after the very busy Memorial Day holiday weekend; everybody in the limo business is extremely busy during this time. The month of December begins with the very busy Art Basel event, then next up comes the busy Christmas travel season, then of course the biggest single night of the year for chauffeurs, New Years Eve. This month is when reservations go way up for the entire month and everybody in the industry is just about ready to get back to work after a long summer hiatus and very slow work.

The next biggest night of the year for the limousine industry is not too far away in that of Valentine's Day and the one night which could very easily compete with New Year's Eve as being the busiest night of the year for the limousine industry. Usually around that same time is the annual Miami boat show which is an extremely busy time for shuttle busses. Soon after that would be the South Beach wine and food fest where all of the major celebrities come down to stuff their faces with free gourmet food cooked by celebrity chefs. Close to the time of the SoBe wine and food fest is Spring Break, with all of the college students coming down here to spend all of daddy's money. As well as Ultra Music Festival, a weeklong celebration of electronic and techno music but I have seen that festival of all musical sounds…'digital', slowly change over to welcome more traditional forms of music and the artists who create it.

Right after Ultra its then time for the always very popular high school prom season, graduation season as well as wedding season and all of the busyness that that season brings. After prom season is the Memorial Day weekend which also lasts about a week and is always a very busy time for limousines. Inbetween all of these winter events are all of the different corporate and medical conventions that come to South Florida for their celebration of Sun and sand in the middle of the winter, as well as the so many cruise ship passengers at both South Florida cruise ports, Port Everglades and Port Miami. Cruise ship passengers literally come from all over the World who very happily come here to sunny South Florida during the winter months in countless numbers and who bring their very generous tipping routines, where an experienced and hustling CDL chauffeur with a strong back can make hundreds of dollar after a full day's work or get a full day's pay after just a couple of hours of hard work.

Chauffeurs who do stick around for the slow summer season usually do get a little reminder of what it used to be like in the busy winter season during the middle of the high heat summer though; that is when the popular Miami Fashion Week and everyone who has a vested interest in that industry roll into town for a very busy week of work. It is the only highlight of a South Beach summer in this industry.

Cash gets thrown around during the very busy South Florida winter Limo season just as if that cash is going out of style, somewhat similar to a number 23 basketball jersey after an unexpected Cleveland Cavalier departure. If you as a chauffeur don't make any money during this very busy time in South Florida it is your own darn fault; this is the time to grab a hold of as much of the cash being thrown around as you can possibly get your hands on because this cash bonanza does not last an entire year. During this busy time of the limousine season it is like having a payday every single day with the large amounts of cash being thrown around from all directions such as from limo companies desperately seeking professional drivers, clients and their generous gratuities and sometimes very quick cash hustles if you know how the industry operates on a whole, all widely available to a keen eyed, alert and very well experienced South Florida chauffeur seeking to hustle up some quick cash.

There is also so much work during the busy winter limousine season that as a chauffeur you will actually start to get quite annoyed with all of the work being thrown your way with the constant ringing of your cellphone from desperate dispatchers looking for chauffeurs to help them fulfill the need to accomplish their daily duty and reservation sheets and satisfy the high demand for sedans and limousines. Working as a professional chauffeur you must learn to balance the demands of yourself, your clients, and the constant annoying of a ringing cellphone from these very hardworking yet very much underappreciated dispatchers; I will be further writing about this proper client dispatcher balance later on in this book.

Since I have been a chauffeur, I have had no accidents, zero traffic points, and zero traffic violations, and that is not due to the fact that I am a perfect driver, quite on the contrary. It is more due to the fact that I always speak very nicely and with honor and respect with any law enforcement agency that I may encounter, and I always deeply apologize beforehand for whatever it is that I may or may not have done upon first contact with the law enforcement officer. It has always worked for me, and it has a very direct and immediate positive benefit. I have gotten out of many a ticket, including speeding tickets by doing this. This is the only professional brown nosing that I have ever done in my life; in this life I have never been anybody's bitch, except for maybe a beautiful woman or two every now and then. This practice has kept my driving record and driver's license clean ever since I had my license returned to me back in 1992; I have truly learned the valuable lessons taught to me over the years about driving privileges in that driving is just that; a privilege and not a right to anyone. Being nice to officers is also the same concept that I use to earn cash tips, just like the Officers that will be reluctant to give you a ticket if you are extremely nice to them, a client will also be reluctant to NOT want to give you a cash tip if you are also extremely nice to them as well and to also have a decent conversation as well as being pleasant with them. In both cases, guilt will be the overwhelming factor for the client or the law enforcement officer to go out of their way for you and to possibly or maybe eventually do the right thing for you because of the friendly and courteous interactions that you had with that particular individual.

This courteous practice while keeping my license clean, it has also kept my auto insurance rates low for all of that time, and has given me a good clean driving record and a good name as a professional chauffeur in the limousine industry. I can be employed as a chauffeur anywhere and immediately with such a good driving record that I have carefully maintained since the spring of 1992, and I have been frequently cold called for recruitment from other limousine companies offering me better pay and/or benefits just so they can have a good, responsible and dependable chauffeur on their team, as all limousine companies ultimately desire to have on their teams. Even the newest and best and most expensive stretched limousine is absolutely worthless without a good and experienced chauffeur to drive it in a very professional manner who always puts their clients and customer service first.

If my courteous interaction with an issuing officer was not quite successful, I will then also try and avoid violations and points on my license by fighting every ticket that I receive in court, whether I was in the wrong or not. The good majority of the time the issuing officer will not show up for the appointed court dates, which has been the majority of my experiences when I go to court with an officer. I even once fought a speeding ticket which I received in Port St. Lucie, Florida, about a two hour drive away from Miami. On that particular court date the issuing officer did actually show up, but it was right around Christmas time. The officer approached me in the hall right outside the courtroom and asked me if I was Mr. Leader, I said yes that I was, and he would then extend his hand to offer me a handshake and tell me Merry Christmas and that he would not be entering the courtroom at the appointed time. I hugged him right away, I thanked him and although I am in no way shape or form gay I would have kissed him if he had allowed me to; even to this very day I truly think it was the best Christmas gift I have ever received from anyone ever and it was probably due to my earlier friendly and courteous interaction that I had with the officer on the I-95 highway. Thank you Mr. Officer Sir, you have been so greatly appreciated.

Aviation has many federally mandated rules and regulations in its books called FAR's that can be dug up if need be, against someone and then those regulations may or may not be used against anyone, at any time especially against any adversary. In my aviation experiences, this has happened to me on several occasions while being employed in aviation, almost similar to what happened when I was working in the gourmet kitchen in Tulsa. I have always thought of this as Ok though, because almost since the start of my aviation career, I've had professional chauffeuring to fall back on, chauffeuring has always come to the immediate rescue for me and my family and in my experience, chauffeuring has never looked down on me, unlike my career in aviation.

Now on the other hand I have also worked for several limousine companies, and I have never to this date been fired from any of them, personality clashes and conflicting egos or not, and there are just as many egos and conflicts in the limousine industry as there are in the aviation industry, maybe even more. For some reason though, those egos and conflicts have never affected my employment status.

Some chauffeurs seem to think they are better than another chauffeur simply because they are assigned to a certain type or different brand of vehicle (to me it is not about the car that you drive but rather the excellent service that you provide and yes, chauffeurs are sometimes assigned to their own personal vehicles to take home with them because it is sometimes less expensive for a limo company to personally assign a responsible driver to his own vehicle rather than to store and house the vehicle somewhere, but that driver must answer his phone at any hour of day or night when the limo company calls you for work or that assigned vehicle can and will quickly be removed from that chauffeur and they may not get that vehicle back for quite some time), or if they are given only a certain type of clientele like strictly VIP's, or even if they own a nice and fancy ipad to digitally display their clients name at the airport greeting area. I've seen a driver or two who have actually dropped and broken their tablets and then get upset with themselves because they do not have a backup sharpie to manually write in a name.

I have also heard of stories about chauffeurs who have stood at the airport greeting area proudly displaying their fancy ipads and tablets not realizing that their batteries had recently died or they forgot to adjust the display settings and their tablet went into sleep mode without them even knowing it, not knowing if their passengers had long ago passed them by as they exited the boarding or customs area.

I once seen this happen with my very own eyes and the chauffeur was quite embarrassed when the actual client walked up to him and asked him to turn on his tablet so that he could see if the name that this chauffeur was supposed to be displaying was his, lo and behold that was the actual client whose name was actually on this chauffeurs tablet that was asking!

This chauffeur probably lost his gratuity for this trip right there and then. I'll happily just stick to my old school sharpie and paper greeting sign; it works just as good as any fancy ipad or tablet that I've ever seen and it cannot fail, unless of course the chauffeur holds the sign upside down or inside out which I have also seen a couple times in my long career.

The airport passenger greeting moment is hard enough as it is because you never actually know the people you're about to meet. It is a nerve wracking time even after decades of experience because you never know who your client is or what type of personality they may or may not have and you will never know how the two personalities of the chauffeur and the client will come together as you basically hold their hand during the long walk out to your limo making idle chit chat, so until that actual moment happens as a chauffeur you are always a little bit on edge until you finally get to shake the hands of your next client and give them a warm and friendly greeting and hopefully get the same in return.

The Seinfeld episode where George Costanza plays like he is the client that the chauffeur was meeting does not help also, because every then and again you always get the wise guy passenger coming out of the secured area acting like they are the actual client but they're really play-ing on the George Costanza role from that old Seinfeld episode. To me it really isn't that funny because you truly don't know how to react to them because you are really truly clueless as to who your client actually is and you truly don't know how to react to that wanna be wise guy trying so very hard to be some type of a comedian. I usually just look them dead in the eye and ask them for the secret password; the actual passengers first name on the reservation. You will usually very quickly know the truth right there and then after that stare down and the wise guy can't give you the proper password. He then usually gets nervous and takes off when it's not funny anymore, running off without even a smile. Somebody somewhere in an airport terminal in this country, even as you read this, is trying to pull off that George Costanza/chauffeur routine and it is no longer funny. To all you funny wise guys out there, the joke is old and so are episodes of Seinfeld, so it's now time for you to find a new joke at the airport terminal.

The truth is however, no experienced chauffeur is better than any other and we as chauffeurs all do the exact same job with the same ultimate outcome; delivering our passengers and clients. There is truly no reason for chauffeurs to be having an ego over one another, but of course there are still are plenty of male egos to go around in this industry. It is a free country after all and we are all free to do and think as we please, even if that thinking doesn't make any sense but to anyone else but ourselves.

Having all of these strong male egos around me in both of these industries; but having ego's only affect me in one of those career industries says a lot to me about the two different industries I've worked for side by side throughout the years as a whole, specifically in regards to my personality and where I am truly called to be for a successful and satisfying career choice.

I have been however, let go as a chauffeur due to a company closure. I have left a limousine company by choice due to an aviation scheduling conflict, and I have also been let go from a company due to a corporate downsizing, in that particular case I was offered the opportunity in a limited partnership. I did not take advantage of that opportunity because of my non-committal type of attitude, even towards chauffeuring. I am who I am however and I am very proud of that fact, with no regrets…ever.

In nearly twenty four years of driving as a chauffeur I have never thought of this line of work as work, I feel more like I'm going to party, or see and do things I've never seen or done before. I also am yet to punch in on a time clock for this field of work, so for that reason I do not have to stare at the second hand of my watch slowly sweeping by for hours on end waiting to punch the time clock out again and finally go home. Quite on the contrary, the time spent driving people around seems to fly right on by when I am working long hours sitting behind the wheel and people watching on South Beach or wherever I may be on that day. The variety of locations I may be at on a daily basis, to me in itself is very exciting. There's truly never a dull moment in chauffeuring, even when you are just waiting for clients.

It also gives me great pleasure in this line of work for me in seeing people enjoying getting excellent service from me; this gives me an extreme satisfaction. I have always loved it when I have taken clients to a long dinner party and when I pick them up after their dinner is over that they are extremely happy and jovial. I really do not know if it is the good service that I have provided for them, or rather just the good alcohol that they have had with their dinner; maybe just simply a combination of both. Whatever the case may be, I am more than certain that if my service to them was anything less than what they had expected, there would be no way that my clients on board could ever be so happy and jovial with lots of singing, laughing and carrying on like big children at a birthday party while on our way back to the drop off point without the excellent service that I provide for them and that they also require and deserve.

I would much rather be put out of my own comfort zone if it would only translate into a client receiving that extra touch of quality service that they would always require and desire. I have many times in this career gone far out of my way to cater to a client so that they may be satisfied, and I have done specific requests that other chauffeurs may not have done, simply to make a client more happy and ultimately satisfied. It truly makes me feel good to provide excellent service to my passengers, whether or not I am to receive a gratuity from them. Tips usually always balance themselves out in the end anyway.

I am very proud to say that in my twenty two plus years of service in the limousine industry, I am yet to receive any type of complaint that have ever been made aware to me from any of my many hundreds or maybe even thousands of paying passengers and clients.

Now that you fully know exactly who I am as an individual person as well as a professional chauffeur, let me begin the stories of my experiences as a chauffeur and continue to share the other parts my life over the past two and a half decades that I can consider interesting and beneficial to all who read this book.

Please continue to enjoy these stories.

CHAPTER THREE
The Birth Of A New Career

Back then in the spring of 1992, when I started my formal training to become a chauffeur for the new company that hired me on, I truly did not appreciate the training I was to receive. In this day and age there is practically no training in the fine art of chauffeuring. Today's first time chauffeurs are simply thrown into a group classroom setting, shown a very cheaply produced training video on the new industry they are about to enter, and are given a crash course on the reading of the paperwork and dealing with the dispatchers, that's all. They are then thrown out in the field to get devoured by all the rich and affluent landsharks and the well to do wolverines of this human world.

Looking back now some twenty three plus years later, I truly now can say that I appreciate the training I had received from this first limousine company that had employed me way back then.

Once I purchased my standard black suit I was then given the standard uniform accessories that we were required to wear for this company, which was an all white multi front pleated tuxedo shirt and a black bow tie; the pleated shirts and bow ties were issued by the limo company to all of their drivers.

The only time that this company was OK with us NOT wearing our standard black uniforms was when we were frequently assigned to chauffeur Cuban migrants whom had only just recently entered the country via the gulfstream current and a raft. This company had a contract with several radio stations where we were responsible for taking the recently arrived Cuban migrants to several different local Miami latino radio stations throughout Miami for a standard on air question and answer interrogation session with the migrants which were then beamed all out to the local Miami Cuban exile community as to what was going on with friends, family and also all of the politic situations going on the communist Island. This was the newest and freshest information that had been available for the Cuban exile community in Miami.

We were told that when we arrived for a pickup at a newly arrived migrants residences, that the migrants were very much intimated by our shiny black sedans with very dark limousine window tints somehow looking like Federales from a Mexican prison, wearing our all black suits and dark aviator style sunglasses, and once we pulled up to their residences to transport them to the nearby radio stations they somehow thought that we were there to lock them up and then deport them back to Cuba. So we were told to simply wear light color Polo shirts and also to try and avoid wearing dark sunglasses except of course for actually driving them and for us to also smile often and to always show a friendly face.

I had never realized how intimidating matching dark sedans and dark sunglasses actually were until this moment. I have never been the type to want to have an intimidating look towards anyone, so pretty much at this moment was when I had decided to stop wearing dark sunglasses unless I absolutely needed to such as when I am flying or when the bright sunlight gives me a headache from a hangover or something like that. As Americans, we usually don't think of this as any sort of intimidation because we're so accustomed to seeing it but these Cuban migrants certainly felt an intimidation factor.

Once the standard chauffeur uniform was issued and all of the proper county licensing was approved by the city and county of Miami, it would then be time for the intensive training to begin.

That training first consisted of me sitting in the right seat of a stretched limousine with an already certified chauffeur with both of us in full uniform; it was simply just for me to observe at first. Today's modern limos mostly do not even have a passenger seat up in the front, rather an area to store excess baggage on airport runs, which for a stretched limousine is a very good idea.

During this first week of training I did not get a paycheck, only sharing in the cash gratuity of the training driver, and only if he wished to share. I, later in the week would be assigned to do everything the regular chauffeur would do except actually drive the limo. I would greet the passengers at their home, their private jet or at the airport arrivals area, or wherever they were at. I would hold the greeting sign at the airport, open and close the car door, hold the umbrella, and brief the passengers as required all while the regular chauffeur just sat back and observed me. I also had to calculate and write up the bill and collect the payment, cash or credit, it was not usually an automatic process as it is mostly today. The regular chauffeur would just observe my performance then he would report back my performance evaluation to the operations department and the driver trainer.

Only when all of my people skills performance criteria were up to standard was I then allowed to go to the next step, which was the actual driving of the limousine. The moment I had been waiting for could not have come sooner. I was excited about my prospect of me being able to be behind the controls of a different type of vehicle than the ones that I had already driven, and one that I would be able to make some money directly off of, and also have a lot of fun while driving it.

Once I passed the personality stage of training, it was then time to learn how to drive the actual stretched limousine. I had to meet the actual director of driver training to do that. He was a very old Caucasian man; I only say this because even back then, it was very rare to see a full blooded Caucasian running small local companies or departments deep in the heart of Miami. He was at least 80 years old, and he looked like he should be on his death bed, but I guess that he must have been driving since the birth of the automobile. I am sure glad that I learned from him though, he taught me to drive well. Even though he was a trainer to chauffeurs, he did not own his own vehicle. He was himself chauffeured into work every day; he was also chauffeured home every day. He lived way out in West Broward County, about 30 miles away from the limo office at Miami International Airport and he lived in a double wide trailer home in a trailer park with his also elderly wife.

My training consisted of me being the actual chauffeur to drive him home for at least three days. These lessons from him were the only actual official driver training lessons that I would actually ever receive from anyone....ever.

This limousine driver training that I was to receive from him was extremely simple however.

He would sit in the back of the limo, fill a champagne flute with water, and place it in a less secure cup holder station rather than the usual flute holder station that you would find inside of a limo. I would then have to drive him the thirty plus miles all the way to his home, to way out west Broward County without spilling a single drop. This drive had a very nice mix of highway driving and Local Street driving to learn on. If I spilled a drop or knocked over the flute, the lesson would be over for that day. I had to do these trips for three consecutive days without knocking over the champagne flute, if I could do that then my chauffeuring lessons would be over and I would have become a certified limousine chauffeur. I was certainly happy that I am a quick learner and I completed the task in the minimum amount of time, because driving to that standard is very time consuming and very stressful especially if someone is judging your driving, and you also get a lot of excessive horn blowing from anxious drivers behind you.

I completely understood the lesson that he was trying to teach me though; that lesson was that a chauffeur's primary duty is to provide a comfortable and luxurious product with a stress free and G force free ride as much as practically possible to his or her passengers, he was teaching me how to deliver that valuable luxury product.

I have never been personally chauffeured around myself, but I do know that a lot of people cannot drive to this standard, and even to this day if I am being driven around by someone and I am feeling too many G forces on my head or on my body, I will soon humbly volunteer myself to take the wheel and ask them politely if I can drive the rest of the way. This is probably my only pet peeve in life. I try to drive my cars like a cruising jumbojet on autopilot; not every chauffeur is like this, I have seen with my very own eyes chauffeurs who drive their limos like they drive their own personal cars. I could never ever do this and Yes, you certainly can say that I am very spoiled this way. Thank you very much Mr. Old Man,

I really do appreciate your lessons that you so patiently taught me; I have truly tried my best to put those valuable lessons to very good use over the subsequent years of my driving career.

When I would get him home finally after what seemed like forever, it was time to take a break and he would invite me into his doublewide and he and his wife would offer me iced tea or lemonade and he would allow me to pick his brain on the limo business. I did this for all of the three days, and he told me a lot of his stories in his many years of chauffeuring. I truly do not remember any of those war stories though, but I do remember him telling me that the reason that they went to that champagne flute mode of training was because the company was paying a lot of dry cleaning bills for complaining clients, because driver's were driving in such a manner that passenger's would spill their drinks on their expensive clothing. He also told me that word was spreading out around town that their passengers could not enjoy having a drink while being driven around town in their vehicles, and that something needed to be critically done to stop that from happening. So the champagne flute drive was the plan that they had finally come up with. That was one lesson that I was taught that made a whole lot of sense to me, and still even to this very day I still drive in this exact manner, although now not as slow but with a lot more finesse. I have since learned that perfect coordination is the precise key to eliminating G forces, not necessarily speed, although speed is also a determining factor.

When I was finished picking his brain for info; usually after about an hour or so, I would then have to drive the limousine the thirty something miles plus back to the base at Miami International airport alone, deadheading as it is called in both of my industries. That drive however was a whole lot less stressful knowing that I didn't have anyone who was literally looking right over my shoulder judging my brand new driving skills, even though I did actually practice what was taught to me.

I do not know if this standard is still set today amongst new limousine companies and their new limo drivers, but I know for me though that this standard will always be set as long as I am able to drive, whether I am driving a limousine or my own personal vehicle. It is not very nice for anyone to get seasick in a moving car, especially passengers paying top dollar for a luxury ride to their final destination.

With all of my newly gained training embedded deep into my brain, it was now time for me to gain my many new experiences as a licensed and qualified limousine chauffeur in Miami and the Beaches.

CHAPTER FOUR
The Fun Begins

Then again; maybe not quite yet.

Right at the start of me qualifying for chauffeuring, I was still not quite ready to have all the fun that experienced chauffeurs have. I guess I was still too young, I had only just turned 23, and I had no experience driving people around town, even though I had just went through all of that exhaustive driver training. The management still needed to feel me out and get to know my driving habits, which is standard procedure for new drivers either a driver being new to a company or new to the industry.

My very first assignments were mainly Saturday morning funerals, weddings, and airport transfers. These are all routine duties for chauffeurs and are usually given to the junior drivers because they are so extremely boring, tips are not usually big, and that same old routine gets awfully old, awfully quick; experienced chauffeurs usually never like the same old routine. These functions are always all the same and hardly ever exciting.

These very routine assignments do not let you get to know the clientele very well, because you spend very little time with the client in these assignments. Airport transfers are usually quick and uneventful. Weddings, even though you are waiting for the client, you hardly ever see them because they are very busy preparing to tie the hitch, and usually you just take them to the reception after the wedding, snap some photos, and then you're done. Funerals are well…you know, funerals. I don't think I need to describe those, you just have to make sure the road escorts are doing their job properly, otherwise you will get smacked T-bone style while going through a red light while you're in the funeral procession.

I've done so many funerals that I have grown to somewhat actually enjoy doing them. It's just another assignment that when all of the other types of assignments are all put together helps me to see the entire cycle of life. I think that chauffeuring is the only job that allows you to see all aspects of life's different stages all at basically the same time, from bachelor and bachelorette parties, baby showers, graduations, to weddings and anniversaries; all of which I have done in my career. Funerals allow me to see the entire cycle of life from the beginning of a family, right down to the end of one's life and in some sort of crazy and funny way, the college assessment test that I had taken years earlier after Pan Am was somewhat correct in its assessment of me because in the years I have learned a lot about the funeral business and I have gotten to meet and know a lot of funeral business bosses and their employees.

The only part I really don't like about funerals is that I tend to get just a little guilty about taking a cash tip from a grieving family. I quickly realize however though, that I have done so many funerals in my career that if I would to have never taken any of those cash tips, my financial situation would probably be a lot different than it has been and more than likely for the worst. So for that reason I have more appreciated receiving those cash tips rather than giving in to that guilt that tells me not to and that feeling is usually put away very quickly. I have also found it kind of funny that those college career assessments must be somewhat correct because they had said that my career should have been in funeral directing. I humbly rejected that result I received but I would end up making a significant amount of money in that business anyway; pay attention to those taking career assessments as they read this.

In the many funerals I've done over the years the most memorable one was one that I just recently did, which was a Haitian funeral in North Miami that had a Mariachi band perform at the burial because the poor old man loved Latin music more than any other form of music. His family honored him well, and all of the guests were all very impressed, and so was I.

I have done so many funerals over the years and I think I can honestly say that it was the best funeral I had ever been to, No...it was by far the best funeral I had ever been to and I have been to so many funerals in my two plus decades of chauffeuring; so many funerals that I think I no longer am terrified of my own eventual demise, hopefully in no time soon though.

When I die family, please have a reggae band playing there for me, thank you.

These regular and routine schedule and assignments for me had now become extremely boring, I had now been doing this for weeks on end, and it was not at all what I had pictured as being a chauffeur. I was patient however, because I knew that things had to change eventually. I now know that for a beginning chauffeur the rookie has to go through a process of having management getting a chance to know the driver's driving habits before they are allowed to chauffeur more higher end clientele and regular clients; this is in an attempt to avoid embarrassing the limousine company with an inexperienced chauffeur making mistakes that only an inexperienced chauffeur can make, which are many.

The first few months for me were not only boring, but they were also extremely uneventful. This is a good thing however for a chauffeur, weeks of uneventful driving for a brand new chauffeur is a bright spot in a new chauffeur's career, as it was for me. I soon would be to receive a commendation for this uneventful driving, which also came due to my no complaints from any of my passenger's. To this very day, I still have that one and only commendation that I have ever received in my driving career.

With this commendation I also received a $50.00 cash award as well as a small promotion. I was asked to now drive the 29 seat passenger mini bus that the company owned. I was told that if I could pass the Commercial Driver's License written exam, they would then allow me to use the company's passenger bus for use in taking the driving exam portion of the CDL test. I happily and humbly agreed. I ran back to the Department of Motor Vehicles to pick up the CDL study guide. I studied it hard for a few days, took the exam and passed both the CDL written exam and the CDL bus driver's passenger endorsement, which now allowed me to take the driving portion of the CDL driving exam.

When it was time to make the appointment for the driving exam, there were no immediate appointments available in the local Miami area. The closest appointments were weeks away, and the company did not want to wait the weeks that the DMV were offering. They needed me to drive that bus right away. After making calls for appointments all over the state, they soon found out that there were no CDL appointments necessary in the city of Key Largo in the Florida Keys, because they had no CDL waiting list. The company asked me if I wanted to take the exam the very next day. I said OK, although to this point I had not yet received any training in driving the bus. However, I had felt very confident in my driving abilities and skills, regardless if I had ever driven that bus before. The company felt that the hour and a half drive down to Key Largo would be sufficient enough for me to learn how to handle the bus, they were very correct. The very next day, me and that old man driving instructor got into that bus and I drove the hour and a half down south to Key Largo. I took the exam and I passed that exam with flying colors. I was now a federally recognized, interstate licensed professional Commercial Driver with passenger and chauffeur endorsements. No training necessary, I could not have been happier and prouder of myself. The old man offered to drive back up to Miami, I said NO. I was way too excited to be chauffeured around for the hour and a half trip back up to Miami, and I needed also to quickly gain experience behind the wheel of that big limo-bus.

It is now required that all CDL's be issued by a fully regulated and licensed driving school. The CDL trainee must also have a licensed instructor's signed endorsement before the driving exam can even be given, which cost new drivers upwards of thousands of dollars. My CDL and passenger endorsement did not cost me a single dime, as a matter of fact; if I remember correctly, I think I got paid very well for it.

After achieving my CDL, the company stepped up the stakes for me. They had gained a little bit of confidence in my driving abilities and people skills, so the next natural progression for me as a chauffeur was to now start driving regular clients and start doing more responsible assignments such as what we call in the industry AS DIRECTED's, or as we label them in the industry...A/D's. This is where you get a little bit more intimate with the clients because you are spending large amounts of time with them. Not just driving them around but actually getting to know their personalities and quirks; doing the clientele favors and honoring their request just as a concierge would do in a top end hotel, except that you are on a much more intimate detail because you are usually right there with the client and not just on a phone with them. As with any usual customer service industry job, this is where and when the real complaints may come in against you and the real criticisms of a chauffeur's personality are truly revealed.

If a certain client does not like or get along with a particular chauffeur, that chauffeur will not get a call back from that particular client; and the limo office will know all about it, and also all the reasons why he or she will not get a call back from that client. This is also where the bulk of gratuities can be made, if a chauffeur plays his cards right with a wealthy client. I've always been a good card player. As a new driver, I felt as if I was ready to take on these brand new challenges in this brand new career.

With these new responsibilities came new experiences and me finding out why limousine companies only give A/D's to the more experienced drivers. I was still only a new driver with a good record in the few short months that I was employed as a chauffeur. Management however was still confident in the skills that they had seen in my skills thus far, that does not mean however that I would not be making rookie mistakes in which I did have plenty of rookie experience and mistakes with. I think every rookie chauffeur will make rookie mistakes, simply because they just don't have the needed experience to get it done right the first time. It's just a matter of making the least amount of mistakes that will least affect your clients.

MY EARLY ERRORS

Just as all early careers begin, there will be mistakes to be made by a professional entering any career. This goes the same way for me and my entry into becoming a professional chauffeur. I had made several early errors that I can still very clearly recall and I will more than happy to share them all with you all.

The key to making early errors in any career is to absolutely minimize the errors, but minimizing is relative and some of the early mistakes that I had made as a chauffeur could have been easily judged as major mistakes by my first limousine employer, but with their help I did get through all of the mistakes to be able to be allowed to successfully continue on in this brand new career for me.

THE FAMILY DINNER

I remember one of my earliest mistakes that affected an affluent family of a client that I had picked up for dinner. This was a family of a very prominent Doctor in South Florida. I had picked the doctor up and his family from a very affluent suburban neighborhood and a very large house, not quite a mansion. They were a family of about eight and I drove them in a ten passenger stretched limousine, including a couple of minor children, not quite teens as yet. They were having some sort of celebration, I don't recall what they were celebrating though, but I do remember having to purchase an expensive bottle of champagne for that trip as per the notes on my reservation sheet.

I had been assigned to take them to Don Shula's steakhouse in the only 18 hole golf course in the Miami suburb of Miami Lakes but that's not where I took them at first though. Instead, I first took them to Don Shula's All American grille in a Miami Lakes shopping center.

Coincidentally, the restaurants are both within the Miami Lakes suburb; which is where the mishap had been born for me. At that time I didn't know there was a difference in the two, but the two are very much different. It is like comparing the national restaurant chain of Joe's crab shack to World famous Joe's Stone Crab on South Beach, I have eaten at both of these excellent establishments and believe me there is no comparison in the two though the names are very similar. The two names sound very much the same but there is a world of difference between the two seafood restaurants; one being a two or three star establishment and affordable and the other is a five star experience as well as very expensive.

What did I know? I hadn't known any better; I was brand new to South Florida and I did not grow up as a fan of Football or the Miami Dolphins and I was still very new to Miami and the name of Don Shula.

I had dropped them off as close as possible to the front of the entrance to the grille; because the restaurant is in a small shopping center, I could not drop them off like a typical limousine would drop off its passenger in typical limousine style; they had to walk a little way to actually get into the restaurant.

Once I dropped the Doctor and his family off, I went ahead and did the typical chauffeur wait routine, found a place to park and chill. Shortly after parking the limo I got a beep on my pager from the limo office with a 911 code which means call the office ASAP, I found a payphone as I had no cellphone then and called the office. The dispatcher informed me that I had taken the Doctor to the wrong restaurant and that I had to go back and take them to the proper restaurant. I rushed right back to the shopping center, picked them up again, and I sincerely and deeply apologized. They were more than OK with the mishap however, they even found it to be somewhat hysterical, simply because of the fact that just as soon as they entered the limo, not only did they pop the champagne bottle, but they also lit the fire and were blazing on the high grade, right there in the back of the limo, minor kids and all. Even back then there was no smoking allowed in the limousines, but like I said earlier, I allow things to happen in my limo that most other chauffeurs would not allow. To me, it is their limo for the time that they are paying for it. They had asked me from the very start of the night if it was OK if they could burn the blunts, I told them it was Ok with me just as long as the solid privacy screen was up and if they made it possible for me to be able to afford a professional detailing of the limo at the end of the night with a nice gratuity from them, which is the standard response to smoking anything in a limo, they said it was OK with them and they would be sure to and they immediately and happily started lighting up.

The only thing they were concerned about after I had picked them up for the second time was that they were going to miss their reservation time at Don Shula's steakhouse, but when we did finally pull up to the Don Shula's steakhouse the maitre'd told them that the grille had already called ahead and told them of my mishap, we were about an hour late to the steakhouse as I can recall.

This was a case in where good ole' weed saved the day for me, because they were extremely giddy and very happy and they never complained, and the dispatchers thought nothing of the mishap. This should have been at least the one complaint in my driving career, but the flexibility with my clients by allowing them to blaze allowed my clients to be happy and satisfied instead of being angry and pissed off, even though I did not properly prepare myself for the job beforehand like a chauffeur is properly supposed to. If they were not smoking the herb however, I can clearly imagine what would have happened if I would have chose to be a very stiff chauffeur and not allow them to light up in the stretch. I'm almost certain that they would have at least called in and complained if only for retaliation for not letting them light up in the limo and I would have more than likely been written up by management for my very rookie mistake and nearly ruining their celebratory evening.

THE LUGGAGE VAN

Another one of my early mistakes was when I was assigned to drive the Detroit Pistons NBA basketball team. Well not the actual basketball team, they had their coach bus for that and I am not as yet licensed to drive a coach bus. I was however assigned to drive an empty luggage van with all of the passenger seats removed for all of the excess luggage that would not fit into the coach, which sometimes happens. Sports teams and the extremely wealthy sometimes have empty luggage vans to hold excess luggage and/or purchases from their extreme international shopping trips, mostly always off of their private jets.

I remember being on the secure tarmac at Miami International Airport and watching the private DC-9 jetliner pull up right next to the motorcoach and my little luggage van. I was impressed that I was there watching all of these professional athletes getting off of their airplane for the very first time. As the luggage van driver it was my duty to just standby and wait until it was found out if I will be needed to transport any excess luggage or not. This particular night I was going to be needed and I loaded up my luggage van with all of the athlete's excess luggage, and I then followed the motor coaches all the way to the Mayfair Hotel in Coconut Grove, which is the capital city of Miami and where the city hall is located.

When we got to the Mayfair Hotel, I pulled my van over to the curbside entrance of the hotel behind the coach and I was so excited to help out, that I rushed out of the van and I somehow locked the keys in the van inside the ignition with the engine running. I had had about thirty pieces of luggage inside the van that all belonged to the athletes and the team support staff. The players and staff were all kool about my error though; they just had to make sure with the front desk that all of the luggage would be brought up to their individual rooms when the van would finally be unlocked and they all left for their rooms.

I called my dispatch office and notified them of the awful situation, but they were no help to me at all. They just told me to somehow get the situation resolved, and as quickly as possible. As the motorcoach pulled off and left me there all alone I remember standing there saying, what the heck am I going to do now!?

I decided to do what I do best when I am faced with a situation…I pounded the pavement. I walked all throughout Coconut Grove looking for I don't know what, maybe a police officer or a fireman. I did not know what I was going to do, but I was going to figure it out. I never saw a police officer, but I eventually did see a fire station in the Grove. It was late at night, and I think all of the firefighters were all sleeping. I did not care, I pounded on the firehouse door to get someone up and I finally got someone to answer. I explained my situation to the fireman that answered the door, but he informed me that they could not help, because they were not allowed to open up locked car doors. I reluctantly walked away and headed back to the hotel, not knowing what I was going to do next.

When I got back to the hotel, I still had not figured out what to do. Soon after however, one of the firefighters from the firehouse showed up with a slimjim. He was told of my situation through the one firefighter that I had spoken too. I was so grateful for him showing up that I could've hugged him. We tried for about twenty minutes to unlock the door of the Ford E-150 passenger van, to no avail. After continuing trying for several more minutes, a rescue vehicle that was dispatched to me from my dispatch office along with one of the dispatchers pulled up with a spare key to the vehicle, they did not tell me they were on the way. I finally opened the door to the van and I felt instant relief; I was so happy that this awful situation was finally over. I remember offering the firefighter the only twenty dollar bill that I had on me. He wouldn't take it however; I was so appreciative of his help that I did finally give him a big hug. I have never hugged a firefighter since or before that situation. This was a very valuable lesson that I learned about chauffeuring that very stressful night and that was to not ever lock the keys in the vehicle again. Ever since that incident, I have always either rolled down the driver side window to at least a height where I can fit my entire arm in to unlock the door if need be, or simply to just not shut the driver's side door completely. It must have been a great idea because this has never happened to me again and I have never again locked a key in a car professionally as a chauffeur or as a CDL driver. I unfortunately have done so privately in my own personal vehicle however.

These two rookie mistakes that I had made were not the only mistakes that I had done early on in my chauffeuring career. I had one other mistake that was bigger than those previous two. This last mistake that I had made actually cost the limo company money for a mistake that was not quite actually my fault but I was ultimately responsible for. This mistake actually took money out of my pocket also.

THE RAP CONCERT

This job was an A/D; I was assigned to pick up a local rap group from the city of Opa Locka which is an inner city suburb of Miami, and take them to the old Miami Arena in the Overtown section of Miami. They were to perform as an opening act for much larger nationally recognized rap groups and artists; I can clearly recall that one of the marquee performers to perform that night was LLcoolJ. I remember simply because I grew up in the same neighborhood as him and he went to the same Andrew Jackson Senior high school as my sister. My sister had told me about this yet unknown Mr. LLcoolJ before he had even released his first album and I tried to get myself in backstage to introduce myself to Mr. CoolJ based on this fact and to also find out if he had known or maybe remembered my younger sister. But my very young and very limited skills as a chauffeur would not yet allow me to possibly get backstage at a major performance like this as yet; as I can very easily do now with over two decades of experience.

I would have to take the group to the concert at the arena, which was in downtown Miami, wait there until the concert was over and return them back to their Opa Locka neighborhood. The minute they got into the limo the weed was burning; although I probably would not have said NO, they did not even ask me as the Doctor and his family had politely asked me. They did however have the knowledge to put up the privacy screen; I figured that they must have been already experienced in the fine art of being chauffeured around town.

We had made several stops throughout the inner city of Miami to pick up I guess what was friends and families, including Little Haiti; all the while that we were driving through the hood, I was performing my chauffeur duties just as if I were driving the Queen of England. I do not think that they liked me treating them like royalty however because they told me that I didn't have to do all of that that I was doing for them, but I saw them as paying passengers and my personal clients just like all of my previous passengers and I continued to proudly do my chauffeurly duties to a very high standard. My high service standards never change based on who I am driving or where I am driving too, all of my paying passengers are all the same to me when I am chauffeuring them around regardless of race, color, creed or lifestyle. My natural love of all people help to keep this very high standard well embedded in me.

Even with all of the trips throughout the inner cities of Miami in a brand new stretched limousine, and with all of the weed smoking in the back, the trip to the arena was pretty much uneventful. I let them all out of the stretch when we finally arrived at the Arena and they all went to enjoy and/or perform in the rap concert, and I patiently waited for their return like any good chauffeur would.

The problem and my very rookie mistake arose on their eventual return to the limo. I was parked right in front of the Miami arena and the arena was packed with people and automobile traffic. I was parked properly on the right hand side of the street with traffic passing by on the left, however that night I broke limo driving rule #1, do not let passengers open the door on the side of oncoming traffic. I was busy talking to some of my passengers in the front of the limo while some of the other passengers were rampaging through the limo, coming and going, in and out. I was up front outside the limo when I saw a small car drive right by the open driver's side passenger door. The car almost made it through but the back bumper of that car just slightly grabbed the open door and pulled it just far enough forward that the passenger door could no longer close.

The car that had just hit my limo just kept right on going, I could not even dream about a car chase through the historic streets of Overtown and I don't think that the driver of that car even knew what they had done anyway. I couldn't believe it; I thought that certainly my short lived career as a chauffeur would now soon enough be over. So much so that I did not even call my dispatch office to inform them of what happened, or even get a police report. I thought that it would be way too much of a mess if I would have called my dispatch office; I just wanted to get this night over with as soon as possible after this unfortunate accident. The police were surely going to be busy enough working a rap concert in Overtown; I just told everyone to get in the limo and that it was time for us to leave. I managed to secure the door as much closed as possible with seatbelts and my own personal belt from off of my suit pants, and I then drove everybody back to all of their inner city residences.

On the way back to the final drop-off point in Opa Locka, after uneventfully driving through all the other inner city neighborhoods, we just so happened to get pulled over by an Opa Locka police officer in his patrol cruiser, what could be worst!? They were all still smoking the weed in the back of the limo, as well as the very visible busted left hand passenger door that was hanging off the side of the limo. As I stated earlier, I am always very kind and polite to law enforcement officers, this case was no different even though my stress levels were now off of the charts. I politely explained to the police officer the whole situation with the busted door simply because I thought that that was the most obvious thing that was wrong with my driving that night and possibly the reason for him pulling me over. After my very long explanation, the only thing that the officer replied back to me was... if that was marijuana that he was smelling. I had immediate flashbacks of that morning in Queens, and my heart started to beat outside of my tuxedo shirt. My brain immediately went into hyperdrive mode because I did not want to go to jail again or lose my hard earned commercial driver's license, and I quickly remembered having this very same conversation with a fellow driver about... if the privacy screen in your limo is up, you as the driver are not responsible for what happens in the back of your limo while you are driving. To this day I do not know if this fact is true or not, but I quickly responded to the officer that I did not know what he was smelling or what was going on in the back; because the privacy screen was all the way up. Somehow, thank God that explanation worked.

I guess that was the right answer, and/or maybe the right response, because the officer let us all go. He did not even look at the damaged door or look in the back of the limo where there were about half a dozen homies from the hood all smoking on the high grade, I'm almost certain they were all extremely nervous sitting in the back of the limo not knowing what was happening between me and the officer and I'm almost certain that they were all getting ready to book on out of there if the back door would have been opened because they were now on their home turf and probably knew exactly where to run to.

I'm sure glad that the officer did not go back there to investigate what he was smelling because it would have been a certain mess that could not have been easily cleaned up. Just like I could have imagined what would have happened after the events with the Doctor and his family. I can also imagine what would have happened if I had decided to give the police officer some sort of bad attitude; it would not have been good for anyone involved in this tense situation, including myself.

I do not know if it was my sparkling personality, or maybe the fact that the officer's shift might have soon been ending and he did not want to get involved with all of the paperwork that would be required to close out this case if he arrested everybody. Whatever may have been his decision to let us go, I most certainly appreciated it, as I'm sure that local rap group appreciated it also. Thank you Mr. Officer, sir.

I immediately dropped the rap group off to where I had picked them up from, I jumped on I-95 to avoid any local police departments and traffic stops and I headed back to the airport to drop off the busted up limo in the garage, there was nobody at the office so early in the morning.

Later on that same morning, I contacted the office and let them know what had happened the night before. They were upset that I did not notify them the moment it happened, but they were happy with me and my 'thinking outside the box' self, because I did not see the reasoning to do such a thing. It was very late at night, the car was running fine, the door was somewhat closed, and all I was doing was taking them home. They came to agree with me and my conclusions and they took it very easy on me, even though I did not follow proper company protocol.

The only negative to this event was that I had to now deplete my $500.00 insurance deductible fund that all drivers were required to have in the event of an accident chargeable to the driver. I had only just recently finished maxing out my funds, which were taken from my paycheck deductions. I do not know why they took my funds though, because I don't even believe they got the insurance company involved because I saw the repairs being done right there in our own garage. That's OK though, I really couldn't complain. It was ultimately my fault like I said earlier. These events this night should have been a career ending event for me or for most other driver's, but for some reason everything went in my direction and nothing negative at all came out of it, and I kept right on chauffeuring with this company. I think the limo company really appreciated the fact that I got the job done, maybe not done right, but done none the less. I got the clients home safely without even a single complaint and this has always been my top priority as a chauffeur; to take good care of my client's accident or not.

These three mistakes early on in my career were the only mistakes that I have made in my entire driving career. I cannot recall making any other mistakes in the two decades that I have been driving since these previous stories. Looking back, I am actually very happy that these mistakes have occurred and that nobody ever got hurt or even complained about the mistakes, as obvious as they were. All in all, I think they have made me a better chauffeur because I have learned from those mistakes and I did not allow them to repeat, it also gave me an eye of what to look for when I am chauffeuring in the future.

Although I had these three early rookie mistakes, they did not in any way affect the way that the company felt about my work performance and they allowed me to keep right on growing in my experiences all while giving me more responsibilities with more high end clients and A/D's. This is when all the fun really began and the juicy limousine stories really started to pile up. These times were truly the start of my long limo career and the true start to the stories that will make this book interesting.

CHAPTER FIVE

Now The Fun Really Begins

I could have or even should have been fired for any one of those early on mistakes or just simply for the combination of all three of the mistakes made together within the same company at approximately the same time, or they could have just simply said that I did not pass my probation period, but the company saw something in me to let my driving career continue to bloom. They chose to let me continue on with my learning and also continued to give me bigger and better responsibilities when it came to me chauffeuring their valuable clients. I truly appreciate what they had done for me, because if they had decided to fire me, I am almost certain that my driving career would not have continued due to my lack of experience and the simple fact that I had been fired as a chauffeur so early on in this brand new endeavor for me.

What limousine company would hire me after all of these little mishaps!?

This book therefore would not have been at all possible to write about without all of the exciting experiences that have happened after these previous stories; I now have many more interesting stories to tell that I will very happily continue to share with you simply because you guys kept me working.

Thank you very much to the management of the old American VIP limousines for not firing me and allowing me the opportunity to benefit from this long twenty three year career that I certainly owe all to you, and the many experiences that I will continue to happily share in this book.

MRS. GRANDMA

Even after all of the early mishaps, the A/D's still continued to roll in for me. I was now getting a little bit of experience and my confidence in dealing with clients started to grow. I started beginning to feel more confident in dealing with high end clients and weekend partiers. One of my earliest weekend partiers I clearly remember simply because she really should not have been considered such as a party person, but she truly was an elderly party animal out on her very own cheetah hunt.

I was assigned one weekend night for an A/D pickup at a house residence in the town of Kendall, which is a southwestern suburb of Miami I was tasked to take the client on an as directed for a three hour minimum which is routine for weekend nights in an 8 passenger stretched limousine.

I arrived at the residence and announced my arrival by knocking on the front door. A somewhat older woman came out of the house and I introduced myself to her as her chauffeur for the evening as I always do. She then proceeded to tell me that she was the one that I would be taking out for that evening and that she would be alone on the trip. I was really surprised to hear this because she was quite older, and she was wearing something that did not amount to more than a simple house dress; she had no fashion sense at all to be partying in Miami, especially for partying on a weekend night and being chauffeured around in a stretched limousine.

I am not the chief of the fashion police though, so who am I to judge?

I opened the rear passenger door for her, and welcomed her onboard of her very own chauffeured limousine, I told her to sit back, relax, and to please enjoy the experience. Once I assumed my driving position up front, I then asked her what the itinerary was going to be for the night. The very first thing that she told me was that it was going to be a very long night. That was because, as she continued to say, was due to the fact that she was very upset at her husband and that she was going to be spending all of his money that evening. OK, I remember saying…I can handle that. She then continued on to tell me that our first stop was going to be a country western bar that was also in the city of Kendall, she gave me the address to the bar and I quickly drove us there. The bar was very close to her home and it was later in the evening with absolutely no vehicle traffic on the road.

As we arrived, I pulled the limo right up to the main entrance of the bar to give her the full red carpet treatment and the experience of a fashionable red carpet arrival. I got out of the limo and I opened the door for her like all chauffeurs are supposed to do. She did not want to rush out, as a matter of fact she politely asked me to come in the back of the limo so that she could speak with me, and I humbly obliged. She continued to tell me that although she was partying; she was also very shy and she continued to confess to me that she did not want to go into the bar alone. I can remember asking her if she was asking me to escort her into the bar. She quickly said yes, and that she not only wanted my chauffeuring services, but she also wanted my companionship as well inside that country western bar.

I told her that it was not permissible for me to go into the bar because it was part of my duty as a chauffeur to stay with the vehicle for security reasons to secure the vehicle and any possessions that clients may have to leave inside the vehicle.

She didn't want to hear that.

She then insisted that I come into the bar with her for just a little while until she settles in with the bar crowd. I continued to tell her not only that I could not but that I also did not want to, I even told her that I was not or have ever been into country and western music or lifestyle. This woman still did not buy that argument and she again insisted, and with this next insistence, she also told me that if I did not come in with her that I would not be receiving a gratuity from her at the end of the night.

I suddenly and abruptly changed my mind and decided that I would comply with her unusual request.

I closed the door with her still inside the back of the limo and I drove the car to where I could safely park it, we then walked into the bar, arm in arm with me in my full tuxedo gear into a country and western bar.

As we walked into the bar I felt all the heavy gleamy eyes in the bar, heavily peering at me because I was in a full black tuxedo and bowtie with my shiny black loafers, everyone else were wearing dungaree jeans, plaid shirts, cowboy boots and hats; country style. I was completely out of my element in these surroundings; I really didn't care however I was doing this for my client and more so for my tip. The folks in the bar did not appreciate me and my spit shined appearance within it; the eyeballs never stopped trying to peer into my soul and things soon after started to get heated in this country and western bar, where I truly hadn't wanted to be.

By this time my client was already enjoying her alcoholic beverages right at the bar while I was standing there beside her, she offered me a drink, but I kindly refused and I reminded her that I was working. She understood that fact and she did not try to convince me to do otherwise. She did however asked me to dance with her, I remember telling her that I do not know how to dance country and western; I can clearly remember her grabbing my hand and pulling me onto the dance floor while she told me that it was going to be easy. I danced with her the best that I could right there on the dance floor amongst all of those wanna be country folk living in the heart of Miami, all while the eyes were zoomed in on us and wondering who in the heck is this black dude was or who in the hell is this couple and what the heck was going on inside our beloved country and western bar.

We danced for a little while, I think that I actually was beginning to enjoy it, but she was much older than me and she did not have the stamina to dance for very long. So we took a break. While we were taking this break is when the trouble started.

A few drunken male patrons approached me as if to start a fight, one of the guys stepped right to me, face to face, nose to nose and his friend stood right behind him as if to be enforcing all that would soon be happening. I've never been known to be anybody's fool, I don't start nothing I can't finish especially a bar room brawl; I'm ugly enough as it is without my face being bashed in by a beer bottle.

I could smell the alcohol perforating from his body is how close he was to me. He didn't say a word, and I stepped to the side as to avoid him. He stepped right back to me, again face to face, nose to nose and also again he didn't say a word. I once again stepped aside in the opposite direction to the last side step. He stepped right back to me, this time our noses touched and he also placed both of his feet, cowboy boots and all, right on top of my shiny black leather loafers as he also stepped hard with both of his feet. I stood right there in front of him and I did not move; only until I could not take his weight on my feet anymore. I forcibly stepped back to remove him and his weight from my shoes and feet, I then turned away and walked over to the bar where my client was enjoying her cocktails. I have always been known to be a lover and not a fighter, and I told her that I would meet her outside at the limo whenever she was ready. She was quite OK with that because the alcohol she already had, already had her ready to socialize with her peers in the bar and I calmly walked out of the bar, without her. If they want me to leave, I will be more than willing and happy to leave, and that would be the end of that confrontation; no words were ever exchanged.

During this confrontation no actions or other physical threats had ever been exchanged, and I of course knew that I was being led like a lamb to the slaughter into a bar fight that I knew I would never win. What this drunken guy did not know was that I was working and that I was completely stone cold sober and that bar fights usually always happens between two or more intoxicated people. I was not going to be stupid and give this drunken patron what he had wanted, then I go to jail and I would really lose my job. I was working and I was actually enjoying the work that I was doing. I was not willing to mess that up for anyone, especially some drunken wanna be country guy in a country western bar in Miami. I have always been a lover and I have never been a fighter. Call me weak and wimpy if you must, but I have no ego when it comes to this type of bullshit; he had all of the ego for me that night. I did not have a problem with that, he could have it all; I'll just take my non-ego having ass back to my limo and go listen to some reggae. That's all I wanted to do in the first place anyway, but it is always in my full intention to give my clients what they want or what they ask for whenever I am at their service.

That is exactly what I did for the next couple of hours or so. I sat in the driver's seat of the limo and listened to my selections of CD's on the limos stereo to pass the time. When my client finally did come out, she was escorted by two intoxicated…should I say, gentlemen? I got out of the limo and assumed my position as to open the door for her, it was not immediately necessary however because the three of them just stood outside the limo and flirtatiously talked, giggled and laughed. I think the guys were attempting to get a free limo ride and whatever else they could hustle up from this drunken old lady. She was really enjoying herself and I was truly happy for her; this should certainly help my gratuity I remember thinking to myself.

After what seemed like forever of all of the flirtatious behavior amongst the three of them, my client finally decided that it was time to leave. I was happy that after all of the begging and pleading that I had overheard, that these two gentlemen were not going to be coming with us. I do think she made the right decision because I was not at all willing to be her chauffeur and her personal police officer all at the same time if these two strange men were allowed to come along with us. I was very much relieved when we did finally drive off without them. I was happy that she was still sober enough to know the difference between what was right and what was wrong, or so I thought.

As we drove off from the country western bar, I asked her what the plans were for the remainder of the evening, she told me that it wasn't nearly over and that she wanted to hangout in the bars of Coconut Grove, not only is Coconut Grove where city hall for Miami is located, but it is also party central with a wide selection of bars and nightclubs. I was surprised with her response because it was very early in the morning already and I was really impressed with her stamina for a more mature woman. As we approached Coconut Grove, we were not quite in the heart of the town center as yet, she asked me to pull the limousine over somewhere. I happily obliged, thinking innocently that she may have wanted to get herself better prepared with her makeup or hair for our next stop on the itinerary.

I pulled over into the nearest empty parking lot and put the transmission in park. She then asked me to come to the back of the limo with her. I innocently and I guess naively obeyed her order and I went out and sat in the back of the limo with her. I really did not expect what was to come next. I can still clearly picture in my head the way she patted the seat next to her as she asked me to come closer to her with that famous 'come hither' look in her eyes. By about this time I finally realized what was going on. I decided to play along with the love game that she had going on in her mind; I came hither and sat right next to her. I can also still remember the awful smells lingering on her body. It was not nice, a combination of alcohol intoxication and personal woman odor is the best I can describe the smell. The odor was a complete turnoff, but I played along anyway; I wanted to try my best to keep my client happy for as long as practically possible for the sake of my tip.

As I came closer to her to sit beside her, she started talking to me in her very own form of pillow talk, smooth, soft and sexy. I really can't remember what she was telling me, it was probably just drunken gibberish, but I can definitely remember her hand going in-between my legs and her caressing and squeezing my inner thighs. This was the beginning of the end of this very awkward scenario for me.

DAMN!!...Don't think of me as some kind of a stuck up snob. I know grandma's need some loving too, but man...why me and why now and why her? I can clearly recall thinking to myself in the back of that limo that morning in the Grove.

I stayed right there and sat next to her for a little while and I let her continue to get her feel on, but when she attempted to kiss me I darted to three seats away. I couldn't bare the torture anymore; the putrid smell of her alcohol intoxication, cigarette smoke, and her dance all night body odor was just too overwhelming for me, and the actual thought of me having sex with her literally made my stomach churn. Sergeant Chubs would not have been able to stand up to the task or her attention at all that morning, even if Sergeant Chubs was forced to; sergeant Chubs had absolutely no interest in her at all. Maybe if Mrs. Grandma took better care of herself, me and sergeant Chubs maybe could have actually stomached the thought. I've certainly driven and seen some very hot grandma's and GMILF's in my long career that I would have been more than happy to give full service and attention to, but this client however was certainly not one of them. It was now time for me to put an end to this awful situation that I had now found myself in.

I sat there in the seats apart from her for a few more minutes as she tried to explain her thought process to me, I didn't say a word to her as she went on and on, no longer in her pillow talk mode, but rather a little bit more assertive tone of voice. The last thing that I can remember her telling me was that I would not be receiving a gratuity if I did not honor all of her requests. I remember saying a simple OK to her, and then leaving the back of the limo. As I assumed my position in the driver's seat as I asked her where would we going to be heading next and she told me "home"...I couldn't be happier. I drove her home back to Kendall, about a twenty minute drive from Coconut Grove and not a word was said during the entire drive back to her home. I didn't mind, I was traumatized. As we arrived to her house I collected the cash for the evening's adventure; she was honest in her words when she told me I would not be receiving a tip, and at least she did not complain to my office. I was Ok with no gratuity from her that night even though I drove her all night long and amongst other things. This was because she gave me a story to tell for the rest of my life, this story to me is priceless and worth all of the hard work I accomplished that evening even without a gratuity.

THE BACHLORETTE PARTY

This last story would have been my first opportunity to actually have sex inside of a limousine, but it certainly would not have been the last time. The next time I was actually offered sex from a client was actually from a group of women, I truly do not know if they were actually serious or not, but they certainly tried.

In my career as a chauffeur I have only actually chauffeured two bachelorette parties, one very recently and the other in the very beginning of my career soon after grandma. Although I have done countless bachelor parties; the one early on bachelorette party was quite a memorable one for me.

I was assigned to pick up the bachelorette from her home right on the beautiful bayside area of what I have always called the Shores of Miami Shores, a very affluent suburb city just immediately north of the city of Miami, and the most eastern section of the village of Miami Shores. As I arrived to pick up the beautiful bachelorette for this night's As Directed assignment, she would inform me that it was going to be a party of about 8 to 10 women in the 10 passenger limo; no men invited. She would then give me the itinerary for the evening; I would be making a few more stops to pick up the other girlfriends and then taking them all to their dinner spot, and then on to club LeBare; which was an all male burlesque nightclub in the city of North Miami Beach.

The pickups of all of the ladies and dinner were all pretty much routine and uneventful, rather boring. All of that would change though when we left LeBare early in the morning very much near closing time of the male burlesque nightclub.

It was very early in the morning and all of the women by this time were severely intoxicated and unashamedly and maybe unknowingly… showing it. Just about all of the women were now flirting with me; I was surprised because none of them had shown absolutely any interest towards me prior to entering the stripclub, just the friendly routine greetings and conversations. I was Ok with that though, I just now had to adjust my personality and turn on the charm in an attempt to make their outing a little more memorable. I did not know exactly where to channel my charm though; there were so many beautiful women to direct it to, this task at hand was certainly going to be overwhelming for me. I had continued to play along with them as I stood at the limo door to let all of the women in; flirting with each one of them as they entered into the limo.

As I stuck my head into the limo to ask for the instructions for the next stop on the itinerary, one of the women grabbed me by the arm and pulled me into the limo, I was thrown onto the floor in the limo and a few of the women groped on me until I was able to pull myself out of the limo. I smiled and continued to play along even though I was somewhat upset about what had just happened, but I did not show it.

I got my instructions to take them to just one single location where they would all depart and then share rides back to the multiple pickup locations that I had originally picked them up from.

As I assumed my driving position, all attention from the women were now solely focused on me. I got every question from these women about my sexuality, from what type of underwear do I wear to how big my package was and how long can I last all the way to what type of women I prefer ethnically; they were all of different ethnicities, I entertained there questions as best I could. Maybe I should not have though.

Somewhere during the ride to the dropoff location, they also begged me to pull the limo over to the side of the road, just as grandma did, so that I could also come to the back of the limo and give them all my own private strip show. They were very much serious, they were so serious that one of the women had reached her outstretched arm through the hole for the privacy window to grab on to me, reaching into my shirt to rub on my chest, and also reaching for Sgt. Chubs, all while I was still driving. I was enjoying all of this attention, but I was also very scared. There would be no circumstance that I would stop this vehicle for anything other than a red light. Being gang raped by these intoxicated women had crossed my mind on several occasions. Again, you can call me wimpy if you must, but I was not at all ready or capable of pleasuring ten women all at the same time.

Maybe they were all just toying with me, but my racing heart and sweating palms certainly were telling me that they weren't toying around. I guess I'll never know.

I finally arrived to the dropping off point as they had requested, un-eventfully and with no harm done. I made sure to hug them all, I got a few kisses and a few of the women still managed to cop a few feels off of me. I was OK with that and I collected my fare and gratuity and we all parted ways with a nice story for me to tell. Although the ladies behaved somewhat badly, it was not the worst that I had seen during a pre wedding party. That would have been when I drove about ten Broward Sheriff's Office sheriff deputies; they got extremely intoxicated and just wanted to start fights by hitting on women in passing cars whether their men were with them or not. They would stick their heads out of the sunroof and spit on the windows or windshields of passing cars when they got rejection from a female, regardless of who was in the car.

This night with these women could have been the second opportunity for me to join the exclusive limo lovers club, but both previous stories were of opposite extremes and I really did not want to deal with either one of those scenarios. My turn would be soon to come though, but why couldn't these scenarios have been a normal and regular situation like the actual first time that I experienced a normal couple becoming members of this exclusive club.

THE PROM

This first time that I actually experienced a couple having sex in my limousine, would have been when I drove a young and rich teenage couple that were attending there high school prom in an upscale well to do community in the city of Fort Lauderdale.

I arrived at the very luxurious home in Fort Lauderdale where I was met outside by the father of the daughter who owned the beautiful home. He told me that I would be taking out his daughter and his daughter's boyfriend to their senior prom. He told me to swipe and imprint his credit card and to leave the total amount open and he would then sign the credit card slip with no dollar amount written on the slip; basically a blank check. He told me to fill out the final dollar amount and to give his daughter the duplicate copy of the finalized credit card slip when the night would be over. He also gave me a nice cash gratuity before the night even began, and he also asked me to take care of his precious daughter. Of course, I agreed to do just that. I remember this trip because getting a blank check from a client rarely ever happens and I cannot even recall ever getting a blank check in my career from any other client again. It is also very rare having just one young couple renting out an entire limousine for themselves for a prom date; it is usually done between several young couples helping to share the cost of the expense of the limo. That however was absolutely no problem for this wealthy family.

I uneventfully took them to the prom and waited until the ceremony was over. After the prom was over, they then asked me to take them on a beachside drive down to Miami Beach. I got on the A1A, the beachside highway and I just drove them down headed towards Miami Beach. As we approached North Miami Beach they told me that they wanted to have a romantic night stroll on the beach, so I pulled over at the fishing pier in Sunny Isles Beach. I drove the limousine right up onto the sand. I opened the door for them to let them out so that they could go and enjoy their romantic walk together.

They did that for the next hour or so, when they returned and it was time to for us to leave, the limo would not drive out of the sand. It was stuck and the drive wheels would just spin in the sand, burying the wheels more and more into the sand. It was time for me to go to work for real. I started scouring the beach for any type of shovel to dig out a ramp for the wheels to catch on to. I found a bunch of wood planks and I filled the hole so the wheels would touch ground and I made a wooden ramp for the limo to drive out of. This whole process took approximately two hours to remedy, but the teenagers did not complain. I think that they were truly enjoying the adventure, and watching me sweat.

By the time I was done it was very early in the morning, close to but not yet sunrise. As we drove off of the beach the solid privacy screen immediately went up, I thought this weird because they had not previously done that at all for the entire night. As I pulled up to the very first red light after leaving the beach, I realized the limo was still moving even though my foot was fully on the brake pedal. My heart skipped a beat; my immediate first thought was that I may have somehow broken the brakes while the limo was sitting wheels deep in the sands. The car seemed to have just kept on moving forward, but not actuality rolling forward. I really thought that something was wrong with the limo, or so I thought.

I soon quickly realized that nothing was wrong with the car, but it was actually the very strong force of this young man repeatedly thrusting himself into the young lady in the back of the limo. I was shocked; I had never experienced any type of force like that inside of a car, and I had not yet experienced anyone having sex in a car while I was driving. I was truly impressed. This young man was making his presence felt by his young girlfriend. The amount of energy he was expending on her was awesome even after the very long night we had just had. He must have been an athlete. I had never felt such a powerful force from a person either before or since this one particular morning. That moment in time was truly a very memorable moment for me.

When I returned them to the house where I had picked them up so many hours earlier, the sun was just coming up and the father was there waiting. In these days there were no such things as cell phones as yet as they had not yet become popular, so he had no idea of what had happened at the beach. I explained to him what had happened at the beach, and he completely understood and accepted the story. I did not charge him for the delay and I gave him his credit card receipt. He also gave me an additional gratuity for my hard work at the beach. I was truly appreciative of that; it was a true workout.

I did however feel pretty awfully guilty about not telling him about the sexcapades that had just happened in the back of that limo on that early morning. I felt guilty because he had asked me earlier to take good care of his daughter while she was under my care, but I may have screwed that up by allowing both of them to explore their sexuality in the back of the limo that early morning. The way that I see it though, is that I did actually take good care of his daughter because I actually did not see the couple having sex, even though I certainly did actually feel them having sex, but there was nothing that I could do about it since I was behind the wheel at the time.

This trusting father did ask me to take good care of his daughter after all, but I do not know if I fully stood up to the task that he had meant for me in taking care of his daughter, because I may have allowed his daughter to do things that were not at all intended for her to happen that night inside of my limo. Oh well, what could I have done differently? Kick them out?

I don't think so.

I have since from that morning; from time to time have wondered what could have happened to that graduating couple, I have always wished them nothing but the best and I at least hope that they're still at least friends.

Being so early in my driving career those were not the only times that I had come across sex in a car. One of the other times I had come across two people comforting each other it weren't as impressive as those last few stories were, rather to me, it was rather quite depressing.

THE NOT SO GOOD DOCTOR

When I had first started with this limousine company, I had noticed one particular chauffeur. He was extremely handsome; I am comfortable saying this because I do not have a gay bone in my body. He was Jamaican-American, tall, and slim, he looked like a taller and lighter version of the famous singer and rock artist Lenny Kravitz, except for the fact that this chauffeur had a shaved head. I thought that he looked exceptional in his long and slim tuxedo suit. I had never up to that point in my life or ever since, been truly impressed by the look of any man; except for maybe that of the dynamic duo that was Miami Vice. He was very impressive to me and we eventually became truly good friends; I even eventually got to meet his very beautiful wife. He was the very first person since I had left my parents home to invite me to go back to Church, as they were both very devout Christians. I never did get a chance to go to an actual church with them though, but I did accept several of their invites for me to attend bible studies that they frequently held in their home and in their friend's homes. I remember going to a few of these Bible studies and I really enjoyed being with them, the fellowship, as well as getting back to knowing and studying the word of the Lord. It was an open invitation for me to finally come back to the Church and the Christian lifestyle that my parents had raised me up in. Unfortunately, it truly wasn't quite yet that time for me to return to Jesus Christ along with the lesson plans that Jesus had for me in my life as yet though.

What was truly impressive about this young man was the car that he drove to the office everyday; it was a brand new 1992 Lexus LS400 sedan. This car had only just debuted in this country a couple of short years earlier and was still very brand new at this time to Americans. People were in awe of this car because they did not yet know this car, and it seemed we were all pretty eager to get to know it better. The chauffeurs were always hanging around that car when it was at the office. I thought this car was truly impressive, both aesthetically and technically. I also thought that it was the most beautiful car that I had ever seen up unto that time, simple elegance both inside and out, and it was also the most impressive man that I had ever seen who was behind the wheel driving that Lexus. My brown eyes would nearly turn green with envy every time that I saw this man and this beautiful machine together.

Never in my life had I ever been jealous of anyone before and never have I been jealous of anyone since, except for what I think was this one particular person and this one limousine story in my life.

He would drive this beautiful brand new Lexus sedan into the office on a daily basis in his well fitted black tuxedo and come and hang out with us regular driver's while we all sat around the office and waited for our next work assignment to come in.

I would always wonder why this rich looking half black and half white Jamaican guy would come over and hang out with us just regular ole' drivers, but all that glitters is not really what it seems I would come to find out as I learned the story behind this very handsome Caribbean chauffeur.

I would later find out, that he was just a regular chauffeur for the company just like the rest of us. Except he was hired out as a private driver, assigned to driving the private car of a certain brain surgeon who had lost his driving privileges due to his over abuse of alcohol beverages while he had been driving on frequent and numerous occasions. He was a convicted drunk driver who still had to make his daily living as a notable brain surgeon.

This chauffeurs one and only job was to chauffeur this doctor around to and from his job at a local hospital in a somewhat suburban city of Miami. The doctor had needed to be driven every day of the week and also when needed on the weekends. This was his only assignment, all day, every day; there were no other assignments for this chauffeur to do. He worked for a weekly salary and a billed gratuity, including overtime for the weekends and evening work.

Not bad...right?

Well, for some odd reason my very handsome Jamaican friend wanted to stop doing this very lucrative assignment for this doctor, he somehow couldn't do this dream job anymore. I never knew exactly why he had stopped wanting to do it and I never asked him why he was no longer interested in doing it. Maybe I truly should have though.

This contract with the doctor was a huge moneymaker for the limo company so they had to keep this assignment going. The company would soon be on the hunt for a replacement driver and the company soon after approached me and asked if I were interested and willing to take over this daily assignment.

Are you kidding me!? An assignment for me to be the lone private driver for a wealthy brain surgeon and drive his brand new private Lexus LS400 luxury sedan all around Miami while also getting paid for it!?

I truly did not believe I could be held up to the high standard that my

Jamaican friend had set, he was so tall, so stylish and just so handsome. His tuxedo seemed to fit him like it was perfectly tailored to his tall slim frame, all I had was a very carefully thrown together thrift store tux. I didn't think I could compare to him, but the company seemed to think so though and I just couldn't say no, even with all of my doubts and all.

I didn't actually believe that they were asking me, but I finally said… Heck Yeah I'll do it!!

If I only I had known what I was getting myself into right at the very beginning of this assignment.

I would now completely understand the phrase of …"All that glitters is certainly not gold".

When I first met the good doctor, he seemed to be very straight forward and straight shooting type of guy. He told me his whole life story right from the beginning, and readily admitted that he was a party animal and a severe alcoholic. He told me that his driver's license was revoked due to all of his arrests for DUI's, but he still had to go to work every day as a reputable brain surgeon. He told me that it was going to be my job to take him to work every day and bring him back home. He also said that I would be responsible for taking him out to dinners at night and evenings out on the town both weeknights and weekends. I agreed to it all.

This was also the time that the doctor had confessed to me that he was openly gay. I had never met anyone to this point in my life that was openly gay, but I was OK with that however because I have never been one to judge anyone for their sexual lifestyle; I for one certainly could not judge with all of my conquests and sexual experiences amounted already at such the very young age of twenty three.

Once the Doc had let everything out on the table, it was now time for me to start a new daily routine with the Doctor. I can still remember the very first day that I had started driving for this doc and the moment when I stepped right into that brand new Lexus sedan to drive it away and the feeling of pure exhilaration and excitement that had come over me in that much of an instant. It was a feeling that I had never felt before, even with experience driving very expensive limousines. The intoxicating smell of the brand new hardly worn out leather interior and all of the sophisticated electronics, this car was just not quite the same as a well used stretched limousine; much better, much more impressive, and a whole lot more sexy!

That routine consisted of me arriving at his West Miami home at around 7am so that we could leave his home at 8am for the approximate one hour morning commute to his office not too far away. I would then drop him off at his hospital office suite and I didn't have to return to his office until his work day was over at usually around 4:30pm.

He gave me his gas card and he told me to be sure to always keep the gas tank on full and then told me to take care of his car and that he would see me later when it was time for me to pick him up. He wished me a good day; he really shouldn't have. That's all I ever had with that car... nothing but very good days.

From the very first day that I was assigned to that job, I quickly noticed all of the attention that car would bring to me. The very first time that I pulled that Lexus into a gas station to get gas for the car, I was in my tuxedo and a beautiful black woman approached me while I was pumping gas, I can still see her face. She told me how good I looked and she handed me her phone number, I hadn't even asked for it. Even though I can clearly remember that she was a fine and beautiful woman, I never used that phone number that she gave me and I never again saw that woman; but that certainly did not stop me from getting to know and meet other beautiful women from all around the city of Miami.

During the time I wasn't with the doctor, I learned that the car was all mine and that no one would ever know the difference. The minute the doctor was dropped off at his office, the tuxedo shirt and bowtie came off and I dressed as if I were Crocket in Miami Vice, dark black T-shirt and black suit jacket Gold medallion and gold chains blinging in the Miami sun. I much preferred that casual style compared to the tuxedo shirt and bowtie. I would then cruise all over South Beach, or wherever the wind blew me to on that particular day and I would talk to and pick up beautiful and sexy young ladies. I was a welled dressed young man, in a well dressed luxury sedan and I was always ready for any action that this combination would bring my way.

The gas tank was always full and I didn't have to pay for any gas at all, I took full advantage of the situation. The doctor loved blasting his air conditioning, but I didn't really think that was cool, no pun intended. I personally liked to roll down all four windows of that luxury sedan and blast the Bose 6-disc CD changer and player multi speaker surround stereo. I had my own personal selection of all types of music for everyone around me and near me to hear, as I would blast my selection of tunes through the streets of Miami and the Beaches or Ocean Drive, or wherever I ended up in that Lexus that day.

I couldn't keep the beautiful women away while I was flaunting in that brand new Lexus LS400 sedan.

I had been driving limos for some months now, but I had never had the attention from women that this car was drawing to me. I think it's because when you are in a stretched limousine, women may know that you are actually working, and that you probably do not own that vehicle you're driving. In that private Lexus sedan however they would have no idea that I was just a regular hard working chauffeur.

Women just wanted to get in that Lexus car and drive away with me, and while we were driving I would of course turn on my charm and then quickly into cheetah mode. If I liked what I was hearing and seeing and I would then eventually conquer my conquests, right there in that doctors Lexus.

This was the first time in my life that I actually realized that women actually like, and are attracted to BLING. There wasn't a descriptive word for that then, but I knew there was something that was attracting all of these women to me that I just couldn't describe. It could not have been my good looks, because I certainly did not get that kind of attention when I got into my little ole' white Hyundai Excel.

I soon learned that women must like to be with a successful looking man, even though they don't know where that success may come from, or even if there is any success at all. I tried very hard to look successful on this assignment; but I truly didn't have any success. I was just an ordinary hourly worker, but they didn't know that, and they certainly didn't care. I didn't care either, because I was enjoying all of these wonderful moments for as long as those moments could have lasted; and moments were all they were. This was because several of the women I drove around actually wanted my contact info for a chance at a second round. Of course I would not give them any, I wouldn't dare show up again to meet them with a beat up old white Hyundai Excel. So, I enjoyed these moments as much and as often as they came to me and then when those moments were over, I went about my business looking for the next conquest to conquer which was never very far away.

My confidence and my ego were exceptionally high at this time in my life, so picking up these women was just too easy for me and I took full advantage of this situation. I pimped out that car for all it was worth; it got me everything I needed for that time in my life… money, women, and free anonymous sex.

When it was time again to pick up the doctor from his office, I would put my tuxedo shirt and bowtie back on and continue to go about my daily routine just as if nothing had ever happened. I would always make sure to keep the car exceptionally clean and smelling like the brand new car that it was, that way the doctor would have absolutely no idea of what I was doing on the inside of his beloved vehicle.

To this very day the good doctor has never known any different about what I've done in his car.

Sorry Doc.

When it was time for the doctor to get off work, I would always make sure to be there on time to pick him up and I always made sure to do everything right to keep this assignment and all the benefits that it bought. I would then usually take him home, where I usually stayed on standby at his house until he decided his evening plans. When he would finally decide what his plans for the evening were I would either go to my own home, or take him out for a night on the town, which was quite frequent.

On the nights that I would take him out, we would always go out with his one main boyfriend. They would usually always have an itinerary such as either to dinner, straight bars, gay bars, gay bathhouses on Miami Beach and nightclubs, concerts and professional sporting events.

Money was certainly no object to the good doctor. Money however was an object and probably also an issue for his boyfriend; his boyfriend was an ordained Catholic priest who served as a priest at a very affluent and prominent Ocean front Catholic Church in a neighboring South Florida city, which I will allow that Church to remain nameless to protect the not so innocent.

These two individuals would party like Rock Stars on New Year's eve night and as if there were no tomorrow, even on weeknights when the doctor had to work the very next morning. We would frequently get home to the doctor's house at 2 or 3 in the morning, and the doctor would be stone cold drunk when we arrived at his home. I would sometimes have to wake him up from the car and carry him inside. I can remember one time I had to put him to bed on his couch on the lower level of his house because his home was a two story home and I was not going to carry him all the way up his stairs to his bedroom.

The doctor would always tell me that I could, and that I should stay the night at his house. This was so that I didn't have to take the almost one hour drive to my home and have to come back so very early in the morning.

I didn't mind driving all the way home at all however, I would drive myself home in my own vehicle at 2 or 3am to get an hour or so sleep, wake up at 6 or 6:30am, take a hot shower, dress back into a nice clean tux shirt, and be headed right back to the doctor's home for my usual daily 7am arrival at his house.

No offense to anyone reading this, but I would much rather do this very crazy schedule than to have to spend the night at a gay man's house by my own choice. Like I said, there's not a gay bone in my body.

I did this hectic schedule quite frequently because I enjoyed the fringe benefits this assignment got for me and a loss of sleep was only secondary to the all the women I was getting to know on a daily basis.

On one of those nights that I had taken the doctor and his boyfriend out on the town, at the end of the evening and before we headed back to the doctors home, we had to stop at the priest's church. He had forgotten something there that he needed for his overnight or weekend stay with the doctor. They were both drunk as usual, but this time was quite different. They started to get intimate right there in the back of that Lexus sedan after we left that Church. They got very intimate, and very audible. I did not see anything, I didn't want to see anything, but I heard just about everything. The sounds that I heard that night have traumatized me forever and I think that I may suffer from PTSD whenever I hear some certain noises; I can never forget those awful sounds. Sometimes certain sounds remind me of that night, that night disgusted me to the core of my soul and I wished right there and then that I had never been assigned to this assignment.

I could not judge those two back there however, because the things that I have done in that car could very easily be rivaled, but at least I did not let them know about it or experience what I was doing like they had just done to me.

I wish they had given me the same option of keeping their behavior private, just as I had given them with my own antics in that car. I guess the Doctor might have thought that since he was directly responsible for my weekly pay and it was his own personal car that it must be OK for him and his boyfriend to do such things in my presence, he was of course correct, but only to a certain extent, but certainly not to that extent.

I have never told anyone about these events in the car that night until now, but I did think about my Jamaican friend and I soon realized that this must of happened to him also and that must have been the reason that he stopped doing this assignment. My Jamaican friend had probably passed judgment on this doctor witnessing something like this. He was a devout and dedicated Christian along with his wife and he probably shared the same or similar stories with her. They probably decided together that this assignment was not proper for his Christian lifestyle and they probably came to a final conclusion that he should no longer do this assignment. Knowing them at that time; it now made perfect sense to me.

This homosexual back seat session wasn't quite enough for me to quit though, the benefits that I was getting I thought by far outweighed this one little torture session they had just put me through. I therefore kept right on doing this same assignment with the doc and his Catholic priest of a boyfriend.

This back seat session and lack of common decency and respect towards me however did now start an idontgiveashititis attitude once again for me and this was near the beginning of the end of what I had thought was going to be a great assignment for me; it somehow was a good assignment, but this back seat event would change all of that.

I continued showing up on time every morning like a good chauffeur is supposed to, and I never looked at him any differently after experiencing that awful night. I also kept right on doing my routine when the doctor was not in the car. This job assignment lasted for probably only a month or so, but it seemed like forever because I was having such a good time. I was always wondering when this dream of a job would all come to an end for me because I knew good things never last for long.

I would have kept on doing this assignment forever if I were allowed to, but I allowed something to happen that I think might have bought it all to an immediate and sudden end.

One afternoon I was driving the good doctor and two of his friends to an afternoon meeting in Coconut Grove, I cannot remember if it was his priest boyfriend or not, but it probably wasn't because I specifically remember them all wearing business suits, which I never saw the priest wear. He was always casual.

While we were driving in the sedan on I-95 southbound, a conversation came up in regards to the disease of AIDS. I can still clearly remember the conversation, someone in the car, it may have been the Doctor, had said that this disease of AIDS could not possibly have come from God. They continued to say that it was because God loves all of his people and that God would not bring such an awful disease to the people that he loves.

The first rule when chauffeuring clientele is to speak only when spoken too, and preferably not at all. I couldn't hold my tongue on this one particular afternoon and I clearly broke that golden rule. Maybe I had gotten too comfortable with this not so good doctor, but I had the confidence in me to speak what was on my mind.

I blurted out loud amongst the good doctor and his two passengers, that God may have bought AIDS to the Earth simply because I believed that God is a sovereign God and God could do whatever he wants to do and he doesn't have anyone to answer to. This very assertive blurt by myself started a very deep religious conversation in that Lexus that afternoon amongst the four of us the whole way to our final destination in the Grove.

This was and still is the biggest NoNo in the chauffeuring industry; obviously I didn't care about what had happened on this day though, because I did actually know this very basic rule.

I guess my idontgiveashititis attitude finally kicked in that one afternoon.

This is the last story that I can remember with the good or not so good doctor, and I don't even remember having any other conversations with any of them after we had left the meeting in the Grove.

The Doctor probably did complain to the head office, it was probably the one and only complaint that I had ever gotten from chauffeuring up until the time of this writing, but I didn't actually hear of it, so officially to me there wasn't any complaint. An actual complaint is when you hear about it from your office and you are asked to do better or something maybe even worst.

It was probably the very first time that I spoke on God's behalf professionally and outside of a Church or Bible group setting, and it did cost me dearly. It certainly would not be the last time that I spoke on God's behalf in a non religious setting and have it cost me financially. I did not mind not driving for the good Doctor anymore, my experiences with him had come and gone and it was now time for me to move on with my new career and gain even more experiences as a chauffeur, that's exactly what I did.

The experiences and the stories were abundant for me and they were also very quick and easy to come to me that very first year of my chauffeuring career.

CHAPTER SIX
Regular And Long Term Clients

I had lost the very lucrative assignment with the doctor, he was a regular as well as also being a long term client, but this limo company had many other regular clients to go around and I was assigned to my good share of them. A few of them I can clearly remember for their very unusual eccentricities.

Before I separately drove these three very different, unique and individual men that I am about to share with you, these three men were already quite known within our office as they were all regular clients and I was pre warned by their previous drivers about what I was about to do for them and that I should also be very careful in what I was about to do for them. But they were very regular clients none the less and they all paid very handsomely to fulfill their regular requirements and needs. Management loved them because they were all very dependable financial income for their bank account. Management allowed them to do whatever they pleased within the limos because they were all cash collect only clients which allowed the company to turn a blind eye. This is where I truly learned to be a professional chauffeur that truly fulfills all of the needs of my clients regardless of what they want or what may happen.

EL GORDO

One of my early clients that I drove on quite a regular basis was this very macho and Latino guy that we in the office had liked to refer to as El Gordo or the fat guy.

Every Friday in the early evenings, the limo company would routinely assign a chauffeur and a stretched limousine to pick El Gordo up at his residence in the little Havana section of Miami, he was very heavy and of central American or Andean decent. I can recall that because he always liked to eat at those higher end nationalities of restaurants Honduran, Peruvian, and Colombian. He was not that much of an old man, but rather relatively young but not at all fashionable due to his extra large size and his non chalant, non caring and free living type of attitude.

I think it was his paydays on Friday's, I don't know this as a fact, but every time that I drove him around I always paid attention to all of the things that he did and I would somehow come to that conclusion in my head. It just seemed that way to me because it was always and only on Fridays, always after business hours and he would spend a whole lot of cash during his regularly scheduled pickup on those Fridays.

He was always alone on these Friday night residential pickups, even in the eight passenger limousine that he was routinely assigned.

He would always go to one of those different expensive sit down restaurant somewhere within the city limits of Miami and usually near Little Havana where he would sit there and eat gourmet ethnic meals all by himself usually for a couple of hours, all while the chauffeur would sit outside of the restaurant and wait for him until he came out after he had his belly full of fine wine and good food.

When he was done with his gourmet feeding and he would stagger out whatever restaurant he chose that Friday evening, it would now be time for whomever the assigned chauffeur was that evening to help him to fulfill his other weekly need, which was to find himself a woman; a temporary woman, not a friend or a girlfriend, not a wife, but rather a lady, a professional lady of the night.

Once he found his way into the car, we would then cruise all the areas where the professional women of the evening would gather. That would usually be to calle ocho in little Havana because it was closest to his residence or we would sometimes go to downtown Miami when he didn't see any of his regular fun loving ladies that night or if he did not see anyone in particular that he had liked the look of on calle ocho that evening.

When he saw a lady that he knew or that he found to be interesting, I would have to stop the vehicle and let them into the limo the same way I would for any other VIP client, so that he could discuss all of the details that the night ahead may entail. They would usually talk for several minutes in the back of the limousine all while I continued to drive around until he would finally make his final decision. If he finally got the deal done that he was looking for. I would then have to drive them to one of the seedy no tell motels in Little Havana or the Hialeah section of Miami where he would spend a couple hours with the lady of his choice for that particular evening all the while the chauffeur sat outside waiting for him to do his do in the motel room.

After his fling I would return the lady to the same spot where we picked her up from, and I would take him back home to his residence in central Miami. This was the only thing we chauffeurs ever did that I've ever heard about with this client. He was well known in our office and the drivers who drove him around would all compare notes on the women, locations and events of the evenings after his dinner. I remember feeling privileged to be able to finally join in the conversations about his adventures; this was because I remember hearing them with no knowledge before I actually got the opportunity to actually drive him myself. I did however only drive him for three or four nights over a few months only, but they were all very adventurous and very memorable moments for me, as illegal as it was. The limousine company obviously did not mind about all of the illegal antics going on with him, because just as I had heard the conversations regarding the fine details of this client's adventure, I am almost certain that management more than likely heard them as well through all of the chauffeurs shared wild stories. Management obviously must have felt this way simply because of all of the large amounts of cash that this very regular client had always bought in on his paydays and sharing his wealth with the chauffeurs and limousine company.

THE RICH CRACKHEAD

There was also another regular client that the company had, that I was forewarned on/or about our probable itinerary before I actually had the opportunity to drive him. I only drove him once but I can clearly remember him because my heart has never raced so fast while driving a client. He also had his own quirky routine and illegal habits. He wasn't on the hunt for illegal sex though, it was not his particular vice, rather he was on the hunt for illegal drugs, and his drug of choice was…crack cocaine.

From the very start he told me what his plans of action were going to be for that afternoon and how he was going to execute those plans. He told me he was in the market to buy all the crack cocaine he could buy at the best prices he could buy it at. I remember him telling me that we would be driving throughout the city of South Miami until he was completely satisfied with all of his drug purchases, and until all of his cash would be exhausted. Like I mentioned earlier, I have never been one to judge and I obliged his request.

As far as I am concerned just as long as you're paying the limo bill and preferably tipping handsomely, the car is all yours to do with as you please; for as long as you're playing your game, and of course for as long as you're paying. Big boys' toy is what I've always called it; you've got to pay to play, and then you can play as you may.

Because he did not fit the mold of a typical drug user or especially a Crackhead, he was a much older gentleman, well dressed, quite tall and lanky and very much Caucasian and he wasn't at all part of the ghetto lifestyle; he mentioned to me that the only way he could ensure that he did not get robbed and that he was getting fair prices for his purchases would be for him to always show his personal weapon of choice to all of the street corner dealers, which was a .357 Magnum handgun, just like the one used by Charleton Heston in his movie roles as Dirty Harry.

It was the biggest gun I had ever seen, he showed it to me before he entered the limousine. He told me that this gun was always going to be in his lap the entire time that I would be driving him. My fellow chauffeurs truly did not warn me about the Magnum part, just the drug purchasing part. He was also kind enough to ask me if this gun taunting jaunt was going to be OK with me. Me, never being one to back down from a challenge, with a nervous grin I told him that if he was fine with it, I would be fine with what we were about to do; so we both drove off into the sunset with both of us ready for whatever action would soon be to come. I remember feeling as if we were now going into the wild, wild, west of some sort of 19th century era of America, with big guns proudly blazing in a horse and carriage.

He was the only client in the back of the ten passenger stretch, and he sat right at the passenger side door with the window fully open. I drove him around in the broad daylight of a sunny afternoon for I what think was a three hour minimum as directed. We made several stops with different corner drug dealers where he made all of his drug purchases; at every stop I would try to sneak a peek back there to watch the transactions going on in the back of my limo. Each time I sneaked a peek that big gun was clearly and plainly visible for all to see, sitting right there in his lap while he doled out his cash and received his goods; just as he told me how it was going to be.

Altogether we probably made around ten different stops all throughout the ghetto street corners of South Miami, that adventure would soon all be over though, uneventfully and with no added drama.

Thank God I made it!

I was incredibly nervous the whole time while driving him around, but I never once lost my cool.

I had always wondered why this person had chose to make his illegal drug purchases this way. I've always believed that it may have been so that he would not have the potential of getting pulled over in his own personal vehicle, and maybe there would be less police attention drawn to a rented stretch limo pulling up to a known drug corner as compared to a regular private vehicle, if that makes any sense at all. Maybe he knew about some laws about limos that I didn't. Whatever the case, he got away with what he was doing that night and probably nights prior and after that night also, I guess you can say he probably knew exactly what he was doing. He was most certainly a professional at his hustle game.

I never again drove for this client because I put it in a written request so as to not drive him again. It was just a little too much excitement for me that one afternoon I think. This is the only time in my career that I had to do a request not to drive someone again simply because I've never in my life particularly liked guns and their close presence, especially in very close proximity to my body. I was just too afraid of the possibility of me winding up with a permanent headache while driving around a crackhead, even if he was a rich Crackhead.

I never did regret driving him around that afternoon though, I considered that assignment just another adventure in my chauffeuring career and another story to share in my life and it gave me a great story to one day tell. I most certainly would not have done that assignment again though, especially with that big ole' pocket cannon of a gun literally sitting right behind my head and with all of the obvious and visible dangers that was closely lurking literally right around each and every corner that we turned in the city of South Miami that afternoon and evening.

THE COCAINE COWBOY

There was another regular customer that the company dealt with on a regular basis and was well known amongst all of the drivers. I was also pre warned about the events that I may or may not have to do with this client. I was also told to collect cash up front from this client and subsequently every three hours thereafter, because this client tended to go on very long and extended multi day jaunts.

But even back then and even to this day, I do not like to collect the fare for A/D's up front; this is for a few good reasons. First, you don't know how much the final bill is going to be until the very end of the job, so you cannot base what your standard gratuity will be based on. Then, I do not like or want to stress my passengers with payments to collect; it is my duty and responsibility to provide my clients with the best possible experience that I can give them…stress free and without hassle and hustle for cash. Thirdly, if you do collect up front even if you know what the total of the final charges are going to be, you are much less likely to receive an additional cash gratuity. People always look for some sort of reason not to give you a cash tip, and they tend to just bolt on outta there if they know they have paid their bill already; when they bolt out of your limo, they are far less likely to dig into their pockets and pull out their hard earned cash that you are out there hustling hard for, because they know the routine of a chauffeur and the fact that you will be standing there with your hand out like a well trained organ monkey. I will be writing more on the subject of tips and tipping later on in this book.

Being the good company man, and chauffeur that I am, I always have to try and balance the two; great customer service and keeping the bosses happy. I had gladly told the company that I would collect up front on the fare and every three hours thereafter just as they had asked me to do, but of course I did not agree with my dispatchers and I was not going about to hassle my client for cash. I decided that I was not going to ask the client for payment up front or even every three hours thereafter and that if he had skipped on the bill at the end of the trip then I would just pay for it out of my own personal paycheck, even if it took me a year to do it.

The way that I saw this decision on my part was a big risk and a gamble for me, but as the saying goes…with no risk, there is no reward. This is what I've always based my cash gratuities on, I give my clients the freedom to do as they wish and this is why I still do not hassle my clients for payment until the very end of the job. I have never to this day had a client skip out on the bill and I think my tips throughout the years have reflected on the fact that I do not hassle my clients for their money.

When I had arrived at this client's home, it was in a Fort Lauderdale suburban city that much resembled an old mid western country town. His house was a modern ranch style mansion, on several acres of land; you certainly would not believe that this guy was a big time drug dealer. He came out of his house and introduced himself to me. He was wearing one of those ten gallon type cowboy hats, cowboy boots, and one of those big cowboy belt buckles, the ideal urban cowboy. Most noticeably about him was not the cowboy getup he was wearing; but rather it was what he was carrying, he was carrying a 1980's style American Tourister type of solid brief case. When I had seen this briefcase in his hands and the fact that I was picking him up at night and well past business hours, I remember thinking to myself that this evening was going to very interesting. Interesting wasn't quite the word to describe the next couple of nights that I would end up spending with this guy.

As he introduced himself to me, I noticed him looking me up and down like as if he was physically checking me out. He actually was, and he also told me that I would do fine for what he was looking for. Except for the fact that he did not like the tuxedo get up that I was wearing.

Right from the start he told me what he was about, he was completely honest and a straight shooter.

He told me quite frankly that he was a drug dealer and that he would be going all around Broward and Dade counties to collect cash from all of his local street dealers throughout the county's and that we would be visiting several nightclubs that he either owned or was partnered in. He asked me if I was Ok with that, and I answered that I sure was. He continued on with this requirement's for me.

He also said that he wanted me to take off the tuxedo shirt that I had on because it did not fit the image that he was looking for. It was a good thing that I loved Miami Vice and Don Johnson's style as Crocket, and it was also a good thing that I had had a lot of experience with the good doctor because that taught me to always wear dark T-shirts underneath my Tuxedo shirt. I took off the tuxedo shirt, and went Miami Vice style with my black T-shirt and suit jacket on with my gold chains and medallion set against that black T-shirt. Yes, he had told me. This is the style that I'm looking for. He was very happy. This however was not all that he was asking for of me this evening. He had other requests of me to fulfill for him before we left for this evenings adventure.

He also told me that he had an unlimited supply of pure cocaine that he wanted to share with me; he said that he wanted a driver that knew how to party and that he didn't want any snobs driving him around. I told him that I knew how to party, but that I had never done cocaine before, which was true, but not fully true. I once was with a woman that had her own supply of cocaine and she also asked me if I wanted to try some, I said no, but she shoved her finger in my mouth that she had just dipped in the powdery white stuff, my entire mouth was numb for what seemed like forever and my tongue has never been the same since. I remember thinking how can anybody ever put this stuff into their brain. That was my only other experience with cocaine use.

I had never really experienced peer pressure before, maybe just a little bit in the days of my then best friend Trefor but I certainly never really considered it peer pressure because it had just come naturally with all that we had done together. This was a completely different situation and I certainly guessed this is what is must truly be like to be pressured. I did not want to lose out on this new experience with this client or the cash that he would potentially bring in for me, but I also did not want to try cocaine. I had heard so many negative things about this drug and I wasn't at all interested in starting, so my brain started to grind, and grind quickly it did. I played the nerd role and told him that I didn't want to do cocaine, but just to be kool and even though I truly didn't want to while I was working, I told him that I would be more than willing to smoke weed if he had it. He sure did, and he had plenty of it too. He gave me a sandwich sized Ziploc bag full of weed and lots of rolling papers, just like that...even before we drove out of his very large gate. Now he was happy and we were saddled up and set for the evenings events. It was just he and I alone in a ten passenger limo as we headed out of his very large property and through his very large ornate iron gates. I had a very good feeling come over me about the evening ahead as we headed out of that big wrought iron gate for the nights brand new adventure ahead.

Our first stops were to several private homes in Broward County where he would go inside and socialize with whoever was in the houses. He did not invite me into any of the houses so I cannot tell you what happened in there. He would usually spend a couple of hours in each house; I guess he was schmoozing with his workers. After he had come out of the first house on the first stop he asked me if I was enjoying the weed, I told him that I was not having any yet because I was driving, he said he didn't care and that he had given me that big bag of weed to smoke right now and not later, while I was with him.

WOW!

He must really like to live dangerously I thought to myself; isn't this the reason that people hire limousine services and drivers for, to avoid being in a vehicle with an intoxicated driver!?

Ok...I had never been a heavy weed smoker rather just a very light sharing and puffing and passing type of guy weed smoker, and I didn't even know how to roll one very well, but I followed my clients request and tried my best to roll one and started to smoke right there and then. I remember thinking to myself who the hell is this person that wants his chauffeur to be blazed right along with him while I'm driving him around, most folks rent limos to prevent this very sort of thing. I didn't argue with him and I followed his orders, that weed would soon be hitting me hard and fast.

I was now driving under the influence of some very strong cannabis and the night was still very young.

I know that there are a few people who are reading this right now and absolutely hating me, I completely understand your anger and your hatred towards me now. I have no excuses for you, but I do have an explanation.

This one moment in my life was not planned and not at all done by my own choosing, but rather a client's personal request. I know that this is not an excuse, and it makes absolutely no sense to do such an idiotic thing, but a client's request is just that, a client's request. It is the nature of this particular business, no matter how bizarre or non-sensical; it is not out of the norm to fulfill a client's request. I certainly do not honor a client's request for my own personal benefit, except for maybe the financial benefit. If you give a client what he or she asks for, they usually will give you what you're out there hustling hard for... money. This was and may still be to this very day be a routine practice and/or special request as hard as that may be to take; I am not going to be naïve and pretend that this practice does not happen even to this very day and I would ask that you the reader also not be so naïve either.

I myself have never had another request like this again and most certainly never again will tolerate any type of request such as this. I will also boldly state however, that I will always live my life with a no regrets type of attitude and that I will always learn from my mistakes as long as God allows me to learn. No one was ever hurt with the living of this story, and I have lived to tell you about it; I am truly sorry.

My confidence that evening was high enough that I could honor this request only because of the prior experience I had had on my New York City to Rhode Island road trip with Trefor so many years earlier.

We had already drove to about three different houses where he had stayed about two hours at each house, it was now about two AM on what I think was a Saturday morning. This is when we went to our first night club; I guess he needed a break from all of his business. I pulled the limo up to the front door of that club VIP style and the door bouncers had opened the rear passenger door for him, I did not have to get out of the limo and do it for him. One of the bouncers then came up to the front window and told me where to park the stretch and that I was free to go inside the night club and drink and do as I please with everything being all on the house. I couldn't believe it. The weed already had me feeling good, but this was going to be even better. I was more than ready and excited to go in.

I went into that night club and I played like a big shot as if I owned that nightclub myself; I think that I was probably actually driving the owner anyway. My ego was as high as the flashing club lights that night. I might as well have owned the place, I was driving the probable owner and he was treating me like high royalty. I walked right up to the bar and ordered my favorite drink at that particular time in my life. A stirred gin martini with a splash of cranberry, and just a dash of orange juice poured into a rocks glass; if it's mixed just right it looks like a nice scotch whiskey. I have never liked the fancy feel of a girly martini glass in my hand and having to do the little martini glass pinky finger thing, so that's the reason why I always have my martini's poured into a manly type of rocks glass. I was allowed to have as many of the cocktails as I could possibly handle. My client had absolutely no worries about me or my partying and me getting high while I was on duty, if you could somehow believe that.

All of these cocktail beverages, right along with all of the strong weed that I was smoking had me flying on cloud nine. I have always been one who has been able to handle my liquor and I kept the martini's flowing, who would or could stop me? I was feeling so good and so high and I was loving my job. What could be better that getting paid big bucks to party, drink, and smoke like a rock star!?

Even though my client was a country cowboy type of guy, this nightclub we were at was basically an Anglo nightclub that played hip hop and rap and all of the popular music at that time, my type of music. I was dancing with all of these beautiful white women as quite a few of them were attracted to me, but I couldn't play with them as I truly wanted to because I was working and I knew that I could be leaving at any moment's notice. It certainly didn't matter to me; I played as much as I could and I was having way too much fun, all while I was working.

I had also already been with the cowboy chauffeuring him around for about 8 hours now and I hadn't yet collected a single dime from him. I also didn't care at all about that; collecting cash from him was nowhere near my mind at this particular time; I was way too busy concentrating on having a good time.

After we eventually left the night club it was back to collecting whatever it was he was collecting from all of these private houses. We had trekked north from central Broward County and we were now in the most northern sections of the county, where he was doing the same routine as he was doing before we entered the night club. This man had plenty of stamina, by this time with the combinations of marijuana and alcohol I was extremely drowsy and was fighting to keep my eyes open. This is when I remembered a trick that I was told by a former chauffeur on how to stay awake when you're drowsy while driving.

This chauffeur had told me about an original energy drink combination prior to what you see on store shelves today; it was the early nineties and energy drinks like Red Bull had not yet been invented. This chauffer had told me to drink plenty of Mountain Dew soda and eat skittles candy all at the same time. He didn't know why it worked but he just said that you should do it because it just worked great. I now know that mountain dew has the highest caffeine level of any soft drink and the concentrated sugar content from the skittles candy are higher than that of any energy drink today and that combination of caffeine and sugar is probably also stronger than any of the energy drinks being produced today. This is basically the same formula for today's Monster, Red Bull and Amp energy drinks; excess caffeine and excess sugar and I had known the effects and benefits well before these drink manufacturers did.

On one of the next long stops, I told my client that I was going to go to a convenience store to purchase something, and he told me that that was going to be fine and that he was going to be at that stop for a couple of hours taking care of business. So off I went to the convenience store to get amped up on caffeine and sugar.

That chauffeur was absolutely correct in his knowledge of this combination of Mountain Dew and sugary skittles candies, this combination worked wonders for me; it was like a newly found charge of electricity running through my already exhausted body. I now felt alive again, even with the cannabis and alcohol still running wildly through my system; I was more than buzzed. I could feel my heart pounding through my chest, and I started to move in hyper mode speed. I truly wish I knew what I had back then what I now know today about typical energy drinks; I would have been more than filthy rich today.

In my opinion, this was the original energy drink combination and I lived off of it back then.

Earlier in that night, soon after the indulgence had begun I had felt like calling it a night because of all the intoxications running throughout my system. Even though I would never have let my client know this fact, I most certainly felt it. But now with this newly found elixir, I had felt fully recharged and I was more than ready to continue on with this awesome adventure; I now had a full strength second wind of life in me.

By the time my client had come out on the last stop in northern Broward, the sun had already began to rise and he told me that he was finished with Broward county and that we would be now headed south to Miami-Dade County.

Our first several stops in Dade County were all on the beach; we started on the north end of the beach and slowly worked our way all the way down to South Beach with multiple long stops along the way where he again took care of his business. Each time we stopped for several hours I had to take power naps, the caffeine and sugar was not quite enough for me to avoid nodding off in the driver's seat of the Limo with the engine running and the cool AC blowing. All the stops had become welcome distractions for me, because I needed those power naps. After about the third or fourth power nap and the wearing off of the weed and liquor I started again to feel like myself again and I soon became no longer drowsy. I did not want to feel like that ever again. I tried my best not to smoke and drink again on this job.

It was OK with my client though, I had already been driving this client for close to 24 hours now, and he knew that I was Kool so the requirement for me to prove my being down for whatever had already been verified by my commitment to do all what he had requested of me.

When the night finally arrived again for the second time around and we were finally in South Beach, I was no longer tired or high. I took him to another night club that night on South Beach but this time I did not go in the night club as I did not want to be tempted with more free alcohol and all of the temptation that the beautiful women would bring to me. So I parked the limo right in front of the club and just stood outside the club and tried to look like someone important as all of the beautiful women strolled by. I was more than happy with just doing that and I did manage to get a few nice conversations with a few beautiful women as I often did when I am people watching and dressed up handsomely like Crockett, even though I hadn't showered in over 24 hours. I stood outside that nightclub for several hours as my client handled his business and I certainly didn't even mind.

People watching on beautiful South Beach, is definitely still one of my most favorite activities to do on South beach, even to this very day; the energy, the beauty of its sites and its visitors and residents, as well as the unique personality of South Beach and all of its beautiful people, has and will always keep me wide awake as well as feeling completely alive whether I'm actually tired or not.

When we finally did leave that night club very early in the wee hours of that morning, he told me that I was doing a great job and that we had just one more stop to make before I would be able to take him back to his plantation style mansion in Broward County and finally call it quits and get some real rest.

That next stop would be in the suburb city of Hialeah, in the most undesirable urban apartment complex that you could imagine. It was the worst property that we had visited in our 30 plus hour jaunt, I was happy that this was going to be our last stop. Before he left the vehicle he told me that I deserved a break after that very long adventure we had been on. He invited me upstairs and told me that upstairs I would be able to choose a woman of my liking without any cost to me for a little bit of relaxation and some adult companionship before we headed north to take him home to his mansion.

With my quick thinking, I played the nerd role once again and I politely refused.

I could not imagine what kind of women he had upstairs in this less than upscale section of Miami, so I told him that I was tired and that I was going to better enjoy another power nap in the car, even though I really wasn't tired anymore. I am not usually a prude, but the looks of the property just gave me a vision of what the women would potentially look like and that vision was not good. I didn't want to take a chance of having to refuse the women and have to disappointingly walk out of the apartment; I might have embarrassed him or his women and thusly ruining my chances of getting a decent tip from him.

I dozed off in the limo until I was awakened by my pager going off with the emergency code 911; I found a payphone and called the company back. It was the limo company calling to find out how I was doing with the client and to make sure that I had collected all the cash that was due for the past 30 some odd hours. I told them that we were doing fine and yes, I had been collecting for the past thirty hours of driving even though I had not been collecting at all as I should have. I was now actually quite nervous because the bill was now extremely high, in the thousands of dollars. When I had made the decision to not collect from this client at the beginning, I had no idea that this trip would be going past thirty hours straight. It was too late now, I was already committed to not collecting from him and I couldn't start bugging him for cash now, so far into the adventure. There was nothing that I could do in this point in time. I just had to completely trust in this client that I had been so close to for such a long time already.

The cowboy had finally come out of the Hialeah apartment well into Sunday morning and it was finally time to take him back to his house. I had still not yet bothered him about the large bill that was still due, but I still did not worry. When we finally did get back to his house and entered through his large ornate iron gates; I tallied up the bill just as he asked me what the charges were going to be for the past couple of evenings. Like I said, the bill was in the thousands of dollars and I tallied the bill with my gratuity already in it. I cannot remember how much the bill was, but it was extremely large.

When I told him how much the bill was, he opened up that large 80's style briefcase that I had noticed a day and a half earlier and the one that he had been dragging around with him for the past couple of days; my eyes became as large as the coconuts hanging from the trees on his circular driveway inside his yard. What I had seen in that old briefcase was two large bags of white powder, what looked like a silver 9mm handgun, and wads and wads of hard green cash. I don't know how much cash was there, but if I had to guess I would say well in excess of ten thousand dollars. Although the adventure was now just about over, that could not stop me from feeling like a character in a Miami Vice episode in that very same moment. He unrolled one of the wads that had been rolled up in a tight circle wrapped together with a rubberband and he counted out the cash for the amount that I had told him. I had given him the amount that was due with my gratuity already included in the bill, but he continued to count out even more cash even after he had reached the amount I had just told him.

Cha-ching, my risk had now been greatly rewarded. This was my gratuity on top of my gratuity, I was most certainly grateful for every single dollar. I had worked long and hard for it. That wasn't the only gratuity that I received from him however, since I was not a real weed smoker and he did not ask for his Ziploc bag of weed back, I decided that I would take the bag to some "acquaintances" of mine from the hood and make some sort of a deal for the remaining amount of weed. I didn't hesitate at all with the first offer I was given and I thought of it as the best offer that they could give me. I can still remember the exact amount…$140. I didn't know the true value of the Ziploc bag full of weed and they probably profited off of me and my gift, but I didn't care, I seen the extra cash as absolutely free money as well as icing on the cake for me and I quickly and very happily accepted the cash offer and I happily went along on my happy way.

I was so relieved that I could now face my limo company with my head up and hand them over all of that cash. I drove right on back to the office and handed over all that I had owed them as well as a nice tip out to my dispatcher as was customary procedure back then and probably still is today at some limo company's. I remember hearing the dispatcher for the first time ever telling me that I did a great job. I certainly felt that I did.

I cannot remember how much gratuity I had received from him for that 36 hour adventure, but I can certainly remember me taking the next four days off so that I could finally get some sleep and recoup my energy and also to spend all the hard earned cash that I had earned in the previous thirty six hours.

These are the requirements of some frequent clients of a limousine service, if you cannot appreciate and honor a client's specific request such as driving for 36 hours straight and/or allowing him to take care of his business regardless of what that business may be. This business may not be the business for you, and you should not even think about entering it. It is a very high customer demanding and customer service industry that you must keep an open mind to the things that you will be seeing and doing as a chauffeur.

THE COMPUTER GUY

This gentleman was the first client that I had for a pre arranged seven day one week long block of time.

He was an extremely wealthy bachelor who also lived alone in a very large mansion in a gated suburban city near Fort Lauderdale.

When I first arrived to pick him up on the first day, he very nicely and politely introduced himself to me and he also gave me the game plan for the upcoming week. He also told me the story of his life thus far.

He told me that he was a computer engineer and that he had made his fortune by designing and building computer systems and networks. At that time in my life I knew absolutely nothing about computers so I did not pay attention to his work description and details that he was describing to me.

I remember him telling me that he was going to be meeting a woman that he had never met before, but had known her from over a computer network and that he really did not know her at all except through computer coded conversations they had shared together. I thought this as extremely unusual, but I as you now know, am not one to judge. He told me that the woman would be flying in from Texas along with her minor children and that it was going to be my job to chauffeur himself, her and her children around all of the South Florida attractions. They had never been to South Florida before and he had wanted to impress her. I found this assignment to be very exciting and I was fully looking forward to this upcoming challenge and adventure.

The first thing I did with the computer guy was to go to Fort Lauderdale airport to pick up his visiting houseguests. He went into the terminal to meet and greet them as I circled around the airport terminal because there were no cellular phones at that time. When they came out of the airport terminal I was greeted to the very beautiful young lady and her two pre teen children. She was about twenty years younger than my client and very beautiful. I got them and their luggage all into the limo and we headed out to experience our upcoming week of adventure. The first stop was to his mansion of a home, where everyone would settle in to their new surroundings. I would sit in the limo outside of his home and be on standby until I was released for the evening and I would then have to be back the next morning to chauffeur them around South Florida.

During that week I remember taking them to many different restaurants for lunch and dinner, I also remember taking them to water parks and more specifically I remember taking them to Miami seaquarium. My client had always paid for me to enter the venues for the main purpose of helping to entertain the children. I had truly appreciated that because most of the venues I had never been to before and I had not been to the Miami Seaquarium since my parents had taken me there as a child so many years earlier on one of our many Miami visits.

What I most specifically remember about this week is that on one particular night, the couple had wanted to become closer and more intimate with each other, so my client had asked me if I was willing to take the children out to the movies, by myself, so that he could get closer to his new ladyfriend.

Being the client pleaser that you now know that I am, I could not say NO, and I happily obliged.

They gave me enough cash for movie tickets and then some and I then spent the next several hours alone with the children driving them to the mall and to the movies; also watching what If I remember correctly were two different movies that we enjoyed together, I also took them to dinner. These kids probably felt like billionaires being chauffeured around alone without their parents, and having a tuxedo clad driver paying for all of their needs for that evening. I truly appreciated the trust and respect that was given me in the handling and responsibility of caring for these two young children, even if it was just for a short time. Even though at this time I was a father, I had really never been a father. But my client and his ladyfriend had seen enough in me to honor me with that mighty responsibility if only for a night.

Another specific thing that I can recall with these clients is that I had taken them to several high end lunch and dinner spots all throughout South Florida and each time they had spent several hours dining as is quite ordinary with fine dining and limousines. But I recall what I think was the very last night that I had spent with them, they had wanted to do something different and not so fancy but just casual. They wanted to do their fine dining that particular evening at their local Taco Bell restaurant. I took them to their local Taco Bell; there is absolutely nothing wrong with dining at Taco Bell. I myself love Taco Bell and I often eat there but I, like the rest of us, have always considered it to be FAST food. However on this particular evening they dined inside that Taco Bell for over three hours. I can understand an hour dining there, but three straight hours? Five people dining at a Taco Bell for over three straight hours, I was totally amazed. So amazed that when they finally exited that Taco Bell, I can clearly remember me telling my client that I have had many clients on dinner receptions that ran on for hours on end, but never have I had a client that spent several hours dining at a Taco Bell. They all just laughed, they did not care about that fact, they were enjoying themselves and enjoying their evening together even if it was just at Taco Bell. This was a truly content family, even if they were not a true family as yet, because of this I also think of them often and what kind of situation they must be in today.

The next day this assignment would be over and it would be time for my client to ante up on the weeklong bill; that for some odd reason, I was NOT pressed to collect like I was for the cowboy. He must have had some type of connection with the limo company. I can still clearly remember the amount of the bill; it was for thirty five hundred dollars. It was a five hundred dollar daily fee which included everything including my gratuity. Mr. Computer guy counted out thirty five one hundred dollar bills and just like the cowboy, continued counting on even after he had reached the correct amount, he then continued to count out another five one hundred dollar bills. Again, my gratuity on top of my gratuity, I was more than pleased, and I remember taking another several days off after that assignment to recoup from all of that hard work and babysitting and to spend all of that hard earned cash. This is the flexibility that I have always loved about being a chauffeur and being self employed, you can always vacation and party at any time after you have worked hard and your cash is right from an unexpected cash tip. There is no other job that I know of where you can do this.

While I am on the subject of gratuities, even though this was a very large gratuity for me, it was not the best that I have ever received percentage wise, to explain better I will now talk on the subject of....

...TIPS

These two previous stories have shown what type of gratuities you might expect to receive as a chauffeur, and no doubt these were excellent examples of great tips. But I did however have to work very hard for those tips; I went way above and beyond the necessary call of duty on both of those two previous chauffeur stories. Even though those were very good tips, tips don't always come like that. Tips are a good indication that you have provided an excellent service for your passengers. Clients are always thinking and plotting on a way to get out of paying a decent tip, so you must always make sure that all of yours bases are covered to at least get a shot at getting a decent tip. Sometimes you can go above and beyond the call of duty for a client and receive nothing but a middle finger from that client for whatever reason they throw your way. Other times you can do just about nothing at all and still receive an awesome and unexpected tip. It is definitely a crap shoot when it comes to tipping while you're chauffeuring, unless of course it is a prearranged or a corporate billed tip that you're working for and don't have to collect the fare.

Although these corporate clients know that the bill is more than likely billed you still always get those individual corporate clients who will always ask you if the tip is already included; I think you have travelled enough to already know the answer to this question sir or mam. This is what I always think to myself when I hear this. We all know that you just don't want to simply just walk away without giving a tip. I always prefer a client who does not tip to just simply walk away then to ask us if the tip is already included in the bill, because if you don't already know the answer to this, now you do, yes it is already included but it's not much at all and it's not always the standard twenty percent gratuity as it is in the rest of the service industry!

Gratuities billed to a corporate account are more of a courteous and professional standard by the corporations and do not actually reflect the actual performance of the chauffeur as it directly relates to the actual client using our services. I have always believed that performance should be measured by the actual cash gratuity given to the chauffeur by the actual client and for putting up with whatever was thrown at the driver on that particular day such as large bags and long waits at the airport or hotel.

I have however received so many cash tips over the many years of chauffeuring that I have actually learned to distinguish the different sounds that different dollar bill denominations can make as the bills are being shuffled around by a client as they are being readied to be handed over to me after a long trip. I consider it to be a great sound especially if it's a really crisp sound and when I hear it I know it's going to be a good day at an end of a trip.

When it comes to tipping, I also never look at what amount of cash is being placed into my palms by my client so as to not pre judge them while they're standing right there in front of me, I will always wait until the final transaction has long been done and over and that's when I'll finally look to see what they have given me then I'll be able to judge my client accordingly; and yes all clients get judged on their tipping whether it matters to them or not. However we chauffeurs will always remember your name and the next time we get your reservation we will then know if we will want to chauffeur you again or just pawn you off to another unknowing driver for them to also get that valuable experience of a bad tipper. On the other hand, if you are an excellent tipper an experienced driver will always seek you out to provide you with his or hers most excellent service; this is the actual definition of tips, To Insure Prompt Service.

A lot of times after I have shoved the cash tip into my pocket, looked the client in their eye, shook their hand and said thank you very much, then later on pull out the cash to see what I had received. Quite often I have been very disappointed in what I pull out. Other times though, I have been actually quite surprised by getting way more than I had actually expected and I would then feel guilty after that because I would now feel that I had not done a lot more for them, like maybe giving them a great big old hug and kiss. This is truly how you feel when you get a very large and unexpected cash tip from an excellent client.

People and how they tip can be a very funny thing and people can also be studied when it comes to their tipping habits as such I have done over the years. When I first started driving a bus I would notice that some of the other drivers would always have a tip jar in the front of the bus. I had always looked down on this practice solely because I have always worked for luxury Transportation Company's and I have never considered tip jars to be luxurious. However, later on in my career when I would become desperate for more cash, I had a sudden change of heart when it came to tip jars. I started to use them when I worked for a certain luxury hotel shuttle on Sunny Isles Beach with the namesake of a certain American multi billionaire, shuttling his guests between several different south Florida locations. These shuttles were totally free and provided by the hotel as a courtesy for its guests; a very expensive courtesy service I tell ya'. No other hotel that I know of in South Florida provides that many miles long free shuttle service to all of its guests. Even with a completely free round trip shuttle saving guests lots of Uber and cab money, these people still refuse to tip. I couldn't be out there driving all day and into the night and not receive a decent cash tip, so I decided that I needed to place a tip jar up front. The tipping would get a little bit better after I did this, but it would still be sometime more before I actually realized that people would tip much more if I started out the day with about ten or fifteen single dollar bills of my own money stuffed into the tip jar; the tipping would only now finally be substantial for an eight hour shuttle shift. People won't tip unless they see other people tip first; funny!

Tipping, or lack thereof for that matter, will always allow you to see people, more so clients, for who they really are and is a very good gauge to see peoples real persona especially when they are in the public eye and claim to be very caring individuals for the people that they may eventually be serving, such as politicians. I had not experienced this next story myself but it was shared with me from another professional chauffeur as we waited and chatted together during our multi vehicle assignment.

This fellow chauffeur had shared with me a story where he was on a sixteen hour long assignment to chauffeur around a visiting politician who was running for a major Florida political office. During the course of that day, the politician had to visit many stops, to do as politicians do, kiss babies and shake hands and brown their noses a little. Of those visits during the course of the entire day, they had visited five different restaurants where this politician had eaten some large amounts of food during all of the five restaurant visits. This chauffeur had become very surprised that after the fifth and final restaurant visit that he had not eaten during the entire course of the day and that this famous politician had not even offered the chauffeur a simple meal or even a simple cup of coffee during any of their many stops that day. This chauffeur had thought of this as extremely hilarious every time he had seen this politician on television speaking of how extremely caring he is for the common Floridian. This chauffeur had actually witnessed the truth about this politician and if this politician had truly been a caring individual; It would have easily been seen during this sixteen hour tour of South Florida. He had also not received a cash tip at the end of the very long day, but he didn't care though and thought of the experience as priceless to know the truth of this long talking politician that very few people had truly known about and he would of course vote accordingly based on the truth that only he actually knew about.

It is also very disconcerting and difficult to deal with non tipping clients especially when you take them on long shopping trips and they return with hundreds or thousands of dollars worth of purchased goods and they find it hard to give you a single dollar bill just to show their gratitude for the time you've spent waiting on them. You can also feel that way when you overhear the conversations of some executives and they're discussing their multimillion dollar deals, or speaking about their kids half a million dollar college tuition, or their discussing what a bargain the thousand dollar meal they just had was, and the steal they got on that five hundred dollar bottle of wine, or even when you transport a busload of $25,000 per plate political donors to a political dinner; but they can't show you the courtesy of even a single dollar bill after waiting on them hand and foot. Even if the tip is already pre-billed, it is still hard to accept if they do not give you even a small amount of cash for a tip. It is understandable though, they already know that we are tipped. These are just certain types of ways that a chauffeur can feel and sometimes expect in regards to tipping, or lack thereof once you are an experienced chauffeur.

Tips may not always be just cash though; I have received other types of tips that I have appreciated just as much as cash itself. Over the years I have been tipped a Kobe steak and Lobster dinner, I've been tipped a couple of lap dances at strip clubs. I have been also tipped many bottles of wine and liquor as well as several cigars over the years, even including an actual authentic Cohiba Cuban habanos cigar. I of course enjoyed every single centimeter of that wonderful cigar. I have once also been tipped a pair of box seats at a professional sporting event which I took my children to in which we all greatly appreciated being there. I also greatly enjoyed knowing the fact that I myself could probably never myself could never have afforded such great front row seats at a professional sporting event.

I will however share with you a couple of good examples of thoughtful and unexpected great tips that were not always cold hard cash that I have experienced over the years of my chauffeuring career.

The first example of a very big tipper only happened very recently to the writing of this book. I had received a call from my dispatch office while I was just hanging around South Beach in my assigned Ford passenger van. The call was for a pickup at a very exclusive gourmet restaurant on South Beach, it was only going to be a dropoff up to the exclusive St. Regis Luxury Hotel and Resort in Bal Harbour, only about a fifteen minutes drive away from the very upscale restaurant. The passengers had already been dropped off earlier by another chauffeur, but I was assigned to just bring them back to the hotel. It was already a prearranged and pre billed pre tipped do not collect job. No collection or tipping was required of the client.

When I arrived at the restaurant, I exited the van and made a greeting sign for my passengers while I waited for them to finish their dinner. When the man whose name was on the sign came out and approached me after recognizing his name on the sign board. He introduced himself to me and he told me that he had truly appreciated the fact that I had come for him, which was truly unnecessary because I appreciated him calling on our service more than he could appreciate me being there for him. But he was sincere because he took out his billfold and handed me over seventy five dollars in cash, he also asked me if that the tip was OK. I said absolutely. This was a great and unnecessary and unexpected tip, the tip was much greater than even the bill, because the fare for the ride was only for about sixty five dollars, with about an eight dollar gratuity included. This tip I had just received was a 100% plus gratuity.

Never had I received a tip like this before and I must say that percentage wise it was the best tip that I had ever received, and it was completely unexpected.

I also specifically remember this gentleman because he was the patriarch of a very large family of about eight or nine people including at least two children who were all in the van, they were all visiting from New York City. This man was funny to me because I can clearly remember that just as soon as everyone was in the van and we drove off, he very non chalantly blurted out to his family… "wow… that was an excellent meal, but who's ready for a number three from Mickey D's!?"

I nearly pissed my pants trying so hard to refrain from laughing my guts out while I was driving this family, everyone else in the van were laughing out loud also. I couldn't believe what he had just said.

The restaurant I had picked them up from is one the most popular restaurant's in Miami Beach's South Beach district and very difficult to get reservations for. Without him even knowing it, he had just let me know and realize, with that one hilarious statement, that all of these fancy dancy restaurants are just only that…fancy, and maybe not really satisfying at all. It made me realize that people may go there, probably only just to say that they've been there and not necessarily to get a satisfying and comforting meal. This was a great head's up statement for me to hear, just in case I ever have the opportunity to frequent these great gourmet restaurants. He gave me more than just a great cash tip; he also gave me a great life tip that I may one day value and appreciate. He was a very down to earth client who all chauffeurs can definitely appreciate. I won't soon forget him, not just only for the generous cash tip, but also for the lifestyle tip. Thank you very much, mister number three sir.

I did not take them to McDonald's that night as he had jokingly suggested, but I did hear him say that he was going to hang out at the bar at the St. Regis when he got back, I don't know if he ordered anything from the kitchen however. I really hope he did, he deserves to be satisfied.

Another great tip that I truly didn't realize was a great tip was back in the early days of my driving career

I had picked up an executive from Miami International Airport, he was traveling alone. I was taking him to CocoWalk in Coconut Grove; this is a shopping and dining center in the heart of Coconut Grove.

He told me that he was a restaurant executive who was here to oversee the establishing of a new type of restaurant concept in Miami. He said that the new restaurant was going to be a restaurant that was solely based on making their very own cheesecakes in house and selling them in the restaurant. He told me that the name of the restaurant was going to be called…"The Cheesecake Factory"; I laughed on the inside.

I couldn't believe what he was saying to me; I could have and maybe I should have laughed at him on the outside as well. I would have, if it weren't for the fact that I am too much of a professional.

Cheesecake…? Factory…? For dinner….? Seriously….!?

I really don't think so, I thought to myself as I laughed out loud internally.

I remember thinking to myself, who in the world would eat dinner at some… "Cheesecake Factory"!?

I swallowed my giggles, and I dropped him off at his then under construction restaurant in the Grove.

He did not give me a cash tip, he really didn't have to, corporate executives are usually always pre billed clients. However, he did give me his business card and on the back he had written a note that I could receive two free meals from the restaurant when they were finally opened. Needless to say, I didn't believe in that restaurant concept. I would eventually lose that business card and never get those two free meals. I have since always highly regretted that. It was only in more recent times and over a decade and a half after that that I finally realized how wonderful The Cheesecake Factory actually is. Over the years I have spent maybe close to thousands of dollars at the Cheesecake Factory. It is now one of my most favorite restaurant chains, with its extensive menu choices and because I always leave there completely satisfied without spending a huge fortune. I truly wish I could get that business card and offer back. I now realize that that personalized business card could have easily been worth around eighty bucks to me and Just like Mr. Mickey D's in the passenger van, also for around a fifteen minutes transfer. This was why this could have been such a great tip for me but yet still a very memorable one.

I thank you very much and I apologize for not believing in you and your restaurant Mr. Cheesecake Factory Executive sir.

Another great tip that I had received was actually not a tip at all and it was very much unexpected, this so called tip was probably the greatest tip that I have ever received for all my time spent as a chauffeur. I will let you the reader, decide if this tip can actually be considered a tip or rather something other.

I had just finished up a late night job and I was extremely hungry as is usually the case for me, this is because I do not eat either before I drive or during an assignment. This helps me to stay wide awake and alert on the road; I have learned over the years that after I eat my digestion after a meal tends to help me get extremely drowsy even if I am already well rested, but if I do not eat I will become extremely hungry but I will not get this sleepy problem. So when I get off of a long job the dinner bell rings loudly in my head and it would now be time for me to chow down to my heart's content, no matter what the time of the day or night.

I went into a Denny's the "America's Diner" chain restaurant that was right around the corner from the Limo office at Miami International Airport for a late night early morning meal; even to this very day Denny's is still a popular hangout for myself because they are just about the only place in Miami that stays open all twenty four hours, and they offer a diner a wide range of choices that I can eat and I usually leave there quite satisfied, not this particular time though.

I sat at the counter as I always do when I am eating alone. This particular time at the Denny's counter was quite different from all of the other times I had frequented Denny's. I had noticed at somewhere around the ten minute mark that I had been there, that I had not been offered any type of services; I started to watch the big clock on the wall. I sat there, and sat there, and sat there for what had wound up to becoming an entire hour without even being offered a glass of water, an introduction from the waitress, or even a menu. This couldn't be real I remember thinking to myself as I calmly walked out.

I was way too tired to fight and argue with the Black Latina waitress that was working behind the counter that night, so I just simply walked out of the restaurant without even saying a word to her or anyone else in the restaurant that early morning. I was way too hungry and way too tired to be shocked, I didn't care about any possible explanations from her or any of her management types in the restaurant; I would just shrug off this horrible experience as an experience and just go on about with my life. I was most upset about the fact that I would be going to bed hungry at this very early hour of the morning, when I got home that early morning I grabbed a snack from my pantry and I went straight to bed.

I know that this is an extreme example of my passivity, but I just didn't know what else to do and I certainly did not want to fight this beautiful dark skinned Latina woman that was behind the counter. As the long minutes went on by, it just became much more difficult for me to speak up about this inconvenience.

If there could ever be a more secure example of my testimony that I am truly a lover and not a fighter, this would be it. I simply had to pray about this awful situation that had just happened to me and let God handle the rest while patiently awaiting an outcome; which is exactly what had happened here. As a true believer and follower of Jesus Christ you must ask yourself what you would have done in this exact same situation or something similar to it.

As time went right on by and this moment in my life was far and fastly fleeing behind me. Some years or months later, I happened to watch a news story on my local television news station. This news story was about a couple of black Federal Police officers in the Washington DC area who were also consistently being denied service at their local Denny's restaurant there up North. Being the undercover officer's that they were, they set up a sting operation to try and confirm what they had been experiencing at Denny's.

This complete lack of service to a certain group of people was soon found out to be confirmed and true due to that sting operation that the officer's had set up. The officer's then filed a class action lawsuit; the law-firm had then asked all who experienced any type of denied service at a Denny's restaurant to write in about their experience so that they could be considered part of that lawsuit. I did what I do best, I pulled out my pen and my legal pad and I started writing right away to detailingly tell the story of my one hour of completely wasted time in my local Denny's restaurant that night after work.

Denny's did not fight in this class action lawsuit if I properly recall.

What type of corporate structure would allow this practice to happen nationwide and why did Denny's do this type of practice, no one will probably ever know. You can't really say that they were prejudiced though, because they had minority's working for them and the beautiful black Latina woman behind the counter was a double minority. I have long stopped thinking about what happened that one early morning, and I do accept the fact I will never know the answers to those questions.

Soon after responding in writing to the lawyers for that class action suit, I would receive a settlement check in my mailbox. I can still clearly remember the exact amount of my share of the nationwide settlement. I had received my check totaling for the grand total amount of three hundred and forty dollars; all would now be right with the universe for me; not bad for an hours' worth of my time I thought.

When I wrote that letter, I had just wrote it to vent about that experience that I had at the Denny's restaurant that early morning and I never really was expecting to get anything in return. I was more than happy to share that experience with the attorneys although I truly wasn't expecting to actually get anything back from them. I was extremely happy that I did though, I had now felt even keeled and whole again because I had always had that experience somewhere close to the back of my mind even though I had still continued to go to Denny's after the event. Now, I had felt like I had gotten that stolen hour out of my life back from Denny's and that I could now truly move on with my life without any concern or thoughts about going to Denny's again, which I still frequently visit for their late night menu and early morning breakfast

This one hour of my time in my full chauffeur's uniform after a long hard night of work out on the town, I can truly say that this settlement check was a gratuity for my time spent. I have always seen it as such, and I have always considered that tip to be the best tip that I have ever received for one hour's worth of my time in the two decades I've spent as a career chauffeur. No one can ever tell me any differently.

Unexpected cash has always been free cash to me and I went out the next day and I spent that cash just as freely as I had received it, easy come and easy go I've always said. Yet I still really do not know if I should thank Denny's for probably my greatest tip ever, so therefore I just won't. I just simply do not know, and I probably will never know what the original thought process might have been behind those decisions of the management of Denny's chain at that time. That check was completely unexpected to me and I would have no idea of how God was going to answer my prayers towards my unfair treatment in that Denny's that night, but obviously God did handle the situation for me and made the situation right although I had long forgotten about the situation when I finally did get reimbursed for my time.

While I'm on the subjects of tips and tipping, over the years I have probably received hundreds if not thousands of dollars in cash tips from all different type of people, I think that I can talk on the subject of who tips the best and who tips the worst based on my years of experience receiving tips.

I can honestly say that in my experience, the best tippers that I have experienced so far are married men travelling with their families; you would think that a family man on vacation or traveling with his family may need the cash the most out of anyone else, but for whatever the reason they are by far the best tippers hands down. They are the most consistent tippers, but not necessarily the biggest cash tippers. The real biggest cash tippers and also just as consistent are businessmen travelling on private jets, I have not had as many private jet travelers as I have had family men so I cannot compare them due to the lack of equal experiences, but I am almost certain that the average amount and average frequency would be much higher for private aviators than family men if I could equally compare the two. Since I cannot equally compare the two I have to go with family men for winning the tipping prize just by actual sheer dollar amount received over the years.

It is really funny how the regular guy tips the best, probably because he thinks that is what the big executive guy does. Little does the regular guy know, until now, that the big guy usually does not tip at all and I think that may be the mentality that got the big guy where he is at today, but keep up the good work regular guy; you are much more appreciated for your kind heart than that of Mr. Big Shot.

Drunken tippers are sometimes also very good tippers, a few times it was almost like stealing candy from a baby and I tried very hard to get outta dodge just as soon as I could, before they actually realize how much tip they have really given me. I always hope that in the next morning during their hangover session that they don't figure out what really happened the night before, this does not actually happen too often but I do remember feeling this way and experiencing this scenario several times in my driving career, but not more than experiencing the appreciation of my very generous family patriarchs.

Then there are the clients that ask you if the tip is already included in the billed amount, knowing full and well that it more than likely already is. What they fail to recognize however is that tip is a very minimal and nearly an insignificant amount and that little bit of cash is only based on a perfect pickup, in which there is none. The billed tip is just for showing up on time and it is hardly ever near the twenty percent standard the rest of the service industry gets; unless the client gives the chauffeur that twenty percent gratuity directly into their hands, a limo company will usually always try to get out of paying you the twenty percent of a four thousand dollar limo bill and simply resort to a higher hourly rate to give you. That billed tip also does not account for the average thirty minute wait time for clients to round up all of their last minute stuff for a simple airport transfer, when they should have been ready hours ago, therefore stealing your precious money earning time away from you and potentially other clients. Or it doesn't account for the back breaking lifting of their heavy kitchen sink that the client decided that they needed to pack into their small carry on suitcase as well as the packing of an engine block in their very large oversized suitcases. A tip is supposed to be the recognition and the personal thank you note for what they've just put you through and not just what the bill says, so now you the client have been officially informed.

On the other end of the pot of gold rainbow are the worst tippers, without any doubt that award would have to go to businesswomen travelling alone. I could probably count on one single finger how many times that I have received a cash tip from a travelling businesswoman. I can honestly say that I have not gotten them as frequently as businessmen, but I have gotten them as clients frequently enough to know their trends when it comes to their cash tipping; hopefully this may soon change with the release of this book. I have come to a sort of conclusion in regards to why this is and the only thing that I could figure out is that most of these businesswomen; unlike Mrs. Grandma, take really good care of themselves when it comes to their hair, clothes, shoes, makeup, and bodies. I can only imagine that these women must think that it is in, you the drivers, complete privilege to be honored with the benefit of driving them around. I could be wrong about this opinion, but it is still the opinion I have based on what I have witnessed over the years.

This is just the opinion that I have come up with after thinking about it for so very long; or maybe they just can't afford to give a cash tip after spending all of their money at the mall to look so wonderful. It's quite OK though, their lovely smelling and expensive perfumes on an early morning pickup is better than any cash tip that any businessman could ever offer; those vapors really gets you going in the morning. It is more energizing and better than coffee and these beautiful women must somehow know this fact I've always thought. Most women probably would not like to hear this opinion solely based on my experience but this is not the case for the regular non-business type woman, regular women both alone and with families tip very often and very well in my experience, this is only directed to the very busy businesswoman with nothing else except business on her mind; maybe this may change a little bit now.

There is also such a thing as what I like to call a reverse tip in which all goes well with the client but the client still somehow complains to management about some minute service item or some other factor to somehow manage to receive a significant amount of cash back from their payment to the company. I had experienced exactly this reverse tip with a group of high powered attorneys who were my clients on a Friday evening that were out celebrating a big courtroom victory previously that same day.

I had arrived at the attorneys law offices on that Friday evening just after the sun had set in a suburb of Fort Lauderdale, it was a group of about seven or eight people who were all celebrating in the limo that night and who had all worked in the law firms office, at least three of them were the actual attorneys.

I had not known who my clients were going to be for that night because I only had an individual's common name on my reservation. My reservation did not say that they were attorneys and I did not know that I was about to be chauffeuring around all of these lawyers and legal types. My energy, attention, and tension levels always change whenever I know that I am driving attorneys for very obvious reasons, but attorneys are sharp minded and very keen individuals who have enough skills to find a way to make a buck where there is no other way, as you will soon see in this sad story.

I had arrived for the pickup on time and as I approached this group that was there waiting for me, I went to introduce myself as their chauffer for that night. I was approached by a man who seemed to be the lead attorney. Very strong, confident and aggressive just like you would want your attorney to be, so I had a feeling he was the head honcho of the group. He handed me his professional business card and sure enough he was the lead attorney in this office and also his name was the name on my reservation for that night.

Part of their reservation was to have on board the ten passenger stretched limousine about five hundred dollars worth of premium brand liquor on ice inside the limo. They had requested about five bottles of different kinds of top shelf Vodka brands, about half a dozen different bottles of vintage wines, several cases of imported beer, several different types of fruit juices to chase with the Vodka and many different types of snacks to keep them busy munching as we headed down south to downtown Miami to attend a Miami Heat playoff game. All of these on board goodies were supplied by the limo company to be charged to the clients Amex business account credit card with an additional fifteen percent up charge as a service fee. As they were entering the vehicle I made sure to let them know that their request had been fully complied with as they gazed at the very well stocked bar inside the limo. The Vodka and beer was on ice just as they had requested and the bottles of wine were also cold on ice in an additional cooler sitting beside me in the front passenger compartment of the limo.

The one and only woman who was in the group had wanted a glass of wine just as soon as she had entered the limo, the only problem would be that we would just as soon find out was that there were no cork puller in the limo or on my person to open the bottles of wine! Wow! I looked and looked all over for one, but I simply forgot the cork puller to open these approximately one hundred dollars worth of top quality wine. The lead attorney would eventually tell me that he knew where he could go get one really quick and he took off to do so. Well this woman, who was now waiting in the limousine for this lead attorney to get back had still needed a strong drink, so she asked me for some ice tongs so that she could get some ice out of the ice buckets inside the limo; she did not want to use her hands to retrieve the ice out of the ice bucket and she also did not want to shovel the ice into the rocks glass provided with the limo, just like everyone else does. This had happened relatively recently to the writing of this book and I could not believe what I was actually witnessing before me because I had never seen or heard anything like this in all of my years of driving. I am near certain that I must have given her some sort of quirky and weird look because she was one of just a few clients that had actually annoyed me.

Well, I knew right away that I didn't have one of those onboard either the limo or on my person because no one in all my years as a chauffeur had ever asked me for a pair ice tongs before. I told her without even thinking about it that I did not have a set in the limo and told her that she should just shovel the ice into her glass. She reluctantly accepted my regretful response and that was the end of that conversation

After about approximately ten or fifteen minutes of waiting and small talk at the limo, the head attorney had arrived back with the cork puller and we would be off to the American Airlines Arena in downtown Miami; a trip that's usually about a forty minute drive away without any rush hour or game time traffic in which there were plenty that evening. But like I said earlier in this book, I do all that I can to avoid any traffic jams even if we have to drive through the worst part of the hood and I got them there as close as possible without any type of delay closest to the scheduled time of arrival. By the time the trip was over and we had made it to the Arena, all of the hard liquor was finished and they had requested even more all to be also additionally charged to the same American Express company credit card. I did not have the hundreds of dollars to honor their service request so I notified my dispatch of their request and they made sure that I had received the additional funds at the Arena to make the purchases for their request.

While my clients for the evening were inside the Arena enjoying the Miami Heat playoff game I dashed off to the liquor store just as soon as I had received the funds from the actual owner of this particular limousine company who had come over to hand me the cash required. I made all of the additional liquor purchases they had requested, I stocked up on more ice and I made sure to purchase an ice tong for the finicky female client. My clients were very pleased when the game was over and they had returned to the limo to see an almost exactly same well stocked bar that they had originally seen when I had first picked them up about three or four hours earlier now.

The next stop would be Red's steakhouse in the SoFi district of Miami Beach, a very expensive and exclusive steakhouse that is known for celebrating for the well to do on Miami Beach. They were there for three or four more hours while they wined and dined and celebrated their big victory. When it was finally time to go, they had thought about me while they were in there because they had bought me out a big bag of gourmet food that I had really enjoyed for the two or three days that it had taken me to eat it all; this is a very rare occasion for a client to do this for their chauffeur, at least in my experience.

It was then time for me to drive them back home to Fort Lauderdale because it was now very early in the morning and my clients had had more than their share of celebrating. The drive back was uneventful and the long night would now be over after approximately nine hours chauffeuring this group of clients. My clients thanked me for a job well done and we parted ways early that morning, I hadn't received a cash gratuity from any of them, but I could not complain about that because there was a billed tip involved, a gourmet meal and a Friday night nine hour as directed time job is a very lucrative night out, even without any significant cash tip and I had also worked prior to this early evening pickup, so I had already had a very good day financially and I headed home to finally get some sleep.

This would not have been much of a story if it wasn't for the fact that a couple weeks later as I had run into my boss who was the same boss that had bought over the cash to me at the Arena. When I saw him again he had informed me that the clients had complained that I did not have a set of cork pullers or ice tongs in the limo and that the attorneys were very distraught over the fact and that they would probably be forever traumatized by it. To settle with them over their discontent about this very minute mixup and to not take a risk at giving the limousine company a bad name and to calm the nerves of these very hyperactive attorneys, my boss had decided to settle with these attorneys by comping them all of the liquor that they had requested to be onboard the limo when I had first picked them up as well as the second round of liquor that I had purchased while they were at the arena watching the Heat play, which was also purchased with the company's petty cash.

What the …..!? Are you flippin' kidding me!?

You comped all of that premium liquor over some mass produced and made in China ice tongs and a cork puller, you can't really be serious!? I just had to ask him…Yes I did he replied; unbelievable.

Those two things together purchased brand new would not even amount to twenty dollars, even in the highest end department stores. Now my boss was comping these clients, that weren't even regular or VIP client's somewhere around eight hundred dollars worth of brand name liquor and all of the amenities that goes with it just because these utensils were not in the limousine!? Before the night had been finished up, everything that they had complained about that was missing had eventually been placed onboard the limousine anyway! This is completely the skills of sharp skilled attorneys who were looking to take advantage of an opportunity they had clearly seen in front of them that evening and this is the power that they have among us to reluctantly pull money out of our pockets, and this same group of attorneys will probably somehow try to sue me for sharing this story.

Lawyers are very smart people and they probably had this all planned out the very second that they realized that there was not a cork puller in the limo when I had first arrived and they entered the limo. Their plot was very successful and I'm sure they were proud of their conquest. That comped liquor was a very expensive haul for them and a very large percent of their entire bill for that night, that would now be reversed and deducted from their bill, which more than covered my billed gratuity and then some, this is what I refer to as a reverse gratuity, and they are the ones that actually got tipped that night. I hope to never see a reverse tip again and that is because I now am certain to always have a matching set of both cork pullers and ice tongs always in my chauffeur case and I don't ever leave home without them

Now you know why my energy, tension and attention span go into full alert mode whenever it is that I'm driving attorneys or even law firm employees, I really don't think any other group of professionals individuals could ever pull off something like this and I have not seen anything else like it since and I hope not to ever see it again. This was very wrong in my opinion and this just may be one of those reasons that lawyers are generally universally disliked in the community, unless of course they are working on your side and doing a good job for you. Their conspiracy had cost this company hard earned dollars and I was certainly glad that my boss was not there to tell me that I would be the one actually paying for their plot; if this would have happened that way I would have been really upset and would have had a certain new type of feeling for all of our countries beloved attorneys at law.

THE REEF

Another long term client I have had is a very private community which is probably the most exclusive community in all of South Florida which is that of the Ocean Reef Club. In my entire chauffeuring career, I have only worked for four high end limousine companies and coincidently, all four of these companies have all had exclusive VIP transportation contracts with this very wealthy and affluent Atlantic Ocean oceanfront community. I had never seeked out companies that were exclusively contracted there, but for some odd and unexplained reason for over two decades I have routinely driven there for the upper end clients in this very private Island community.

This island community is called by another name by some of the driver's that I have met down there throughout the years, such as the land that the banana built, or Chiquitaville simply because the island community was founded and developed by the founder of the Chiquita banana empire and even though he may not be here anymore, his extended family still retains a very large share in this luxury oceanfront development. This far and remote community to me will always be the land that the banana built because of this fact and I often see it as such when I drive through its lush manicured tropical grounds.

This beautiful community is located in the very isolated northern end of Key Largo, Florida. This is a also a community where several of our American Presidents have actually stayed and vacationed while in South Florida and the Florida Keys, including the currently elected American President who actually recently stayed there at the Reef to the very day of me writing this book and also this chapter.

I first accomplished training and started chauffeuring to the Ocean Reef Club back in the spring of 1992 right after I started with the first limo company that I worked for, and to this very day of me writing of this book I am still a frequent and at least weekly chauffeur working to service this very exclusive island community and the well to do clients residing or vacationing there.

Over the years I can honestly say that the Ocean Reef has been my single biggest and most consistent client. I have even very recently, actually also during the time of writing of this book; I have been assigned to chauffeur the Board of Directors for this very large and wealthy community. I was assigned to take the entire Board to a very high end restaurant opening for dinner in downtown Miami, an hour and a half drive away, where the Board spent over five hours wining and dining in what else but only luxurious Miami style of dining with water and city views right along with fine international food and fare.

I have always really enjoyed overhearing the conversations of the comings and goings of people that I drive; it's like eavesdropping without really eavesdropping. I have always called it free life lessons even if I don't always totally understand the conversations; if you pay close attention there is always something to be learned in the conversations of the well to do. This ride was no different from any other and I learned a lot about the happenings at this place where I had spent so much time in my life and where I had frequented for so many years but had known so very little about. When I did finally drop them back to where I picked them up from the Reef, the chairman of the board handed me over a very decent cash gratuity. I was truly quite surprised by this because he truly didn't have to do this, over the years I have made a small fortune from the Board's business decisions and they also know that the chauffeurs always get a billed gratuity on our jobs. This community is probably my limo company's biggest single transportation contract, currently accounting for millions of dollars of annual revenue for both the limousine company and the very many chauffeur's driving there daily to service that Island community and its many patrons. I did greatly appreciate it though, so thank you dearly Mr. Chairman Sir.

I can confidently say that in all of that time in between; the scenery while driving directly to Ocean Reef has not changed at all in all of those previous years; not even any of the only two roads leading directly into the Ocean Reef community has changed in all of those decades either.

The one and only sleepy fishing town establishment of the Village of Card Sound has also not changed at all either, right along with its two only business' in the small isolated community; a small seafood restaurant and bar named Alabama Jack's, and a boat that doubles as a crabshack where you can buy fresh gulf blue crabs and stone crab claws when they are in season. As well as the well worn toll booth shack that has also never changed since the time that I have been going there. The only town residents are several liveaboard power and sailboat owners who dock their boats right along the banks of Card Sound canal and a few houseboats and stilt raised homes right along the canals shore edge.

The only toll road in all of the Florida Key's; Card Sound Road Bridge have not changed their toll amount either in all of that time, it has always been a single dollar for any two axle vehicle and it doesn't accept any type of auto pay account. If you pay that one dollar toll and cross over that bridge; you are now committed to only one of two possible things; either fishing on Card Sound Road or you can continue your ride on to Ocean Reef. Once you have crossed the tollbooth though, there is now nothing else you can do except one of those two options. Because there are no establishments between both of the incoming roads directly leading to the Atlantic Ocean frontal community, and there are several security cameras on these miles long roads to actually see who's on the roads. I've always considered these roads to be actually like ancient moats that I like to call land moats because there is nothing else surrounding entry into the Reef, all for the purpose of securing the King's castle with high tech surveillance cameras all around to also monitor entry and egress there as to help keep out the riff raff from this lovely, very wealthy seaside community.

Card Sound Road can be easily identified by being the road that is directly opposite and perpendicular to the Last Chance Saloon and it's always proudly flying Jolly Roger flag, a proud reminder that you are now entering what was once considered pirate country. The Florida Keys once used to be the home of pirates and profiteers' and it is still a land of undersea salvage and treasure hunters. The Last Chance Saloon is a country and western dive bar and package store that is the very last establishment before the very long and lonely twenty plus mile road section of US1 which leads directly into northern section of the city of Key Largo, Florida. There is truly nothing on this road except for a couple boat marinas between the Last Chance Saloon and Key Largo, hence the great name of the bar. This establishment also has not changed in the time in all the years that I have been driving to the Keys, either personally or professionally.

All over South Florida there has been change that can clearly be seen by anyone that has spent any amount of time here. Card sound road however has not changed at all, even the only parallel route of US1 into the Florida Keys have changed quite significantly over that time, but nothing else at all has changed that has anything to do with the drive into this very affluent and beautiful community setting. Not even the designated driver's bathroom at the Ocean Reef Inn has been changed in all of that time; I know this because it is the most consistent bathroom that I have used in two decades, not even the bathrooms in my multiple homes that I've resided in since that time has been this consistent.

In all of the Florida Keys, there are only three 24 hour fully manned and gated communities that I can speak of. One of them is the Ocean Reef community which has five large gated lanes, two for exiting and three for entry for member's and invited guests or hotel guests to the one and only Hotel in the very large community; The Inn at Ocean Reef, and also of course for the chauffeurs who are pre scheduled to be there. If you do not have a reason or an appointment with residents to be at Ocean Reef, you will not be welcomed in, your name and destination must be in their security database, for it's a very private community and I am certain that is the way that they the members of that community want it to stay.

The other two other gated communities that I can think of in the

Florida Keys, are the Air Force base in Boca Chica, and the Naval base in Key West, and I have heard that the security at these bases are not as good as the security at Ocean Reef. I really do not know if that statement is true or not, but I do know the security at Ocean Reef is quite intense; for as long as I have been travelling there, I stilled get grilled by the gate guards like some terrorists trying to sneak onboard a jumbo jet without a ticket. That's Ok though, over the years I have made quite a lot of income from these well secured and extremely rich folks down there.

Ocean Reef is a very beautiful community with it's gorgeous and pristine golf courses, it's well manicured landscaping, very private airstrip with lots of big private jets, fancy megayachts in the Marina, and waterfront homes and mansions with breathtaking Ocean views. I have always wondered about these folks that I was bringing to Ocean Reef though. For the majority of the years that I have been bringing them there, I couldn't understand them; there was something about them to me that just did not quite add up. For a good amount of the last twenty years since I've been driving there, I have tried my best to figure it out with these folks and I never could; to me it was a very good thing that I have always had love for all people, because the confusion about these Ocean reef folks had my brain doing somersaults about them.

The frustration I had about them would frequently set in with me when I was assigned to an Ocean Reef run, I of course would never let that frustration show though. That frustration had all of a sudden changed recently when I had finally figured it all out with these very special folks while I was taking an Ocean Reef family to their Ocean Reef home from the Fort Lauderdale International airport.

I had picked up this large family during the winter months just as I have often done in the years past to take them to their winter retreat at Ocean Reef. The ride from Fort Lauderdale to Ocean Reef is usually about an hour and a half to about two hours depending on the traffic, so I always forewarn my passengers before we leave the airport to sit back and relax for that long ride ahead of us. After I give them plenty of warnings about the long trip, I would then normally ask them my standard question which is if they have been to Ocean Reef before, just to see if they are accustomed to that long ride. This particular family told me that they have ever been coming to ocean reef for over twenty years continuously every winter, so I now knew that they were fully knowledgeable of the long ride ahead. When I hear this, it usually gives me a sense of relief because they already know the routes to the Reef and also the traffic trends getting there which may relieve some excitement and anxiety for my clients on the trip down to Key Largo.

This family was a friendly family and they conversed with me the whole way down to the Island community, I have always appreciated when I can speak openly with my clients because it always shortens the trip by the amount of the conversation, it makes my job much easier and it also helps to keep me alert and awake and of course may help with a gratuity or maybe even a better gratuity.

As we got closer to the Reef, our conversation turned to talking about the rest of the Florida Keys, the father of the family boldly stated during this part of the conversation that in all of the twenty plus consecutive years he and his family have been frequenting Ocean Reef, they had never been outside the Ocean Reef gates to head south of Ocean Reef and deeper into the more southerly Keys while vacationing here.

WHAT!! Are you f#[+!^g serious!!! I immediately thought to myself. I couldn't believe what I was hearing

With that one bold statement I no longer had concern for my Ocean Reef people; I now knew exactly who they were. I had now figured out what may have be concerning me about these Ocean Reef folks over all of these years and that is even though they are actually in the Florida Keys, they are certainly not **OF** the Florida Keys. I had finally figured it all out with that one simple statement; they are just simply transplanted northerners who bring not only themselves, but their northerner's way of life and lifestyle with them. They probably would not actually blend in with the native Keys folk and their Keys lifestyle very well.

You see, if anybody knows the Florida Keys; the Florida Keys folks are the most laid back, relaxed, open minded people, life loving people in all of the country. That is why I call the Florida Keys the American Caribbean because of not only the gorgeous tropical scenery, but also for that laidback and carefree attitude of the people that is so prevalent down there.

I once overheard a cellphone conversation in my limousine from a local Key West resident that I was driving telling someone on the other end that he does not even sober up from the night before unless he knows he's going to be making at least $300 for that day; must be nice I thought to myself. Right along with me laughing out loud on the inside; this is how resident Keys folk make you feel. They will have you laughing with them all the while you'll be envying their carefree way of life and humble style. So this is what these Ocean Reef folks are missing in the people that are much more southerly in the Florida Keys while they stay locked up behind their large continuously manned gates.

I love Keys folk dearly, I have a special place for them in my heart and I pray one day that I may become a neighbor to all of these wonderful Keys folk. To say that you have been coming to the Florida Keys for over twenty years and have not actually seen the Florida Keys or the wonderful folks of the Florida Keys to me is just ludicrous, and shows me that you actually have no interest in to what the Florida Keys truly have to offer.

Before I dropped the family off at their private home on Ocean Reef, I had gotten comfortable enough with this family to have literally begged them to go outside those large Ocean Reef gates and to see the rest of the Florida Keys, the father did tell me however that they did not actually have the time this time to go outside the gates, and that he would certainly make sure to try again the next time they would come to Ocean Reef; I think I know what that truly means. I truly hope that one day that they do actually go outside those gates though; I guarantee you sir that you and your family won't ever regret it.

A perfect example of the difference between Florida Keys folk to all the other folks of South Florida is the fact that I have been driving countless and all types of shuttles between two or more locations during my driving career here in South Florida including professional sporting events like PGA tours and US open tennis and also shuttling for luxury hotels. Never though, had I ever driven a shuttle deep inside the Florida Keys outside of The Ocean Reef until very recently. On this particular shuttle I was shuttling folks between a High School parking lot where the Keys folk would park their cars and I would shuttle them a short distance to a local community church in the Keys for their annual arts and craft fair.

The entire distance of this shuttle was approximately three round trip miles; it was an eight hour shift shuttle assignment for two shuttle busses. During this shift I collected in cash tips one hundred and twelve single dollar bills and one five dollar bill for a grand total of $117, this was besides my normal pay and billed gratuity. All of these gratuities were also accomplished without a tip jar, for I have rarely ever used a tip jar during anytime of my driving career; I just so happen to personally think that it cheapens the luxurious experience of any client that I am driving, even in a shuttled minicoach. We were also provided with our choice of lunch straight off of their charcoal grill at our breaks with unlimited cold water bottles and caffeinated drinks.

My shuttling partner on this day did even better than me in his own cash tips than I did, he would later tell me. Never in my experience of driving a passenger bus and shuttling passengers have I been shown this kind of gratitude and appreciation. These however, are the hearts and minds of the residents of the Florida Keys. If you have never experienced the Florida Keys, everyone who reads this should look to try and experience these truly wonderful people down there if they ever have an opportunity to do so; I will highly recommend visiting the Florida Keys to all who have the ability to do so, it is just simply a different place.

In all my years of shuttle services, never had I received more than maybe about twenty or thirty dollars or so in total cash gratuities on any eight hour shuttle, with the average being somewhere around five or ten bucks per shift when on the more northern shuttle routes in the greater Miami and Fort Lauderdale areas. This is clearly the generosities and hearts of the people of the Florida Keys shining through; I will always remember the warm and friendly faces of the people on my bus that day, and I look forward to one day being your new neighbor down there in the beautiful Florida Keys.

Although I can honestly say from my many years of experience at the Reef, that it is probably the most perfect Utopian society that they have down there, I still truly wish that Ocean Reef could be more like the rest of the Florida Keys. I know however that this will not be ever possible; it is just wishful thinking on my part. I can't help but to imagine though what the beauty of Ocean Reef would be like if they all had the laid back, loving, caring and accepting to all lifestyles that is so abundantly prevalent in the rest of the Florida Keys. But I also think that without the tight and strict security controls of who enters Ocean Reef, Ocean Reef may not have all of the beauty and tranquility that it does currently have and has had for the past several decades. I'm just imagining out loud what such as exclusive place would be like if they were to suddenly become inclusive to all and to everybody. I truly wish that I could tell everyone reading this to visit The Ocean Reef community the same way as I have said for the Florida Keys in general, but I really don't think that can be a possibility in my lifetime.

THE HURRICANE

The last long term client that I will mention, was not really a single client at all, but rather maybe hundreds of clients all within a nonstop forty eight hour sprint to evacuate all of them from their beachfront condominiums in the evacuation zones east of US1 and away from the oncoming and historic Hurricane that was named Andrew back in the summer of 1992.

I was extremely happy that I had had previous experience of driving nonstop for a continuous thirty six hour stretch, because I now would have and I used that valuable experience to help me get this mission at hand accomplished. I still remember the day that the limo company requested that all the driver's must be available for work when the three day forecast for Hurricane Andrew with its high intensity wind speeds put South Florida square in its cross hairs for eventual landfall. South Florida immediately became a haven for intense hurricane preparation activities, one of those activities being transportation contracts being issued to limo and bus companies to evacuate all of the elderly and retired community members off of their beachfront properties and all the properties that were east of US1 in both Miami-Dade and Broward counties. I can still clearly remember that task had seemed like it was a nonstop, impossible and never ending job for just the few days that I did it.

During that forty eight hour shift, I was tasked with driving the 27 passenger minicoach and making several round trips away from what was thought to be going to be ground zero for Hurricane Andrew. I made one round trip to Orlando, Two round trips to West Palm Beach and a couple going to Stuart, Florida. All of the people that I was taking away were all going to local hotels that still had the rooms available for all of my clients that they had already prearranged. During that forty eight hour stretch I did not sleep, only powernaps whenever I could, and of course lots of Mountain Dew and Skittles candy. I had now come to depend on this combination of caffeine and sugar, even when I was not working long endless hours because I just simply liked the pep and the energy spike that it had now frequently given me since the time I had learned of this amazing concoction.

When I had finally arrived back to the base at Miami International Airport after my final run was over, I was the last driver back, it was already late in the evening and Andrew's winds were already picking up his strength and speed. I can clearly remember that it was around 11pm on the eve of Andrews historic landfall. I parked the bus inside the garage and then I parked my little white Hyundai Excel right behind it also inside the garage, I had to squeeze it in tight as there was no more room for any other vehicles in the garage that night. I did not want to drive the 10 mile ride to my little apartment due to the worsening weather, the driver lounge had had a convertible sofa bed which I pulled out and went right to sleep, it took me absolutely no time at all to enter lala land, as can be imagined after driving for forty eight hours continuously. Nothing could keep me from falling into a deep sleep, not even caffeine and sugar, or a major category five Hurricane howling just outside the office door. I slept soundly right through all of Hurricane Andrew.

The next morning when I awoke, I went outside the office door and I simply could not believe what I was witnessing; there was nothing but complete destruction and devastation everywhere, it had looked something like a war zone or a nuclear disaster. The garage door that I had closed about eight hours earlier was now blown into the garage and sitting right on top of my Hyundai. The first thing that I remember thinking was how in heaven had I slept right through all of this!? That entire two story garage and office building could have fell right on top of me and killed me. I would've died in my sleep and never known it or felt a thing as I made my way up on to heaven.

Outside the garage was completely desolate, the normal buzz of

arriving and departing jet engines directly up above was now gone because I was certain that the airport had not yet reopened and was still
closed with all of the catastrophic destruction all around. There were
no people walking around the area because I was in an industrial area
and no one was coming in to work on this particular morning. There
was no auto traffic because there were downed power lines and downed
trees everywhere. I could not believe what I was actually seeing; I was
in complete and utter shock. I would soon realize however that I had
to just shake off this shock and move on with my life even through this
devastation; that's exactly what I did.

The very first thing that I had to do was to get my car out of the
garage; it was enveloped by a two story garage door that was still partly
attached to the two story building. I worked extremely hard to get that
door off of my car, but I still had to clear the roadway to drive onto the
main road so I could get out and check on my home. I had to move pow-
erpoles, trees, and all sorts of debris to clear the way for me to get out of
the industrial area and when I finally did get the street clear enough for
me to leave, I still had to weave and bob all the way home to North Miami
where my apartment was located.

North Miami was not hit that hard, except for the fact that there was
no electricity for the next several weeks. There was no damage to my
small apartment and all would soon be OK. The only real problem that I
had was that I had no gasoline in my little white Hyundai's gas tank and
all of the gas stations could not pump any gas simply because they did not
have electricity to pump the gas out of the ground. I had to drive about
thirty miles to central Broward County where I finally found a working
gas station, but I remember for the first time ever in my life that I had to
wait on a very long line just to purchase gas, and I was extremely lucky
in the fact that my little white Hyundai's gas tank had just ran empty just
as I was approaching the gas pump. I had only seen long gas lines before
as a child when I was living in Queens; I had remember seeing the long
gas lines of the energy crisis of the late seventies because we lived on a
major street where I witnessed miles long gas lines. This empty gas tank
lesson was a very valuable lesson for me and I now fill up my gas tank
each time we are issued a hurricane warning down here and when it's
more than obvious that the Hurricane is fast approaching South Florida.

After the aftermath of Hurricane Andrew there was no work for anybody in the limousine industry for anybody to be had anytime soon. I do not even recall how all of the elderly people that I drove off of the beach got back to their homes, so the industry in south Florida took somewhat of a little break, including a break for myself. I truly think that it may have been a well deserved break, but there was eventually more work for chauffeurs to get back to sometime after the shock value of this terrible storm had passed. In my long driving career I have had very few clients that I have driven for hours or even days on end, a very powerful client named Hurricane Andrew just so happened to be one of those clients that kept me extremely busy for a good couple of days both before, as well as for a couple of weeks after that horrible storm in the summer of 1992.

VIP'S AND SUPER VIP'S

One of the benefits of doing an excellent job as a new chauffeur is that you will eventually be rewarded with and the next most natural progression after doing well with regular clients, and that is finally being assigned to drive a VIP or a Super VIP client. This will usually only happen when you have a proven track record of dependability and professionalism; and even then driving a Super VIP is still not guaranteed. Only if all the circumstances fall into place that will allow a new chauffeur the chance to get that very important assignment.

As I mentioned earlier in this book, the very first rule in chauffeuring is to only speak when spoken to. Well of course that rule will also ring true with VIP clients, but closely behind that rule is the second rule of not being a star struck driver. What this means is that there should be no autograph seeking or photo requests with the VIP and celebrity clients. I have never wanted to take photos or ask for autographs with any of the clients that I have driven. I only just recently during the time of this writing have had the opportunity to chauffeur around recording artist JCole who happens to be the artist who sings one of my all time favorite rap songs and performs in my one and only all time favorite rap music video of "Can't get enough", probably because it best describes the way I was feeling back in my youth.

The contents of that music video also contains all that I hold dear to me as a Caribbean born man, tropical sights, beautiful women especially the sexy Ms. Rihanna; chauffeuring him around for an entire evening and into the wee hours of the morning did not even phase me though. I had a great opportunity to see him perform that song live that night right while I stood there backstage being only about 5 yards away from him. I did not even make an attempt to ask him for some sort of a photo or even an autograph; I wasn't at all interested. However, I will be very tempted to break those golden rules if I ever get the opportunity to chauffeur around the greatest athlete there is in that great ex-number 6 of Miami Heat fame, LeBron James; just because it will make my son extremely proud of me, he wouldn't really care less over a JCole photo or autograph.

I do not ever live my life with regrets, but if I were allowed to have just one regret it would be the time I had come very close to asking a certain female celebrity VIP client for an autograph which would have been more than cherished by me simply because of the certain circumstances of this particular situation that I was in with her as I spent the day chauffeuring her around. I will write more about that one particular Super VIP circumstance that I was in later on in volume two of this book.

Over the years I have had my fair share of VIP and a lot of Super VIP clients; I will share a few of the stories here in this section of this chapter. I will also have several more VIP stories as the book progresses on, as I am telling my stories in as much of a chronological order that I can properly recall.

Super VIP's usually don't tip, but what they do actually do is give you lifelong stories to share with friends and family as which is obviously the case for me here in this book. These stories in most cases can be more valuable as unforgettable life experiences more so than any cash tip could have ever done.

By now you must be curious as to what the difference is between a regular VIP client and a Super VIP client may be, well early in my career this is the way it was once explained to me by a fellow more experienced chauffeur than I was at the time as being basically this…

If a driver were to get into an automobile accident while having a VIP client on board and that client were to actually get hurt, word will eventually get out via the media and that VIP client may get local or national news headlines or coverage, maybe sometimes not at all depending on the level of their VIP status. However, if you get into an accident with a super VIP client on board and they were to also get hurt, that media coverage will expand locally, nationally, and more than likely internationally across the World, that is the major difference between genuine VIP and Super VIP clientele; just simply how much of the world will follow the news of your mishap on the road with your client and/or their other passengers if you were to somehow deliver them some type of reason to have a more than memorable experience that is not so positive for them by having a major accident. Very much like the recent accident that involved the actor/comedian Mr. Tracy Morgan.

Limousine company's however can and often do label their own regular clients in house as VIP or Super VIP clients, depending on how much business that client may be bringing into that company's bankroll. For an example the not so good doctor that I wrote about earlier was a VIP client at that company, even though if we were to have gotten into an accident with him on board the story probably would not have even made a local medical journal.

I have driven all of the different types of VIP clientele mentioned here throughout my years and just about each time I was forewarned that I would be driving a VIP client beforehand. A few of these examples of my very early VIP experiences will be such as the following.

THE COUNTRY WESTERN SINGER

One of the very first VIP's that I was assigned to, actually happened not too much after the evening with Mrs. Grandma, I remember this because the stories are almost quite similar and I remember thinking to myself, if this situation that I once again find myself in, is a normal routine amongst women and limos.

When I was assigned this first VIP client, I was not informed that this was actually going to be a VIP client that particular time for me. This often happens sometimes when a new chauffeur is first assigned their first VIP client, and may also happen on subsequent VIP assignments. This happens to help to avoid the chauffeur from getting celebrity shock while on the VIP assignment and causing a nervous and jittery chauffeur, which has actually happened to me in my career which I will describe in detail a little bit later on in this book.

As a professional chauffeur you are not supposed to take photos or ask for autographs or anything else that a regular fan would do with a well known celebrity. You as the chauffeur are there only to provide a very private luxury service for them and take them away from the outside World where they are quite often and regularly bombarded by their fans and people who seek fanfare and autographs from them.

This first VIP client for me was a woman who had told me that she was a Country and Western singer who was chartering the limousine all to herself; she was on tour and was to perform in a concert the following night. If I were ever to be tortured to remember her name, I would be tortured to death because there is no way that I could remember her name as I have never followed country music. This night that I was chauffeuring her she had just finished up with rehearsals and sound checks earlier in the day and she wanted to go out and relax on her own as I recall her telling me after she had introduced herself to me as a recording artist.

I, as I would normally do to all As Directed clients on a weekend night, asked her what the itinerary was going to be for us for that evening. She replied to me by saying that we were going to be heading to an alternative lifestyles nightclub located in South Miami, just like Mrs. Grandma I also picked her up in Kendall.

When I had drove her the very short distance to the nightclub, she also like Mrs. Grandma asked me to go inside the nightclub with her. She also just like grandma told me that she was extremely shy, and she did not know anyone in the nightclub and she did not want to go inside alone. I really did not want to go inside an alternative lifestyle nightclub at that time, so I decided that I had to make up an excuse as to why I couldn't. Don't think that I am some type of closed minded prude that would not go in and experience an alternative lifestyle's nightclub, because I had already partied in such a nightclub a couple of times previously with a couple of women that I was seeking after, this was for the sole purpose of wooing those bisexual women into liking me because I was interested in getting to know them much better, if you know what I mean. That is the only way that I was ever willing enough to go inside of a gay nightclub; if it will impress or loosen up some beautiful sexually open minded woman that I am interested in for the sole purpose of pursuing the fantasy of a potential ménage a trios, which I have successfully accomplished a few times after partying with them in these alternative lifestyles nightclubs.

My excuse this night was not really an excuse at all though, but actually the truth; the problem truly was that the nightclub was extremely crowded and the parking lot was packed with parked cars. I had nowhere else to park the 10 passenger superstretch limousine. I had to park the limo there in the parking lot and at the same time had to block in about three or four cars because I had to park perpendicular to them, for that reason I had to stay with the limo so that I could move the limo at anytime to allow people in or out of those parking spots. I really could not leave the limo this time as I had done with Mrs. Grandma, with Mrs. Grandma I had perfect stretch limo parking at the bar. I explained this fact to her and she completely understood what I was saying so she made her decision and went in by herself, all shy and alone.

She was not in the nightclub for very long and she would soon come outside quite happy with a lot of new friends and an entourage because she came out with a bunch of people; I really thought she told me that she didn't know anybody inside that nightclub. I always figured that her celebrity status must have been recognized inside the nightclub or that maybe she had noticed people from the earlier sound checks that she was at. They had all looked like they had known each other for quite a long time with the way they were acting and carrying on before they all climbed into the limo; or maybe it was just the alcohol and whatever other party favors were being ingested by this group of party people that night.

They all got into the back of the limousine; I think there were at least six people that went back there if I can remember correctly, both men and women. I was standing at the right rear door assuming my professional position as if I were the keeper of the gate just in case someone needed to get out, I could hold the door open for them. No one needed to get out of that limo anytime soon though; they were having too much fun as they soon after started to light up in the back of the limo, I could see the lighters lighting up right through the side tinted windows. I do not know what they were burning though, because I do not recall the smell of anything like marijuana emanating from the limo. That was not the issue I was having with them though because I was already well accustomed to clients lighting up in the back of my limos. My issue was that whenever they lit their lighters up back there I could almost clearly see what was going on in the back of the limo, more specifically on the floor of the limo. What I saw through the dark tinted windows was a full blown orgy going on with the women on the floor of that limo. I could not tell which woman was which or who was doing who, all that I could see were the fine silhouettes of beautiful women slithering around on that limo floor. Every time someone would light up that lighter, which was quite frequent, I would see a different sexual position going on right through the very dark window tint. It was like watching a black and white porno flick, all in slow motion; I couldn't stop watching what was going on and thought it to be quite exciting as I witnessed all of the action going on in the back of that limo. It was also very exciting watching my very first VIP client getting it on hotly and heated with what seemed like to me was complete strangers; I guess I could be wrong and they were all already familiar.

I couldn't help but to think to myself that if I had only found a proper parking space for this limo and went in that nightclub with her, I could have quite possibly been back there with them watching the show in high definition and in living color instead of monochrome black and white through limousine tinted windows. It was just a little thought that had always crossed my mind from time to time over the past twenty years of my life; no big deal at all, I'll get over it one day soon.

I stayed right there at the passenger door the entire time that I was assuming the position while they all partied literally like rock stars inside of the limo; I stood there and acted like the guardian of the gate. I kind of felt left out and like the kid that was not invited to the popular kid's party. By the time they were all done with their letting the good times roll, they all just went their separate ways and left just as easy as they had came. It was now right back to me and my VIP client all alone together once again.

She had not known that I was able to see all that was going on back there as I stood guard outside the limo, so it was really awkward for me to be alone with her once again now knowing the actual type of woman she had truly been and with me being the type of guy that I was at that time, VIP client or not. I remember not having much of a conversation on the ride back to the hotel because I was afraid of what it might lead to so I kept it strictly professional and I took her right back to where I had picked her up from. She would never know that I actually knew what was going on back there because I would never tell her. I then collected my fare and gratuity from her for the evening's adventures and I went right on with my career and life and chalked this little adventure up to experience. This was a little lesson for me that even VIP clients are just regular people like the rest of us; they are human and have their very own needs and urges just like the rest of us. This experience put me in a place where I could not be intimated or nervous dealing with VIP clients.

THE VIP PARTY

One certain VIP client that I was assigned to wasn't actually a celebrity VIP, but a VIP locally here in South Florida that the company had familiarality with. In this case, I was notified that he was a VIP client and to treat him accordingly. I happily obliged as I always do, even though I treat every single one of my clients like VIP clients. Most limo companies however don't want to hear that statement from a chauffeur and expect you to either step your service up for VIP clients or reserve a little extra something for them, I have never really understood this statement in all of my years chauffeuring because to me that would mean that I would have to step down my service for regular clientele; I have never agreed with that philosophy but I do understand their point of view. I still treat all my clients the same regardless of VIP status because everyone who does tip, tips the same; VIP or not. It all depends on who you drive and you will never know who the real tippers actually are. To me good tippers are the real VIP's, sorry bosses. When a client shows up you can never know who they actually are, maybe they should be labeled a VIP but they choose not to. I have twice in my professional driving career had a family give me a cash tip that was at least equal or more than the actual service fare and both times they were just simple Ford van transfers, and none of these clients were ever labeled as a VIP client. These are of course the real VIP's in my mind and they of course deserve to be treated as such; management decision to do so and label them or not.

This night I was assigned to pick up this VIP client at a private yacht in a marina located in Broward County. I was picking this client up off of his private yacht. When I finally found the pier that I had been searching for, he was there waiting for me with a beautiful, svelte, tall blonde woman at his side, he was much older than she was because she had looked like she was right out of high school. I thought, in my then limited experience, that she was probably a professional woman of the evening because of her non-chalant easy type of demeanor; and I had enough experience already and I had already seen enough professional women by this time to know when certain women are working girls or not. Over enough time, an experienced chauffeur will soon eventually get to realize all of these minor details about their clientele and the people that they drive; it's just something that naturally comes with the territory of partying with people and watching their sometimes extravagant lifestyles.

She was very beautiful, very well dressed, and extremely shapely. I could not keep my eyes off of her but I managed to keep my eyes off of her just enough to let my VIP client introduce himself to me. He introduced himself to me as an executive at the very popular Miami Subs fast food chain of restaurants. I was impressed by this because Miami Subs has always been one of my favorite fast food spots since I had arrived in Miami, I was happy to drive him around and I was determined to do an excellent job.

He also told me that we were going to be headed to a very exclusive VIP party at a very exclusive VIP nightclub on South Beach. That nightclub was going to be the brand new Amnesia nightclub that had just recently opened with much fanfare in the SoFi district of Miami Beach. I had seen all sorts of television news reports about its grand opening and I really never knew why this particular South Beach night club out of the many, was such a big deal, but I was very happy and excited when I found out that was going to be our destination for the night. I then loaded the both of them into limo and off we went leaving the marina for the short ride down to Miami Beach and the exclusive South Beach night club.

Just as soon as they got in the back of the limo and I started driving away my intuition about this woman was probably proven correct, although of course I could never be certain. I watched the glass (sound only) privacy screen go up, it was obvious to me that this gentleman was not at all familiar with driving in the back of a limousine because I think what he really wanted to put up was the solid (complete privacy) screen. This is because they immediately started sexually going at each other and this very young woman took off her long and beautiful dress and would soon be straddling him on the back seat of the limo and I could see everything including her beautiful young body and perky breast. I could also see all that they were doing through the combination of the glass screen divider and the driver's rear view mirror. I couldn't drive straight and I tried my hardest not to crash the limo because my full attention was now focusing on the rear view mirror to see all that was going on in the back of the limo. I saw everything just as if I was right there with them due to the mood light setting they had set in the back. They went on for about half of the trip down to South Beach and I enjoyed watching just about every moment of it. I would find it amazing that they had not noticed all of the erratic driving that I was doing; but then again they were extremely busy doing what they were doing back there and they had no idea what was really going on around them while they were in the complete bliss of the very exciting heat of their moment.

When they had finally finished giving me their peep show, I was then able to get them to the night club in a safe and timely manner because I was no longer distracted by all of the sexy antics going on in the back.

When we had finally arrived at the night club, my client was suddenly surprised when he had seen the line to get into the nightclub; the line was literally bent around the corner. We drove past the nightclub entrance and drove around the block, he would then hand me a single one hundred dollar bill and told me to go give it to the bouncer at the velvet rope so that he could get extra special VIP entrance. As we came back around I stopped the limo at the valet stop and told the valet folks that I would right back. I approached the bouncer at the front door and behind the velvet rope; I outstretched my arm as if to shake his hand with the folded up bill inside of my palm. I told him that this was from my VIP client in the back of my limo, and I asked him if it was OK for my client to jump to the front of the line and head right through the velvet rope, he said that it was quite OK with him and he unclasped the velvet rope and signaled to the back of the limo to wave them in. I then ran to open the passenger door to let out my client and his beautiful blonde escort. They went into the nightclub ahead of all of the other people on the line in front of them and I went to find a place to park the limo. I had figured that the bouncer did not know that my client had actually paid the tip, so I should be just as good to get inside the club ahead of the pack. I found a legal spot for me to park the limo and I went right to the front of the line to see the bouncer that I had just handed over a hundred dollar bill to; just as I thought he undid the clasp for the velvet rope and let me right on into the nightclub, it was now once again time for me to party like a rock star.

Or maybe not.

I had been well adjusted to partying with my clients already, but I had to remember that it was only when I was invited to party with them. This particular client did not even know that I would be inside the nightclub and I tried my best to avoid him and Blondie, so I knew that I could not party like I had been already accustomed to by drinking and doing all the other things that I had been doing with past clients.

So for that reason I behaved myself and I just watched the hot scene with all that was happening inside this VIP party. The nightclub was packed with a much older crowd that I would normally see in a South Beach nightclub, and it seemed like there were a lot of important people in there because everyone was extremely well dressed and everyone just looked so important and sophisticated. I had no clue of what type of party this was or what was actually being celebrated. The nightclub had a different couple of levels inside the night club and it also had an inside and outside area where people would both dance and lounge amongst themselves. I just walked around the very large nightclub in my bowtie and tux and I just enjoyed the scene and the people watching that came with it.

I have never been a celebrity hound and I have never been able to actually recognize the faces of celebrities directly in front of me unless they are major celebrities, but I would later find out later that night, that the nightclub was filled with all types of major celebrities; I had only clearly recognized two.

I was hanging out on the balcony level of this nightclub looking down onto the dancefloor when I had noticed a man dancing with all different types of beautiful sexy women, the women were all excited and actually literally lined up to dance with this gentleman; as I looked closer and focused in on this very tall gentleman I finally realized who this man was, it was Erving "Magic" Johnson. He would dance with each one of the women for a few moments and move right on to the next one, and each one of the women all had broad wide smiles and grins and they all seemed to be so happy to have the chance to grace the presence of this multi millionaire of a professional athlete.

The women were all impressed with this giant of a man, but I truly wasn't; I think I was hating on Magic.

At this particular time of my life I had been a somewhat judgmental person; it was still the very early days of HIV and Aids and not too much after Mr. Magic had made his official announcement to the World. I have never really judged anyone externally but I would certainly judge everyone internally, but I really don't know why because with my own personal bad behavior when it came to women I could have been just as easily judged by anybody. I was certainly doing the exact same thing that Mr. Johnson was probably doing to potentially catch that same bug, and yet I still felt free to pass judgment on him.

On this particular night I had passed that judgmental treatment right onto Mr. Magic; the only thing that would cross my mind when I saw this scene was that this man had already announced to the World that he was HIV positive. Didn't all of these beautiful women who were all lined up to make his acquaintance know this fact!? I was thinking about this to myself like as if you could catch that bug by just being close to someone's proximity, as in a dance partner. I was also thinking that this was not fair and that all of these beautiful women should be lined up to dance with me, even though I wasn't even as tall as Mr. Magic, or I wasn't even close to being a thousandaire and I didn't even have the freedom to be dancing with them as I pleased like he was.

Maybe it was jealousy more than judgment, or maybe it was just a little bit of both. Whatever the case was, I know for sure that I was being judgmental towards you Mr. Johnson, and for that reason Mr. Magic I must apologize to you, I had absolutely no right to judge you especially when I myself was doing the same things that you may or may not have been doing when it came to women. You are truly a great man, you are truly blessed and you have done amazing things for the community in a whole. I am truly sorry for my judgment towards you that night sir and I pray that you can forgive me.

Looking back over my years situations like this have made me understand why we are called not to judge anyone. I was wrong to judge Mr. Magic on this night, but I had not as yet learned that lesson as I have passed more judgment on certain people who have passed through my life, in which I will share with you later on in the coming chapters.

Back in my early days of my chauffeuring when cell phones were not as yet prominent as they are today. I would have to make pre arranged meeting times with clients when they were having dinner or at nightclubs or events, and it would usually be within eyeshot of the same place and location where you had dropped them off at. So, on this particular night I had done just that and I would start heading out to the parked limousine approximately thirty minutes prior to our pre-arranged meeting time.

As I was leaving to head out to the vehicle, I decided that this was the time for me to use the restroom and relieve my bladder before the long drive all the way back to Broward County.

As I was entering the men's room to take care of my business before leaving the nightclub, was when I bumped into the second celebrity face that I had clearly recognized that night. It was a certain local South Florida native who was also alumnus at a certain major South Florida University who had now rose to that of national fame and fortune as a current professional athlete.

He was a very happy individual when I saw him, as well as also being a very drunk individual at that time and a superstar professional NFL player, who I would easily describe as being one of the absolute best at what he did as well as also being one of the most controversial wide receivers in the history of the NFL.

This Superstar was now being held up and supported by two of his faithful entourage members because he clearly could not hold himself up with his intense intoxication. Although he was quite out of it at the time I saw him, he still portrayed himself as a very friendly celebrity athlete with a broad and jolly smile on his face, open to freely talk whatever, all while being very talkative to me as he made his way into the mensroom. I decided right there and then that I would try to take advantage of this unique moment and try to quickly pick his brain a little bit about football, his football career and about life itself in general.

We did manage to have a small conversation about football while we both relieved ourselves at the adjoining urinals despite his intoxication, but I had to end that conversation quickly when I looked down and noticed that he had pee'd all over my brand new shiny black wingtip shoes. I jumped back and went to wash my hands and attempted to wipe off all of Mr. Wide receivers urine that had been sprayed and showered all over my recently shined new shoes.

I left the restroom with Mr. Wide receiver and his helpers still hanging out there in the mensroom talking a lot of smack and laughing hysterically amongst themselves. I can still remember thinking to myself right there and then that Mr. famous Wide receiver pissing all over my brand new wingtip shoes was going to make a very good story for my kids one day as I walked out of that very exclusive South Beach Amnesia nightclub mensroom. I don't know why I had thought that thought right there and then though; I hadn't thought that thought in any other of my many memorable life experiences.

I went outside the nightclub to go and get the limousine and I pulled it right up to the front of the nightclub and I was allowed to wait there because the night was just about over and no one else was arriving at the nightclub and also for a visual show for the nightclub because nightclubs usually enjoy having fancy cars parked at their front doors for attraction and show just as long as there is no patrons coming and going. I stood there outside the limo and just outside of the nightclub and watched people come and go while I waited for my clients to finish up their evening in there.

As they arrived back to the limo, I loaded them in and we uneventfully drove back to his private yacht in Broward County and that night would soon be over. Needless to say, on our way back to his yacht, we did stop at a twenty four hour Miami Subs restaurant where they purchased a late night snack and he also offered to buy me a late night snack in which I happily accepted. I enjoyed that Philly cheesesteak sandwich he had bought for me; which I had always thought of as the best outside of Philadelphia. I was also quite happy that I now I would not have to go to Denny's for breakfast on this particular morning as I was still quite upset with them for what had recently happened there.

THE MIAMI DOLPHIN

Another early VIP client that I was assigned to was a professional football player who was a player on the Miami Dolphins NFL football team. I was told that I was going to be chauffeuring him around for an entire evening of celebration due to the fact that he had just been resigned to a long term contract with the team and that he had just received a very significant signing bonus. I was told by management that I should do all that I can to help relieve him of his financial windfall by giving him all that he had wanted. My client for this evening, who shall remain nameless, did not know of this fact or ever had knowledge of what the limo company had known about him, and he himself never told me of his financial windfall; I guess the limo company knew of this fact from recently published sports reports. I was more than happy though, to try and oblige the company's request and also the client in this very special endeavor.

The first part of this assignment was to fulfill his request to stock the ten passenger stretch with all kinds of Champagnes, alcohol, and provisioning. When a client pre request that we stock the limo with all of the provisioning that they will require for the evening, it is a cha-ching moment for any driver or Limousine Company. This is because that request will be fulfilled, right along with at least a twenty percent markup of the final supplies bill that will then be added to their bill or credit card at the end of the night. The driver also has the option to make that twenty percent return themselves if he or she has the cash to supply all of the needs of the client. I did not have the cash to supply his needs for this evening, so the company gave me five hundred dollars in cash to get all that he had requested for his limousine. With the limousine now fully stocked with liquor, snacks, and ice the party was now ready to begin, I would now be off for the start of an interesting evening and to pick up my millionaire VIP client.

I picked up my client from one of the very popular hotels that was situated on Miami Beach in what is known as Condo Canyon, because of its very high density of high rise condominiums and luxury hotels all cramped into a near one mile stretch along Collins Avenue.

That is the area between forty First Street to the south, and sixty Third Street to the north, directly along Collins Avenue on Miami Beach. I will not say the name of the popular hotel because some folk will try and interpolate times, dates and locations to attempt to try and figure out who my client was for this evening.

When I picked him up at his hotel I was warmly greeted by himself and also his wife or Fiancé and their very young children. I couldn't help but to notice that she had a very large diamond engagement ring on her hand. Mrs. Dolphin player however would not be attending this celebration event with us on this particular night. I think she was just there to tell me to take care of her man and to make sure that I was actually capable of doing just that. As I pulled off and away from the hotel she yelled out to me to make sure that I bring him back safe, the look she had given me was as if she was trying to get some kind of reassurance from me that I would not allow her man to get into anything that he should not be getting himself into; but how could I have done that? I myself was thrilled to be celebrating with a multi millionaire professional athlete. I couldn't reassure her of anything, I can't even reassure myself of anything. So I gave her one of the nicest and brightest smiles that I can give someone and a great big thumbs up to maybe somehow re-confirm to her that all was going to be al- right as I drove off into the sunset with her cash cow of a professional athlete in tow. My adrenaline and excitement flowed out from looking forward to this long upcoming night on South Beach or wherever we may have been headed to.

We drove off with him in the back of the 10 passenger limo all alone, but of course it did not stay that way for very much longer. We went to pick up all of his boys who were all staying at different hotels along Collins on South Beach. As we picked them up each time the itinerary would come more clearly into clear focus as they all started to discuss what the evening was going to look like. This was going to be an evening of whiskey, women and stripclubs, nothing else. I do not think any one of them were actually from Miami because they could not tell me exactly which stripclub that they actually wanted to go to, as there are plenty to choose from in Miami. When they finally told me of what the actual itinerary was going to be, I was to be correct in my assumption and they informed me the whole night was going to be spent at a stripclub; I took them to the most popular stripclub that clients had already requested to me in my then very limited experience.

I was happy to take them there not only to be going to a stripclub with a pro athlete, but also to collect my "head count cash" as I call it. This is the cash that a chauffeur will collect when he or she brings a party to a stripclub, usually between five and ten dollars a head depending on the night of the week and how busy the stripclub actually is. When we arrived at the first stripclub I let my patrons out, had the valet count my heads, parked the limo and then went in to collect my cash. You also get a free meal and soft drink and free entry into most stripclubs when you are a chauffeur. While I was enjoying my free meal and drink at the bar, and after some time my client approached me and told me that this particular stripclub was too soft for their taste and if I had known of anything harder in which they could better enjoy themselves; I told him that I did and I hurriedly finished my sandwich to go and bring the limo around to the front of the club.

I took them to the next stripclub that I thought they would like, and I again was looking forward to another dose of head count cash from the front door, but as I pulled up to the next club, one of the clients came up to the privacy window and asked me if this club was going to be the same type and style stripclub as the stripclub we had just left. I said yeah, that they were somewhat similar with the same type of patrons and type of female attractions. He would then tell me no, that was not going to work for them and they were now requesting to go to a stripclub that was a little bit more raunchy and as ghetto as can be.

GHETTO!? You ask.

Why didn't you guys say that in the first place!?

Now I finally knew exactly what they were looking for and I took them to the raunchiest, and most ghettoist stripclub that I knew of at that time. I had never taken any of my clients there before; I never had a request to go there by any other client before and I truly didn't know what to expect. I didn't even ask at the door if they provided head count cash for chauffeurs, so I didn't receive any, but that would be quite ok that I were not to receive any from this stripclub as you will soon find out why.

I once used to frequent this very same stripclub on my own and during one particular visit I was shocked to see one of the dancers running around and actually squirting her breastmilk from her very own lactating breasts onto various patrons; this is how raunchy this particular nightclub was. Don't judge me though; I didn't go there with the intention of seeing this type of activity, I just went to do what guys normally do there. I do not think you would ever see this type of activity in any of the two stripclubs I had just previously taken them to; they for sure would probably get slapped with some type of assault lawsuit, but this would not be a problem here at this particular urban and not very suburban stripclub.

I took them to club Rolexx, a stripclub in an unincorporated section of Northwest Miami-Dade County, in other words we were in the heart and soul of the Miami ghetto, exactly what they had requested of me. They had loved the choice I had made for them because the energy level had almost instantly changed for them and change for the better.

They were now very noticeably excited, more than the other stripclub we had just left. So much so that Mr. NFL asked me to join them in the stripclub if I would just simply take off my bowtie and tuxedo shirt, here we go again, nobody likes my bowtie I thought to myself, but I was more than happy and ready to oblige and I was once again very proud to sport my all black T-shirt, my shiny gold chain and my beloved Crockett Miami Vice style of dress in this the most ghettoist of a ghetto stripclub.

As we were all walking into the stripclub together I was surprised when my client would hand me over three one hundred dollars in cash; he would then also tell me not to worry, that was not my cash tip for the evening but rather cash to tip out the girls of my personal selection for lap dances at the stripclub as I saw fit.

WOW...are you for real, I remember feeling, but not quite saying so to my client. This can't be for real.

Of course I couldn't say no, right!? My company bosses told me to get out as much cash out from Mr. NFL as I could, obviously that doesn't mean that the Limo Company actually had to get any. Now I was somewhat shocked and also truly excited. With my belly full from the last stop and lots of cash now in my pocket I was also now ready to party for real and so looking fully forward to the adventures that this night would bring to us coming right up ahead and in front of me.

As we were entered the stripclub and searched by security at the entrance, I overheard my client request a VIP table and VIP service in the VIP section of the stripclub, this night is going to be interesting I remember thinking to myself. Interesting would be the very least that I can remember this night would eventually wind up becoming as we made our way to the private VIP section that we were being led to.

When we all grabbed a seat and assumed our positions in our VIP section, the VIP bottle service soon began freely flowing and I had a glass of champagne but I sipped on it very slowly remembering that I am actually working and that I should not fall into the trap that the cowboy led me into. After the VIP bottles were flowing it would soon be time for the women to start flowing through the VIP, it would soon be a nonstop parade of women coming into our VIP section, only the ones that were invited to stay would be welcome to stay for drinks and lap dances, it wasn't very long before they had half a dozen women grinding and gyrating all over them. I would soon be asked why I didn't have any woman gyrating in my lap; I just responded that I had not yet found one that interested me for an intimate lapdance. The truth of the matter was that I was holding on to those three hundred dollar bills for dear life because I felt that I was working for this hard cash and was not at all willing to hand over this hard earned cash for nothing else but a striptease. I was enjoying being the voyeur that I was being that night and even though I didn't know it at the time but I was also building up my memory banks for a future reference like this book.

Mr. NFL was a very big tipper this night, I had witnessed him making rings out of one hundred dollar bills and placing those hundred dollar bill rings onto the left hand ring fingers of the girls that had danced for him; I even heard him ask one of the dancers to marry him for the night, he probably asked all the girls he tipped that night that very same question. We were there for several hours but I can't remember exactly how long though. Mr. NFL was spending hundreds maybe thousands of dollars per hour in there and I also couldn't imagine how much cash Mr. NFL was tossing around that night; but if I had to guess, I would guess somewhere at least around ten thousand dollars, probably much more, in liquor, limos and lap-dances. I guess that wasn't much as compared to the multimillion dollar signing bonus that he had just received, but to me it was a small fortune none the less and I really enjoyed watching all of it fly away in one evening. Never before and never since, even to this very day had I witnessed so much cash flying away at such a fast rate of speed and without any type of regret or remorse. For anyone that has never witnessed this type of hyperactive behavior before, it is definitely a memorable sight to see.

As the night was winding down and coming to a close, Mr. NFL, by this time very intoxicated had leaned over to me and told me that I can choose any one of the strippers that I wanted for the rest of the night to take back to the hotel, but the most that he was going to spend on her was five hundred dollars.

I was shocked to hear this generous offer from him for two simple reasons. One, was for the fact that I had yet to spend a single dollar out of the cash he had already given me before we entered the club and yet he was going to spend another five hundred dollars on me, or rather her. The second concern for me was… wasn't his wife or at least fiancé back at that hotel!? I thought to myself. I didn't dare ask him that question; I just played right along with my client, what else could I do, give him some sort of lecture on money and morality?

Nope, I don't think so.

I just selected the girl that I wanted to spend the rest of the night with; I can still remember her name and what she looked like, as they also made their choices for the rest of the night. We loaded up the limo and headed right back to Condo Canyon. The celebration continued in the back of the now extra loaded up limo on the thirty minute long drive back to Miami Beach.

As we arrived back at the Condo Canyon luxury hotel, Mr. NFL paid the valet attendant to park the limo right in front of the Hotel and we all went into the hotel together. I would soon find out from overheard conversations that Mr. NFL had reserved another suite on the same floor as where his wife and children were more than likely sound asleep. We all went into that suite and the party continued on for the rest of the morning, where the ladies continued on with their dance routines amongst other acts that they were happy to perform. They also darted off to more private rooms in the suite whenever necessary with their temporary significant others. Although I had made my preferred selection of a sexy woman, I didn't do anything with her or any other of the women, I was just there admiring and enjoying the fact that I was partying like a rockstar when I was actually just simply there earning a paycheck and a very handsome gratuity. Although I would never actually complain about working and partying all at the same time; of course this is basically what this career is basically all about if you're ever lucky enough to be chosen to by any of your client to do such things.

I would certainly never work as hard as I did this night and then simultaneously hand over all of the same exact money that I had been currently working for at that time. So for that reason I kept every nickel that Mr. Dolphin gave me that night and besides, by this amount of time already in Miami, I had already had amassed my own selection of lady friends that I could call on at anytime that nature arose for me and it would just cost me a nice simple evening on the town with a movie, liquor and maybe some dinner; If even that much. Sometimes, we may have been on the exact same page and just simply decide to stay in and enjoy each other's company in the privacy of my humble apartments.

It was very early in the morning when everybody's energy level was completely depleted and all of the partying had actually stopped, I approached Mr. NFL as he was nodding off on the living room sofa and I asked him if my services were still needed for the rest of the morning. He told me that I was no longer needed as he shook my hand, thanked me for a job well done and handed me over another five one hundred dollar bills. This night will be one for the ages I can clearly remember thinking to myself as I rode the elevator down to the lobby level and exited the hotel. I drove out of the hotel driveway with very bright sunshine lighting up the brand new day. I went home to finally get some well deserved sleep and took the next few days off from driving so that I could recoup from this very great adventure and to spend all of that hard earned cash that I had earned from the new experiences that I had just gladly had all the while thinking... what other job in the world can you get to do and enjoy this type of lifestyle!?

THE REALLY BIG GAME

This VIP assignment was actually two VIP assignments together at once, I hadn't known that fact however when I had received this assignment on this day. It was also a very historic assignment because it happened during a very historic day in the sporting history of American sports and this is why even to this day I still know the exact date of this particular VIP assignment.

I was assigned to pick up a certain nationally recognized television sports broadcaster from Miami International Airport. I remember when I was waiting at the arrival gate holding the passenger name greeting sign, one of the passengers coming off of the airplane had known exactly who I was waiting for because he called out my client's entire name and was extremely excited about it, although I was just holding up the name sign with just my client's last name with no first initial just as I have always done throughout my career while greeting clients arriving from a flight.

This celebrity newscaster's name will remain nameless though, however what I can say is that when I had heard on the news of a certain scandal that this particular celebrity was going through a few years later, it did not surprise me at all of what I had heard of the scandal because when this particular person first entered my limo, the very first thing that he had asked me was if I had known where the "women" were at. This has always been a certain code word amongst chauffeurs, or taxi drivers and their clients to suggest that they are looking for women of the evening that they can be introduced to at their hotel for an evening of consensual adult entertainment.

At that time in my career I did have a couple of woman friends that knew of the type of work that I was doing and the type of clientele that I was getting from time to time; although they were not professional women of the night, they had still suggested to me that they were more than willing to entertain certain type of men for an evening if the price was right. They had also asked me to contact them with the client if the subject matter had ever come up with any of my affluent clients. But I was not at all the type of person that was wanting or willing to become a pimp to someone, especially someone whom I had considered a friend and I could never actually see myself as a pimp no matter how much cash would be involved for me at the end of the transaction. I never did contact any of them when this certain subject matter actually did come up with any of my clients, which has been surprisingly quite frequent.

Although throughout the years I have known a few drivers, both men and women, who have had this type of service arrangement set up for their clients who do ask that type of question. My thing however when it comes to sinning, as we all do, or actually sinning publicly in which we do much less, is that I have always been willing to commit a sin for myself for my own pleasure or gain but I have never ever been at all interested in leading someone else into sinning; I tend to always follow my guilty conscience to do the right thing when it comes to my friends but not necessarily for myself, If that makes any sense at all, I'm just simply being honest.

So I just politely told Mr. Broadcaster that I did not know where any of the women were at, and with that subject matter squashed, we would then go about the business of documenting and broadcasting this potentially historical sporting event that was right in front of us.

At that particular time I truly did not know that I would be part of this historical night, but when I did finally find out and realize that it was very historical night I became very proud and told the story to a few of my sporting friends who had always enjoyed this story and were also somewhat proud of me.

When I had first picked up Mr. Broadcaster, it was very late at night and I had to just take him to his hotel room at the Doral golf resort in Doral, a suburb city of Miami just adjacent to the Miami International Airport. This first night of three was just that, a transfer to his hotel room and that was all; I was done for this first evening as this was a three day as directed assignment.

The next morning I arrived back at the hotel to drive him around town as he was setting up to document the upcoming night and the next historic day that was fast approaching. I mainly took him to a broadcast studio where he was getting setup for filming and editing for the upcoming documentary. When the second night had rolled around it was now time to start this adventure. I did not know about anything that was about to happen so there were no nerves involved at this time.

Mr. Broadcaster then told me sometime in the evening of Saturday October 10th 1992, that we would be heading to Fort Lauderdale International Airport to pick up the multi sports superstar Mr. Deion Sanders off his private chartered jet, which would be arriving very early in the morning because Mr. Sanders had just finished playing a Major League Baseball playoff game with the Atlanta Braves that very same night, and that he was travelling here to South Florida to play a regular season NFL football game with his other professional sports team on this Sunday...the Atlanta Falcons. Mr. Sanders was trying to set a professional sports record by playing two different professional sporting events in the very same 24 hour period. This to me was really no big deal, what was a really going to be a big deal for me was that I was going to get to meet and drive the wonderfully famous Mr. Deion Sanders.

You see for me growing up baseball was everything to me, not only baseball but specifically the New York Yankees. I played baseball, I watched baseball, and I went to Yankee stadium and watched live games out there in the bleacher sections in the Bronx; I loved baseball and I still do to this very day.

Although I was now living in Miami and just beginning to come around to liking the Florida Marlins, I was still a diehard New York Yankee fan and I had still followed the Yankees even while I was living down here in South Florida. (Even though I will always be a lifelong Yankee fan, during the 2003 World Series between the Yankees and the Marlins however was the one and only time in my life that I had been completely neutral in a professional championship baseball game but by that time I had fully become a Marlin fan after their 1997 World Series win and their impressive 2003 post all star game play, which I once described to someone as being…"on par" with the New York Yankees.) I also had known that Mr. Sanders had played for the New York Yankees for a couple of seasons prior to his current team of the Atlanta Braves, but to me he was still an impressive New York Yankee, and I was going to get to meet him, and drive him, a real live Ex New York Yankee superstar, and he was going to be in my limousine. I was now extremely excited and the jittery nerves would soon set in, I was happy that I didn't know this fact until we were well on our way to the airport to pick him up; I would not have been able to stand the pressure of this assignment ahead if I had known about it beforehand.

As we arrived at the Fort Lauderdale airport private aviation terminal to pick up this super VIP client, we were allowed to drive right onto the tarmac, right along with several other television crews who were already there also documenting this potentially historic event and we all watched as the charted Challenger jet pull right up onto the tarmac. When the plane had finally parked on the ramp and the flight attendant opened the passenger door, she would then step to the side and there he was, he came right to the jet's door to flash his style. He was like an angel at heaven's gates; I remember clearly that he wore an all white track suit with a lot of jewelry including two massive diamond earrings each one on both of his ears. With all of the lights of the cameras and camera crews, this was the ultimate definition of what is bling bling; I can never forget that sight. He was so bright on that dark night that you really needed dark shades to block the brilliance that he bought in the darkness of that early morning night. The bright brilliance had looked like a heavenly angelic vision shining brightly right here on this Earth and I was in total shock and awe of the vision before me.

I pulled that stretched limo right up to the base of the airstair door and Mr. Broadcaster and I were standing right there at the limo passenger door to greet him, and I also wanted to shake his hand. As he came down the airstair I held the limo door open for him and I stuck my hand out as to shake his hand, and to also introduce myself to him as his driver back to the Doral. He whizzed right on by me without saying a word or even shaking my hand, OK..Kool I thought, he must think that I want an autograph, he should know as a professional chauffeur I'm not supposed to do that, but then again does he even know that I'm going to be the chauffeur? I don't know, however maybe we can have a good conversation in the limo on the ride back to the Doral. I kept right on standing there as he had left his beautiful wife or girlfriend in the airplane and I offered her my hand as she exited the aircraft, to help her come down the airstair of the aircraft. She herself was extremely beautiful, but not quite as bright and brilliant as Mr. Sanders had displayed himself to be this particular morning; he was definitely a very proud Peacock of a man I had thought to myself. This must be the reason that they call him Mr. Neon Deion I remember thinking.

With everyone loaded into the limo and with all of the luggage in the trunk, it was time for me to get in and start the drive back to the Doral resort with my two extreme VIP clients in the back of the limo, I could not have been prouder. The exact moment that I had climbed in to assume my position for the ride back, the solid privacy screen went straight on up, you could tell that he knew what he was doing and how to work a limousine unlike Mr. Miami Subs. I couldn't see anything and I didn't hear a thing, hey, at least my jittery nerves were now quelled. There would be no introduction to Mr. Sanders or conversations with him for me on this early morning, nice knowing you Mr. Sanders. I uneventfully took them all to the resort hotel, let them all out, I said my goodbyes, and once again I received no response from Mr. Sanders; I really didn't care though. I was very happy and proud to have gotten him to his destination safely and without complaint. I would then make my arrangements and meeting times with Mr. Broadcaster to meet with him later on that very same, now gameday Sunday morning.

I went home to get just a few hours of sleep and it was just as soon enough time for me to come back to pick up Mr. Broadcaster. That morning I had just taken Mr. Broadcaster back to the broadcast studio where he would spend the morning editing and producing the documentary of Mr. Sander's historic day getting the broadcast documentary ready for the national afternoon broadcast. I was invited into the television production studio where I intently watched how television production and film editing all comes together behind the scenes which I have always since appreciated; thank you Mr. Broadcaster.

When Mr. Broadcaster was done in the studio with the film production, I took him back to the hotel where he picked up his belongings and checked out of the hotel. I would then take him to Joe Robbie stadium where the Miami Dolphins were set to play against Mr. Sanders and his Atlanta Falcons that day. Mr. Broadcaster was there for a little while, I guess to do some sort of NFL pre-game show and I would then take him back to Miami International airport where I dropped him off and he gave me a very handsome gratuity for all of my work over the past few days. He also gave me his Joe Robbie stadium Press Pass for that day and he told me that it was still valid for that afternoon's big game. I thought that this was even better than the cash gratuity he had just given me, and I rushed back to the football game with no client on board, parked the limo in limo parking and entered into Joe Robbie stadium before halftime proudly displaying my hard earned press pass, all the while wearing my tuxedo shirt and bowtie. I then proceeded to strut my stuff around the football field sidelines where all the players were either standing around or playing on the field like a very proud peacock all without anyone ever even batting an eye at me; Deion Sanders had nothing on me on this particular day. Although I had no bling on me shining, I most certainly felt brighter than Mr. Sanders was shining on the previous morning when he departed that jet. I remember thinking to myself there on the sidelines of the field that day, that this was certainly not a bad way for me to get to go to my very first professional NFL football game. I have not yet ever been to another professional football game since that very memorable Sunday in the fall of 1992.

When I had finally had my fill of strutting my stuff down and around the sidelines, I walked out of the stadium tunnel and I sold the valuable press pass I had just received from my client; not bad at all for attending my very first professional Football game I had thought as I walked out of the stadium with all of my extra cash and an experience of an NFL sideline strut; I would have probably stayed if it was an MLB Yankee game and reveled in that atmosphere. I had wondered how many other chauffeurs have ever actually done this before just like what I was doing right now I would ask myself. I sold the press pass for a very decent price, which I had considered a part of my gratuity, to a couple of very excited fans who told me that they were going to take turns strutting their own stuff down there on the sidelines. I stuffed my hard earned cash into my pocket then went home to do my favorite solo bedtime activity; taking an afternoon nap.

Although I was right there at this potentially historic day in American sports and especially right there on the sidelines of a professional NFL game and amongst all of the players, I would never again get to see or speak to the marvelous Mr. Neon Deion Sanders; that was quite OK though, this was an experience that was well worth not getting some stupid handshake. That potentially historic day in American sports did not actually turn out to be however because although Mr. Sander's did make it to the MLB playoff game, he did not actually play in that baseball game that day; I believe he was benched on that particular day in Atlanta, or he did not play in that regular season Miami Dolphin NFL game, I can't remember which it actually was. But the day did not end up being a historic day in American professional sports anyway.

CHAPTER SEVEN
Back To Aviation

All the while that I was still enjoying my new found career chauffeuring; I had never forgot my career roots in aviation and I had always been looking for a way to get back into my first love. During one of my job searches, I came across a startup airline that had just been founded by an ex Eastern Airlines airline pilot. He was looking for an experienced mechanic to do the routine and non routine maintenance on the three small airplanes that had founded the new fleet. He hired me on as an aircraft mechanic to work on these three small airplanes he had leased to service the Bahamas from the Miami International Airport. I was one of only three mechanics to be hired on at this brand new startup airline in South Florida with chartered flights all over the Bahamas and government contract services to the Island nation of Cuba.

Since I have the knowledge of the exact date of one of the last VIP jobs that I had accomplished as a chauffeur, which was actually with Mr. Sanders, and I also still have my very first paystub from the startup airline that I had been hired onto at the new startup airline, I can say that the date was January of 1993.

I can also say that the time in between those two specific dates were more than likely uneventful times that I had spent working as a chauffeur. This is quite routine in the chauffeuring business, with the fact that you can go several weeks or months without any memorable or interesting storylines to talk about as you drive. Then all of a sudden and without notice you could be hit all at once with many consecutive fun and exciting assignments to talk about that you could possibly one day be sharing with your children or grandchildren.

I can still remember the day that I had walked into the limousine office to tell them that I was leaving and heading back into my chosen career field of aviation. They were all quite surprised at my hasty decision, but I had to do this; "my future and my career is in aviation" is what I had told them as they tried to convince me to stay on as a chauffeur. They were of course upset with me, as rightly they should have been; I did not know at that time but I was leaving right at the height of the busy travel and tourist season in South Florida. I had not given them any prior notice that I was leaving and they were now losing a CDL driver that they had invested in, which is a very valuable commodity for a South Florida limousine company. Looking back, I should have listened to what they were telling me, but of course because I was already a professional aviator, I was judgmental towards professional drivers and I hadn't quite yet appreciated what a career as a chauffeur in Miami could bring to me. Aviation would of course do much much better for me and my future family than driving professionally ever could; this is what I would have naively thought to myself. I would walk out that office door and leave that limo company after their long pitch for wanting me to stay there, without any hesitation at all on my part, and I would anxiously restart my aviation career the very next day.

I was very happy to be back working in aviation maintenance after a more than one year absence, and I was proud to be one of only three other mechanics working in the maintenance department at this brand new start up airline. I was trained on the aircraft that I would be working on and in no time at all I would be supervising myself on the routine inspections and performing the pre departure checks that would be required before the early morning departures of the Bahamas bound flights.

This is where I had also began taking field trips to fix broken airplanes that were sometimes stuck and grounded throughout the Bahamas, Florida and also Cuba. While I would either fly over there to fix the broken airplanes, or fly back on an empty leg on a non revenue flight, I would always let the captain know that I was already a licensed private airplane pilot and that I was more than willing to help them fly because these small airplanes did not have co-pilots or autopilots for the long flights over to wherever it was that we here headed to. The pilots were always willing to let a fellow pilot help them out and give them a little break on sometimes hours long flights throughout the Bahamas and Cuba.

This is when my flying bug had hit me once again after receiving my first piloting license that I had received shortly after the closure of PanAm. I had not flown since receiving my private pilot's license because I could no longer afford to do so and chauffeuring had taken up the majority of my time and concentration. I had forgotten how enjoyable and pleasurable flying over the turquoise waters of South Florida and the Bahamas was, but I was quickly reminded on these long trips and I wanted to once again pursue flying as a fulltime career. Although I was enjoying my fulltime job as an aircraft mechanic; I must soon try to figure out a way to pursue furthering my flying career. I would once again turn to doing what I do best.

I once again pounded the pavement, but this time I figured out that I could work part time only for a flight school in exchange for my maintenance labor hours. Only if they would allow me to exchange my maintenance hours for actual flight time hours on the same airplanes that I would be working on, all the while I would remain working on the same commercial airplanes that I had been working on already at night and work at the flight school in the mornings.

It did not take long at all for a flight school to take interest in my plan and a flight school would soon take the bait and accept my offer. I couldn't be any happier; life was perfect for me at this time. I would work my fulltime schedule from 7pm to 3:30am in the morning then go home get about 3 or 4 hours of sound sleep and be at the flight school by 8am and work there until noon or whenever scheduled work would be completed. Then I would go home and get some much needed rest until the start of my evening shift. I did this for months on end and I was able to accumulate a lot of flight time and air experience on my own, including the flight school allowing me to fly one of their airplanes all the way up to Atlanta, Georgia to partake in my sister's wedding. I could not have begged for a better arrangement in my life. That would all soon change though, like the saying goes, all good things must soon come to an end. That is exactly what happened to me in this, my most idealistic situation.

I had worked for that same airline for more than a year and had fully enjoyed the experiences I had gained and truly appreciated the growing and learning that I had acquired from being employed there. I watched the airline grow in that time from three small airplanes to a large scheduled airline with dozens of airplanes in the small amount of time that I had worked there. The only problem was that they could not maintain proper maintenance leadership, and they had gone through several directors for the small maintenance department in the short amount of time that I was there; the last one they hired would wind up having a slight problem with me.

As I went in for my morning shift at the flight school one particular morning, I went into my boss's office to make my usual pot of extra strong coffee to get my juices flowing for the long day ahead. Lo and behold, the boss from my fulltime job is there in the office conversing with my boss from part time job. They had known each other very well from previous employers, he was just as surprised to see me as I was to see him but we had a good conversation about that fact and I really didn't think that he had thought anything of it at all, and I certainly didn't think anything of it at all, I should have though.

This is when all of my problems at the airline started for me; very strong male ego's would soon prevail and instead of communicating the fact that it may have been a problem or maybe even a conflict of interest by me working for the flight school, problems and issues magically started appearing for me at the airline. Manly ego's would soon take effect, and not for me and the positive things that I was doing for my career, but rather surprisingly, against me. I had been there for more than a year, without any previous issues or problems even working throughout the state of Florida, the Bahamas and Cuba working overtime whenever it was required of me without any complaints or issues from my part; I had really enjoyed doing my part for this growing airline; not everyone would see it that way though.

Soon after the surprise morning meeting at the flight school, for the first time ever the new airline boss whom I had spoken with in the flight school office had all of a sudden ordered mandatory overtime for all overnight shift employees in which I was one of them. Instead of getting off at 3:30am as I normally and routinely would, I would now be getting off at 6am.

Are you F'n serious!? Why must people always attempt to steal someone else's joy? I could have very easily and happily work mandatory overtime prior to start of the 7pm shift, but the airplanes would not have been
there at that time; 7pm was the start of the airplane arrivals from their
day long Caribbean treks. He could have also been man enough to come
and speak to me face to face, man to man and just let me know that he
had an issue with me working another job or the possibility of a conflict
of interest. I'm sure we could have worked something out, I'm open like
that, but NO… the male ego must always prevail.

This is not going to work for my beautiful schedule; he is purposely
throwing a wrench in the gears of my life's master plan I remember
thinking. How can I beat this crappy setup coming from this lousy ass-
hole of a man!?

I complied with these new rules for the first few nights, but of course
there was absolutely no way that I could keep up with it and maintain
this mandatory schedule. I again would soon have a severe case of idontgiveashititis; on the third night I decided on my own to leave at the
previously scheduled time of 3:30am. When I got home that morning
around 4am, I had a message on my telephone answering machine from
my supervisor on the shift I had just walked away from, whom by the way,
I had previously trained in all manners of our airplane's maintenance as
he had just graduated from his beloved aviation college with his beloved
aviation maintenance degree. I can still clearly remember his message
to me "you had better have just went out to get something to eat and
you are on your way back to the hangar." Is what I can clearly remember
him saying on my home answering machine. No, I was not just getting
something to eat, I was just now getting ready to go to bed, I gotta go to
work in the morning; see you when I see you boss man.

The next few days I would come into both jobs and work both sched-
ules just as I normally had with no issues at all, but on the third day at
the airline they called me into the office. They needed those three days to
put together their paper package of made up discrepancies against me, in
which not a single one of them were about me walking out of mandatory
overtime.

They had fired me, a year and a half with no issues at all, and within
only weeks of me running into the new boss at my other boss's office

I would be let go. As I was not making very much money on the part time job for the flight school, I also had to consider giving up that job as well to comply with a potentially new airline full time work schedule; in other words I had just about lost two jobs at once with this, what I would consider an unjust firing.

That would be quite OK though, when I walked out of mandatory overtime that first morning, I knew I had to get a quick backup plan, just in case. So I had called my old friend from Aviation High School who had went to Tulsa with me; my good friend Alberto Barnett. Al had left Tulsa well before I had left and he had relocated to nearby Fort Lauderdale; he had been living in South Florida for about five years already and was working as a jet aircraft mechanic for a jet cargo airline here at Miami International Airport. I had already hooked Al up with a few around the town limousine rides at no cost to him when I was first working as a chauffeur and I felt that he had owed me a favor or two and the least he could do for me was to put in a good word for me so that I could get hired on at his airline as a mechanic.

When I had telephoned Al looking for that job, he told me that I had perfect timing because he had just been upgraded to flight crew member as a flight engineer on a DC-8 cargo jet, which is the person in the cockpit who operates all of the systems and controls of the aircraft such as the cabin air conditioning and engine fuel management. Al would inform me in that telephone conversation that he would be leaving his mechanics position and there would now be an open position for an additional jet mechanic. I jumped on this brand new opportunity in front of me and I started complying with the hiring process right away.

I would soon after be hired on as a jet airplane mechanic working on the DC-8 jetliner; life will always go on in a positive direction just as long as you don't give up on it and let it potentially ruin you.

When I started at this new job, the only schedule that was offered to me was also an overnight shift but from 11pm to 7:30am, I had tried very hard to maintain my part time job at the flight school but it would eventually become just too difficult to work all throughout the night without any sleep and then work and have the energy required to work in the bright daytime sun and heat of South Florida. I had needed to be on the school's flightline early in the AM because the airplanes were all dispatched for various flight training lessons and I had to be there at that time to ensure on time or as close to an on time departures as possible. Because of the high energy nature of this task, I would soon have to give up my flight school job and the beautiful flying that came along with it. I would now decide to fully concentrate on the new full time job that was at hand, it was a brand new challenge for me so concentrating on learning this new airplane and its complicated systems would not be too difficult for me to focus on.

I was already well into working at this new airline for over a full year all while enjoying the work there and learning the new equipment that I was fortunate enough to get to know and become familiar with.

Almost as soon as I put in enough time and I was getting just comfortable enough at this new company, two drastic things would happen there almost simultaneously that I saw as completely negative for me at the time but looking back at those two events actually turned out to be more than a blessing for me.

The first thing that was changed was that my overnight schedule of 11pm to 7:30am for five days a week would be suddenly and abruptly altered. My new schedule would now be from 7pm to 7am; a 12hour shift with four continuous days off that would always alternate. I didn't like this dramatic change at first, but I would soon learn to love this beautiful new schedule because with the alternating days off I would always be guaranteed a full weekend off every now and then from 7am Friday morning having Friday night off all the way to Monday night off not having to be back at work until Tuesday night at 7pm.

This new schedule was also good for me because the airline would soon after ask me to upgrade my position from a regular flightline mechanic to a flight crew member as a flight mechanic who would be responsible to travel with the airplanes throughout their scheduled flight routes to guarantee on time and continuous deliveries without the concern of a delay due to a breakdown of the aircraft and to change critical aircraft parts and service the aircraft systems from the aircrafts onboard supplies store better known as the fly away kit. I would do this type of work and travel for the airline on my regular days off for great overtime and travel pay. I would do this assignment mainly on my weekday days off because I always wanted to enjoy my full weekends off in sunny South

Florida. This is the time when I began travelling as a flight crew member throughout the Caribbean and South America including my own home town of Port of Spain, Trinidad and Tobago; I had really appreciated being able to travel internationally and especially having the ability to see my extended family over there at absolutely no cost to me, an excellent and great job to have with the employment benefits to match. This is definitely what I had thought about this new position that was given to me.

This job had also given me the opportunity to see my grandmother on the last day of her life. I had been working down in Trinidad when I had an opportunity to go see my grandmother in that little humble home that she had lived in for so very long. When I went to see her that day, she was on her deathbed and I had not seen her since my preteen years. I clearly remember seeing her big ole' grin when I had walked into her bedroom. My aunt had told me she had not smiled like that in a very long time and she had been very impressed to have seen her do that within my presence; I was glad that I was able to as well because I will never forget the energy and the love she showed me as I walked through that door. The happiness would be short lived however, because as I had arrived back home to my beautiful waterfront Miami apartment the very next day, I had come home to my telephone voice answering machine with a message from my father telling me that my grandmother had just died.

Why didn't I like this change of schedule again? This job was truly a God send for me, just because of this one single wonderful opportunity that it had afforded me to be able to see my grandmother after so many years of being absent from her, and on the last day of her life on this Earth. It was as if she was waiting on me just to say goodbye before she decided that she would finally leave this Earth and this one particular job had everything to do with that happening. May you continue to rest in peace Granny. I know that you are up there still grinning that big ole' grin you showed me when I last saw you.

The second drastic and dramatic change that happened to me right about that time was due to my fault and my immaturity at that time. A couple of years earlier while I was enjoying my... by now long gone chauffeuring career I had never paid taxes on my income as a chauffeur and my 1099 income statement had been turned over to the IRS just as they were supposed to; right along with me not paying out my income taxes to the US government. I had also never stopped my unemployment compensation from my layoff status at Pan American World Airways. I was an independent contractor and my employment status was never relayed to the proper authorities to readjust my employment status. Those "icing on the cake" unemployment checks just kept right on coming in and I never made any type of attempt to stop them from coming, so they just kept right on coming for the whole year that I was eligible for benefits.

I know I was wrong, don't judge me. We all make mistakes; just make sure to learn from them.

Well what the change was, was that the IRS and an IRS tax collection agent walked right into the office at my new airline to get my attention. They came to collect all of the money that was due to them.

What could I say or what could I do?

I couldn't do anything but admit my wrongdoing and that's exactly what I did. I did not even put up a fight; whatever amount they had came up with I wouldn't argue I would just accept it like the man that I was. The amount they had came up with for the unemployment taxes, the 1099 at the limo company, late fees and of course penalties were well in excess of ten thousand dollars. The IRS had agreed to give me two years to pay it all back and set up a two year payment plan for me, which in turn turned out to be more than half of my income at this new airline, even with the overtime and travel pay that the airline was allowing me to have. I had to figure something out so that I could continue to live, again.

It did not take me long at all to recall all of the adventures and all of the money that I had made as a chauffeur almost a few years earlier now, so I decided to go back to where I had gotten my start as a chauffeur to find some part time work. I had figured out that on my long weekends off from the airline I would be more than happy to work as a chauffeur because to me it wasn't really work at all; it was more like getting paid to party for me as I had recalled my first year of driving professionally. On my days off for the airline in the mid week I would travel overseas to collect overtime and travel pay and I would chauffeur again on my weekends without it actually feeling like work I would convince myself to think. This should be a really big cash boom in my income in order to help me offset the new mandatory IRS payroll deductions that would be now taken directly from my airline paycheck.

This was now a new plan for the ages; so why was I so upset for all of these sudden and drastic changes!? This plan that I thought up would eventually wind up working so well for me that I was actually able to soon after starting this plan, be able to move back to the tiny Island community and rent a waterfront apartment with perfect bay views of beautiful Biscayne Bay and the gorgeous Miami downtown skylines.

When I had gone back to my old limousine company to reapply for a part time driving position, I was shocked to see that they were no longer in business and the garage where I had spent close to a year of my life was shuttered and empty. I didn't think anything of it though, I had known of a few other small limousine companies that were even closer to the little apartment where I lived since after the days of PanAm and where one limousine company in particular were always proudly displaying their inventory of super stretched Lincoln limousines and Lincoln towncar sedans right along a major stretch of highway US1 in the city of North Miami, better known in Miami as Biscayne Boulevard.

I had went to that specific limo company for an application for the sole reason that I also lived right there in North Miami at that time and the offices were only a few miles from my tiny apartment.

When I entered the office, I would tell them that I was looking for part time work as a chauffeur, and when I told them of my previous employer and experiences they suddenly took a keen interest in me and they hired me right on the spot without any follow up interviews or application forms. I think it was because they had already purchased all of the assets from my previous limousine company and they had probably saw me as an additional asset that they could claim and say they had also acquired from them.

I would now have to renew all of my professional licensing and I reactivated my pager; it would now be time for me to once again get behind the wheel of a chauffeured limousine for a brand new employer and to gain brand new experiences as a part time chauffeur, in which there would now be plenty of brand new stories for me to acquire and share, in which I will now continue to do as such and share these incredible limousine stories with you.

CHAPTER EIGHT
Round Two

When I had started working for this new limo company, I had noticed that they had taken an immediate liking to me. This limo company was a family run business with all of the head officers who were running the show were all blood related; fathers and sons, brothers and uncles, wives and sisters.

I was also very happy that I no longer had to wear some stupid bowtie and pleated white tuxedo shirts, as the company had their own company brand necktie that they issued to their drivers. All the drivers had to do was provide their own standard white oxford shirts and the standard black suit.

Over the years speaking to other drivers who had worked for this company I had heard a lot of stories about the origin of the success of this company. When I was first hired on, what I had originally heard about this Italian family was that they were partially founded by the Italian Mafia and that they had still had ties and connections with that organization all while I was working there. That did not bother me at all though hearing about that, just as long as my legal paycheck would clear the bank. I really couldn't care any less about how they were originally founded. I would later hear from other drivers that the patriarch of the family had actually made his fortune in the upstart valet parking business of South Florida, and had then eventually branched out into the limousine business. Whatever the case might have been, this family was good to me and they treated me as such.

What I had noticed right from the start was that they had assigned me to drive the matriarch of the family along with their teenage children to the family's private yacht in Islamorada, just south of Key Largo in the Florida Keys on a very routine and almost on a weekly basis. I would pick the family up on late Friday afternoons or early evenings after business hours and then drive them down there and come back alone to the office to drop off the vehicle. I didn't only think that the family had liked me for the only reason of allowing me to have the responsibility of driving the family down to the Florida Keys so often, but rather that as I arrived to pick them up for the long trip down, they would always allow me to sit and wait for them as they got themselves ready inside of their beautiful waterfront home in Keystone Point, a very upscale waterfront community in North Miami. They did not want me to sit there and wait inside the limo like chauffeurs normally and routinely do while they had gotten ready for their weekend.

When I would wait in their lovely home I would always admire the tropical foliage surrounding their beautiful home and I loved their collection of a few exotic tropical birds and listening to all of the beautiful chaos of the noises these birds would all harmonize together. This beautiful musical orchestra of these tropical Parrots has always made me know that I would also probably want to have a collection of tropical birds to harmonize in any home that I may one day eventually own; to me it was a certain type of natural peace and comfort to listen to in one's own home.

Another thing that I had noticed about this new limo company was that even though they were a whole lot smaller than the limo company I had previously worked for, they had a whole lot more very exclusive clientele. This company did not do as many weddings, funerals, and proms like the first company, rather they had a large client list of truly exclusive VIP clientele who were always ready to party, spend their money and flaunt their wealth. I did not get this interpretation from the first limo company I had worked for and this is probably the reason why they had succumbed to company closure; I was now very excited to be able to work here even if it was just on an alternating weekends and on a part time basis.

THE RICH DAD

One of the earliest clients that I had remembered working for at this new company was for what I was told by the dispatchers was the wealthiest man in Broward County at that particular time. This truly incredible assignment was to just be a standby driver for a party that this man was having at his gorgeous intercoastal waterfront mansion in the very exclusive upscale community of Lighthouse Point.

I was assigned to just simply drive anyone home that was too intoxicated to drive themselves home and to simply standby until that request would come through.

This wealthy man was a genuine real deal of a great man; he invited me to standby inside of this beautiful multi story mansion instead of having me standing by inside the confines of the ten passenger limousine all alone by myself. Of course at first I did let him know that I had to stay with my vehicle, but he wouldn't hear anything of the sort. That excuse did not make any sense because I was parked inside of his secured multi car driveway, he insisted that I get out of the car, shut the ignition off, and come and join the party inside of this, his very large mansion. I now could not say no to my client anymore.

As I entered the mansion I was awe struck at what I had seen inside, the back of the home did not have the typical type of solid wall you would see in any other typical home. This back wall of the home was made entirely of transparent glass with a wonderful view of the intercoastal waterway and his private yacht docked at his very own pier, dock and his own professional marina equipment. The view on the backyard patio was to die for where there was a constant parade of very expensive private yachts slowly cruising on by and that was also where the professional outdoor cooking station was located at, right along with the professional chef and his professional cooking team, where they were hard at work putting out a delicious gourmet meal for all of the guest to enjoy that day.

As he led me to the back patio where the official party was in full swing, I did not know what the celebration was for, but he had kindly introduced me to family members and guests at the party as if I were an actual family member invited to the party. When he was through with introducing me to all, he would then cut me loose and he gave me permission to wander around the mansion on my own; he told me that I had free range of the mansion and that I could take a self guided tour to anywhere I had wanted to go; he must have seen something in me to give him that amount of a trust level for someone he just met.

Are you kidding me!? I'm a black man if you haven't noticed sir, I remember thinking to myself; haven't you seen any of my type on any of the local TV news reports, I would continue to think to myself.

Of course, I didn't say that out loud. Rather, I gladly took on the challenge of his generous invitation; I would have to take this challenge, I had never been inside of a mansion before!

Before I branched out on my own for my solo tour, he told me to help myself to the bar; I said OK and thanked him as I walked back into the mansion. My first stop was through the very large industrial style kitchen, the kitchen was larger than the size of my little efficiency apartment in North Miami. As I walked out of the kitchen I walked into what I deemed must have been a sort of living room, however it wasn't your typical living room, this living room had a bar, a very large bar that can be easily rivaled against any bar in any night club in South Florida. Not only was the bar very large but the stock of liquor bottles and all the bottles of wine was just as impressive, it was a full bar with hundreds of different bottles of different brands of alcoholic beverages. I couldn't believe what I was seeing and that he had told me to help myself to it; I was more than happy that I have never been any type of an alcoholic personality because I surely would have gotten myself into a whole lot of trouble that late afternoon. I had just simply helped myself to a simple soft drink as I had clearly remembered my chauffeuring days of past and more specifically that wonderful cocaine cowboy from a couple of years earlier.

My next stop around the mansion was to the indoor gymnasium, it was a full gym with all sorts of exercise equipment. No gym membership was ever needed in this household, they had more gym equipment than the best equipped public gym as well as being fully air conditioned. I remember being impressed by that because I had seen home gyms before, usually outback or inside of a garage but never had I seen a fully air conditioned home gym inside of the actual home; very impressive I had thought. After roaming around the first level of the mansion and awing over all of the luxury accommodations that came with this house, I would then make my way up to the second level of this luxurious home.

On the second level of the home, I saw the master bedroom with all of the personal belongings of the homeowners and the spectacular water views that the second floor allowed; all of the same waterfront view of the intercoastal waterway and the yacht docked out back. I remember thinking about the ability that they had had at waking up every morning with those spectacular views; I certainly would not need coffee to wake me up with that wonderful view, life in itself would wake me up with a life like that.

As I continued to tour the second floor, I also looked through all of the additional bedrooms for the children that had lived there. Each one of the rooms were decorated to the individual child's liking and they all also had bright sunshine shining into the rooms, right along with the same wonderful water views. I had truly realized how trusting of me that my client truly was when I had opened one of the bedroom doors to see one of his teenage sons laying there alone on the bed and quietly reading a book to himself, I apologized to the young boy as he looked over to me surprisingly, I then quickly closed the door and continued on with my unescorted tour.

Wow, I remember thinking to myself after that somewhat embarrassing moment. What is it that this client sees in me to allow me to have full run of this mansion especially when he has family members still lounging around in their personal spaces!? I didn't think long about it though because I had to get back to the business at hand once my tour was completed. I did however appreciate the trust that he had extended to me and that made me realize that I must be some type of special individual that allowed me to be such a trustworthy individual; or maybe he was just watching my every single move on some closed circuit security cameras with a full security team watching over me, I don't know.

I had truly appreciated the invitation to do this self guided tour of this very expensive home simply because it had been a lot better than just sitting inside the limousine for hours on end waiting for this party to end as is usually the case for chauffeurs who do private parties for high end clientele.

After my special tour, I had returned to the back patio area where the family and guests were all gathering and I spoke to my client about the wonders that I had seen and told him that I had truly appreciated the trust that he put in me, he told me that it was no problem and invited me to lounge on the patio with the rest of the party. I was once again impressed by his actions and I lounged and I ate and I drank as if I were a guest myself. Why was I not doing this chauffeuring job for the past couple of years again? I remember asking myself; this is the life to experience all of these wonderful experiences.

When night time had finally rolled around and the party was finally over I was of course one of the last to leave the party because of what my assignment had entailed of driving too intoxicated people home. When it was actually time for me to leave I had realized that I had not driven anyone for the entire evening and I had just hung out, lounged and did nothing else but enjoy myself for the whole time that I was here at this rich man's party. When I had finally left the party, he sent me home with a very nice care package of gourmet food and a very handsome cash gratuity. What else could I have possibly asked for on a job? Assignments like this have made my driving career interesting and unforgettable thus far.

THE RICH COUPLE

In working for this new limousine company it had seemed to me to be a pretty regular trend towards families allowing me to enter and also tour their beautiful homes because this next story has almost the very same circumstances as the party at the mansion except for the fact that it was not an as directed.

On this one particular assignment, I was simply assigned to do an easy home to airport transfer to the Fort Lauderdale International airport from the very exclusive community of Golden Beach in the extreme northeastern corner of Miami-Dade county right on the Atlantic Ocean; these are the only single family homes directly on the Atlantic Ocean in all of Miami. The one and only exception to this fact is the Versace Mansion on Ocean Drive in South Miami Beach, which is now a specialty hotel. All of the single family homes directly on the Atlantic Ocean are not really homes, but rather very large mansions; including this home that I was assigned to pick up this rich couple for an airport transfer.

As I pulled up to this oceanfront mansion, I was allowed into the wrought iron automated gate and was told to park in the driveway of the multi car garage. The lady of the mansion would then come over to the Lincoln sedan and notified me that they were not quite ready to leave for the airport as they had just arrived from work and that they still needed about an hour or so to get ready for their weeklong trip. She would then invite me into the mansion to wait while they finished their preparations for their trip.

While I entered the foyer she had directed me to the immediate right which was the media room, which looked more like a small movie theatre which was completely blacked out with dark movie theatre style curtains and with the same movie theatre style seating, a large projection screen and projector also with multiple television screens in the front end of the room.

The Mrs. would then hand me a very large component box that looked something like a thicker version of a modern day computer tablet, except at that time there were no computer tablets yet invented. I was told that it was the remote control for all of the media systems in the room. At that same time I was also once again told that I was free to take an unescorted tour of the oceanfront mansion as well as to help myself to whatever I had wanted from the state of the art refrigerator in the professional gourmet kitchen.

Again Wow…I must be a really special person because I once again thought to myself that these folks must not watch their local TV newscast and they also must not notice the brown hue of my chocolate skin. But I still felt more than wonderful to be so fully trusted on a first time meeting basis; then again it just might be the trust of those expensive security systems that were guarding these multimillion dollar mansions.

How and why must these very welcoming committees be so welcoming to me so very often I would contemplate to myself; but I certainly would not turn down a free and open unescorted tour of a beautiful oceanfront mansion like the one that I was currently in right here and right now.

As the lady of the house went upstairs to continue her trip preparations

I decided to put down the very complicated piece of machinery that was the media remote control and take her up on the unescorted tour. The first place that I had went to was the very large professional gourmet kitchen; I can still see and remember all of the shiny new kitchen appliances in the gourmet kitchen; I think it was the first time that I had seen a kitchen with all matching stainless steel appliances, the kitchen was extremely well maintained and professionally kept. Even inside the refrigerator was spotless and all of its contents looked so very scrumptious and appetizing; I just took out a soft drink again and passed up on all of the tempting looking food that was sitting very neatly inside the refrigerator.

I had not been invited to the second floor of the mansion as they were still getting ready for their flight so I stayed on the first floor, but I did not need to tour much of the first floor because attached to the kitchen was the back patio along with the view; the view of their swimming pool as well as also the Atlantic Ocean. I did not have to tour any other part of this mansion; I was at home right out here on this beautiful deck with its incredible views. I sat out there on the patio as if I were at my very own home, so much so that I completely lost track of the time and only realized that I was actually working several minutes later. When I had realized that I was actually on a job I would then run back to the media room to try and learn to work that remote control while I passed the time as they continued to get ready.

By about the time they couple had been ready to leave, I had just about figured out the basics of the remote control, but when they had come downstairs with their luggage I dropped that challenge and went out to load up the luggage into the Lincoln sedan. This would be the end of this tour as I did not go back into that gorgeous mansion again and I took them to the airport for their Southwest Airlines flight; I was truly surprised that they were travelling with Southwest because I truly did not know or believe that multimillionaires actually travelled on Southwest airlines. They would also give me a very handsome cash gratuity, and I even got a chauffeur's ultimate form of gratuity by the couple requesting me for their airport pickup one week after I picked them up at the mansion. This is a chauffeur's ultimate sign of a job well done by having a returning client request you by name; the greatest thank you that a chauffeur can ever get. I picked them up one week later and bought them back to their ultimate in a luxury home. Thank you rich couple for the honor of the unescorted tour and the trust you gave me to roam your home. I pray you are still together and that God continued to bless your family.

MY CO-WORKER

On one particular evening I was assigned to do a long VIP as directed assignment for a regular client at this new limousine company. The assignment was to chauffeur around a single gentlemen who was also a very regular client of this limousine company who would routinely be chauffeured around town for usually about 8 hours straight usually on a Saturday night.

I pulled up to the very large house in a suburb city of Miami which I will not name to protect the innocent or not so innocent. When I had exited the vehicle to knock on the door to let the client know that I was there and to introduce myself as his chauffeur for the evening, as he answered the door, I was completely surprised to recognize the client as one of my co-workers of the airline where I was currently employed for as a fulltime mechanic and flight mechanic. I was in immediate shock and I got instantly nervous because I did not know if he would have recognized me; I was very happy at that time that I had always wore a baseball cap to protect my skin from the sun and also to mask my already fast receding hairline. I also would never clean shave my facial hair like I was absolutely required to do as a chauffeur, this gave me some comfort that he probably would not recognize me and also that he did not work directly with me.

As time seemingly took forever to move on that evening, I slowly came to conclusion that he did not recognize me and that he wouldn't recognize me just as long as I did not talk about myself and my other career so I gradually started to relax my jittery nerves as the night continued to wear on.

This gentleman would be my one and only client in the ten passenger stretch limousine the entire night. I had taken him at first to a private house in a city way down south of Miami, about an hour away from the pickup point. This is where he had spent the majority of the evening. I stayed outside of the private house where I heard a group of men inside of the house playing poker and making lots of noise laughing and joking; I am almost certain they were all somewhat intoxicated with more than likely free flowing alcohol inside of the house because they had just sounded as such. The entire time my client was there enjoying himself inside of the house, I just sat outside in the limo listening to my collection of reggae CD's as I would normally do on long as directed assignments.

We had stayed at that house until about 3am that Sunday morning and when he was ready, and we were to finally leave that house way down south; he would then tell me where the next stop was going to be for us on that very early morning as directed assignment.

He bluntly told me that he wanted to get a woman of the night and that we would be searching for her around Biscayne Boulevard in central Miami, a known hotspot for this type of illegal activity in the city of Miami, again almost an hour away from our location down south. When he had told me this, I had once again gotten extremely nervous and jittery because all that I could think about was getting busted by the police in the course of picking up a hooker, and that Mr. Co-worker would of course now eventually find out who I actually was and who I actually worked for on a full time basis; him. Mr. Co-worker right there in the back seat of my limousine searching for hookers. I would never live down this crazy story amongst my coworkers if we were to somehow get busted by the police on this one unbelievably easy but crazy night. As I would normally do for all of my clients, I honored his request, although I could have easily and justifiably said no to his illegal request of me; it is just in my nature to serve in a service industry even if it could eventually cost me dearly.

When we had arrived to downtown Miami and started to cruise Biscayne Boulevard we made several circuits of the approximate seven mile strip where the ladies of the night would usually frequent. He would end up speaking with a few of the ladies through his rear seat window, but he never actually found a woman or let any one of them into the

limo. When I would stop the limo to have him talk to the potential ladies, I would just about to start to sweat profusely even in the cold air
conditioned limo; I could not stop looking at all of my rear view mirrors
looking for anything that might even come close to looking like a city
of Miami police officer on road patrol. I was really anxious for this long
night and this very awkward situation to finally be over.

The sun had finally started to show just under the horizon when he
finally gave the command to take him home, he did not find a woman this
night and I couldn't have been happier. I was tired of doing the circuits
up and down Biscayne Boulevard looking for hookers and I just wanted
to go home to bed.

When I had finally taken him back to his multi story home in that
Miami suburb city, I had went to the back of the limo to let him out as
I always do and to expectantly collect my cash gratuity. After that long
probably about ten hour night, this client, a co-worker of mine from my
full time employer, had the nerve to tell me and I quote…"I can't give you
a tip right now because I am down to my last million dollars." These are
words that I will never forget and will never leave my brain because this
statement was shocking to me solely for two reasons.

First, Mr. co-worker lived in this huge, close to the size of mansion
type of home seemingly all alone and Mr. co-worker was just looking
for hookers for half of the night who I'm sure do not take any type of
plastic credit card, which obviously means that you do have some sort of
cash on your person, otherwise you just risked both of my professional
careers at the same exact time for absolutely no reason at all. No other
case of having a non-tipping client has ever disturbed me as much as this
non-tipper had, simply because I went so far out of my way.

Secondly, Mr. Co-worker you are just a simple co-worker working for
a relatively small cargo airline, how do you get to live in this very large
mansion style of home and still have anything near one million dollars in
your bank account on a relatively small cargo airline's employee's salary.

I had thought about this situation for a very long time, especially
every time that I ran across Mr. Co-worker at work. I made sure to keep
my cap on at all times near his vicinity at work, so as to not have him be
able to recognize me. I would also make sure to come to work unshaven
and not "Limo Clean" as I have always called it ever since I started to do

both careers simultaneously; I would never be limo clean while I was at work in aviation.

I had also thought about that bold early morning drop off statement from Mr. co-worker for a very long and hard time after the fact, until I had finally had the opportunity to find out what was actually going on at that small airline which is no longer in operation and has been out of operation for over a decade.

This is what actually happened to make me no longer question what was going on with Mr. Co-worker.

One afternoon while I was working on the flightline for the airline, probably on overtime duty, I had received an incoming flight that had just arrived from Bogota, Colombia. I was doing my normal arrival inspection on the massive DC-8 all cargo aircraft, all while all the cargo was offloaded and customs and inspection officers had combed through the aircraft and cargo for any type of illegal contraband. None were found and I was finally allowed to go onboard the aircraft so that I could complete my interior inspection of the routine arrival check.

During the accomplishment of my interior inspection, I noticed that the hydraulic system of the cargo door required servicing due to the fact that the door actuator fluid level was on the low side. I was on the aircraft out on the flightline while the servicing fluid that I needed was inside the hangar about half a mile away. I was lazy and the Florida sun was extremely hot as usual, I did not want to walk all the way to the hangar to get the servicing fluid that I required to service this cargo door, so I went to what we call the aircraft's fly away kit, which is an area in cargo aircraft where all essential parts and servicing items that the flight mechanic can use to get a grounded airplane back up in the air. It is supposed to be only used in the field at outstations, but all the mechanics routinely broke that rule to make their job a little bit easier as I did this particular day.

I felt lazy that day and I didn't want to walk all the way over to the hangar supply stores, so I went into that fly away kit to get the one quart can of hydraulic oil that I needed to service the cargo door. As I opened the can of oil with an old school type of can opener which makes the triangle shaped hole in the top of the can, instead of fluid being in the can, a big puff of a white cloud came up from out of the can. I thought nothing of it at first, I had honestly thought that since this flight had just arrived and the cabin was extremely cold, this led me to believe that the fluid in the can may have just simply frozen up and maybe needed a little thawing out. I waited for a few minutes with the can in the hot Florida sun but I saw absolutely no thawing out of the oil. I decided to go back to the fly away kit and check out the other cans of oil sitting there in that fly away kit. I opened another can of oil and the same thing happened and I now noticed that this puff of white was also under extreme pressure; this was not a case of frozen oil I immediately thought. I shook the other cans of the quarts of oil in the kit and there were no sloshing around of the fluids as there would normally be, rather very solid and very heavy cans. This is when I realized what was going on and what I had found; it was cocaine, pure white powdery cocaine flown in directly from the jungles of Colombia all stashed in a case of 24 sealed quart cans of hydraulic oil.

With all this uncut and undetectable cocaine literally in the palm of my hands; the K-9 dog team had already searched the arriving aircraft. I had instantly felt like I was in another hot scene of my favorite television show Miami Vice and I now had immediate daydreams of buying an H1 hummer, the same one made famous by Mr. Arnold Schwarzenegger and what I would potentially look like behind the wheel driving through Ocean Drive in South Beach on a busy weekend night.

The H1 Hummer had become my dream car at that time because this airline I was working for had previously shipped a few of them out of the country and I helped myself to a quick drive on the airport ramp with one of them during a midnight shift at work when no one was looking just before it had been prepped for loading into the aircraft. This is when I had instantly fallen in love with this very masculine and very sexy all at the same time type of machine, for the little bit that I had driven that vehicle I had felt like a man's man behind that wheel. But I still could not bring myself to come up with some sort of a master plan to get these 24 quart cans full of pure Colombian cocaine outside of the airport fence; the 24 quart cans were completely and professionally sealed and the cocaine was completely undetectable as proven by the fact that the search dog had missed it. Those cans would have been extremely easy to move off of the ramp because the cans had already been sniffed by the US customs search dog and also thoroughly visually inspected by the US customs officers, so therefore I am certain that no one else would have had any type of suspicion, except of course the people who actually owned the shipment.

I did not want to think of another possibility of potentially getting a permanent headache. So Instead of taking that risk, I did the next best thing that I could think of at that moment; I notified my immediate flightline supervisor to inform him of what I had found. I had felt at that moment that I called him, that if he had wanted to sneak the case off the ramp and into the Miami streets that I would have been more than willing to oblige and share in the potential proceeds. That did not happen though and he would take the better option of making the call to law enforcement. My supervisor did the right thing by calling the powers that be in the company as well as the US customs officers back over to the DC-8 cargo jet to show them exactly what they had obviously somehow missed during their earlier search of the aircraft.

It had turned out to be 52 kilos of uncut and pure cocaine with a street value worth over five million US dollars at that time, which was what the US customs department would eventually report. I thought that I would get some sort of cash reward once the investigations were completed since I had turned it all in as some sort of motivation for doing the right thing by turning it all in; however they had told me that I had needed to turn in the conspirators to actually get a reward, like if that would ever really happen. So for that fact all I got was a pat on the back, a thank you and nice job from the United States Customs and Immigration service; I couldn't take all of that wonderful gratitude from the US government to the bank though and I went back to work as if nothing had ever happened, always thinking of what could've been.

Approximately two weeks after my little cocaine find, the same co-worker that I had driven all around all that night looking for companionship would put out a companywide memorandum notifying all employees that we were no longer allowed to go into the fly away kit for any reasons at all to remove any type of servicing necessities to service the aircraft while on the Miami maintenance base. This is all that I needed to hear; with that memo I would no longer be wondering as to why this simple co-worker could live in a mansion and be down to his last million dollars as he refused to give me a cash tip after a very long and hard night of driving for him. I could be wrong and I might be passing undeserving judgment on Mr. co-worker, but I don't care, it finally made me stop the long and hard wondering that I had constantly been doing about how this man could possibly do what he does and live where he lives; I would finally have the peace of mind that I had long been looking for ever since I had dropped off this simple company co-worker at his suburban mansion and heard what he had told me about his sobbing and heartfelt financial situation.

He could have very easily been joking around with me that early morning, but I did not see it that way, I had driven him all night and he did not show me any appreciation, there was no reason to joke around and he genuinely sounded sincere in what he had said to me in his statement about that he only had one million dollars left in his bank account. This incredible experience would now be finally over for me with this companywide memo, some months after it had started.

THE SECRET CELEBRITY

Like I mentioned earlier, this second limousine company that I worked for had specialized in Super VIP clients and this was the majority of clients that I had been assigned to while employed there and this next story was one of those a prime example of the clientele that they were accustomed to acquiring.

I was assigned to pick up a certain up and coming celebrity female Super VIP client for a transfer from Miami International Airport to an Art Deco hotel on Ocean Drive in South Beach. The limo company had known that I was a full time airport employee and that I had a full access Identification badge so that I could go right to the gate of the arriving aircraft without any security hassles. They had truly appreciated the fact that they could provide this excellent service from aircraft door to hotel door VIP service for their VIP clients; it simply stepped their game up just that little bit more above the other competition.

I went through the security checkpoint with no problems as I had done so many times before; but I would soon realize that something was going to be very unusual about this particular assignment because of what I would I would soon see; this what I would see was not normal and therefore this assignment is not starting out on a normal basis was my simple reasoning behind my feeling unusual.

As I was waiting for the little shuttle train over to the gate area for the American Airlines flight, I had noticed someone that I was very surprised to see. It was the same Mr. Co-worker of my airline company that I had driven months if not weeks earlier; I again didn't want him to recognize me so I stood way back and away from him and I stayed at full attention to do what I could to avoid any type of contact with him.

Although I had worked directly with him as a moonlighting chauffeur once before, I still didn't want him to actually concretely recognize me and know for sure that I truly was moonlighting on him as a chauffeur, so I did whatever it was that I had to do to steer completely clear of him that early evening.

As we both got off the little shuttle train and made it to the gate seating area I would realize that he was taking an outbound flight out to somewhere for what seemed to me like a business trip because of his dress and attire and that he was not actually maybe stalking me; this was the confirmation to me of my practice of not being limo clean when I was at work on the airport. I just decided that I would have to stay fully alert until he boarded his airplane and left or until I had left with my Super VIP client; I would certainly keep my eyes wide open in his direction as to try and avoid any and all contact with him.

When the arriving flight had finally arrived and my celebrity VIP client had stepped out of the jetbridge I immediately recognized her even though she was completely dressed down and what I can only think and describe as purposely unrecognizable. I had already known who she was, but because she was so dressed down I or nobody else would have probably recognized her without a complete staredown. She was still beautiful and absolutely gorgeous and I was more than excited to meet her and to especially drive her to her final destination. I wish that I could mention who this celebrity was, but the privacy of this unbelievable story will not allow me to do so, so please just enjoy the story as it is written.

She was the first passenger off of the aircraft as she was more than likely travelling in the first class compartment and was also escorted by one of the female flight attendants, the flight attendant had shaken her hand and said goodbye to her as if she was showing her the appreciation for having the opportunity of meeting her.

As I was holding the code named greeting sign as some celebrities who do not want their names to be recognized often do, she would recognize me and acknowledge me as being her. I kindly introduced myself, and I told her that I was going to be her driver to her South Beach hotel like I would normally do. She was travelling alone and had no other entourage; this to me was very unusual because women of her beauty and stature usually have some type of entourage or at least a bodyguard for some sort of protection from all of the celebrity hounds at airports. I certainly did not mind having her all to myself though so that I could use my charm to get to speak with her and actually get to know her in the short trip over to South Beach. The charm absolutely worked, because we spoke, laughed and joked around like we had been friends for years and she was very honest and open towards me all before we even made it back to the parked sedan. No one had recognized her as we walked together through the airport terminal and we made it back to the Dolphin parking garage and the sedan uneventfully, right where I had had my very first Miami International Airport conquest so many years earlier.

As we finally got into the sedan, the conversation and debauchery would continue in full swing, so much so that during the drive over this super VIP client would tell me that even though she was a celebrity she did not enjoy being around people that she did not know, but we had clicked so well that she felt as if she had known me for years. I did not mean to put on that sexual "cheetah" charm that I wrote about earlier, rather just the same professional charm and personality that I extend to all of my clients who I am chauffeuring. She would also continue to tell me that she was actually extremely shy and that she does not like to spend time alone in hotel rooms all by herself. This statement by her kind of made me figure out that limos and single females wanting company must be some sort of trend because I had so many times before experienced these invites quite often in my so short chauffeuring career. She then further continued to tell me that she had to do all of her business the next day and her business would not start until late the next morning and that she didn't have plans or intentions to go anywhere else for the long evening ahead; she wanted someone to help her pass the time at hand.

She politely asked me if I would like to keep her company for that one evening, she also continued to promise me that it would only be for that one evening and that there would not have to be any type of formal commitment after the fact. My heart immediately started to race and my once dry palms started to immediately sweat, but I didn't let her see the nervousness that was fastly accumulating inside of me.

Are you kidding me!? Are you seriously serious, I would think to myself!!

This beautiful gorgeous VIP celebrity woman tells me that she wants to spend time with me alone for an evening without any type of commitment afterwards!!

This seriously can't be for real! I thought t myself.

But it certainly was for real; I struggled to continue to keep my calm kool, and I play acted like this wasn't the first time that some beautiful celebrity woman had approached me and asked me to spend an evening with her, although it most certainly was.

I was of course more than happy and excited to oblige with this special request of her driver though.

I made sure to put the shock factor; that I was in no doubt feeling at this time, far away from my personal being and I made sure to continue to keep up the same intense energy level and flirtatious actions and behavior that had gotten me to this spectacular point with her thus far. Right along with that same touch of courtesy and professionalism that had probably built up some sort of trust.

When we had finally pulled up to the oceanfront hotel on Ocean Drive after what seemed like an hour's long drive, I helped her with luggage and she told me to wait for her outside of the hotel in the sedan while she checked herself into the Hotel. She would soon after come out after checking in and she would then give me the spare key to her hotel room; I told her that I had to return the sedan to my company's office, this was because I was not as yet experienced enough to have an assigned vehicle to myself and I told her that I would soon be back with my own personal vehicle in a little while. She then leaned into the sedan to give me a very nice long kiss square on the lips with a little bit of tongue action just to say goodbye for now and to give me a hint of what would be soon to come.

Don't judge me; I'm in the customer service industry first and foremost and I was just servicing my VIP's customer's special service request. Don't feed the hate that you feel; Love will always conquer any hate.

I must have done about one hundred miles an hour speeding back to the office because I didn't want her to somehow change her mind if I took too long to get back to her. I parked the sedan at the office and I threw the key to the dispatcher on duty without even speaking to him; I then jumped into the white, in mint condition 1976 Datsun 260Z 2+2 sports car that I had just recently purchased with all of the cash that I was making at both the airline and chauffeuring. I rushed back to the South Beach Hotel and I parked my car right on Ocean Drive and made my way up to my awaiting princess for the night.

By about the time I had gotten back to my VIP client at the Ocean Drive Hotel, it was still pretty early in the evening somewhere around 8pm, we talked somewhat for just a few minutes in the Hotel suite but then the tension in the air was just too intense after that initial introduction kiss on Ocean Drive and we had to finally just break the ice and all of that very thick tension filing the room; we attacked each other ferociously and enjoyed each other's flesh in almost an instant and for the remainder of that entire evening and into the morning. I had definitely been a fan of this very beautiful celebrity prior to this wonderful fun filled evening and I could now obviously consider myself very much a groupie.

We continued this passion well into the night and I stayed there with her until I knew that she was fast asleep which was somewhere around midnight, not long, but long enough for us both to enjoy ourselves and also for me have a story to tell my grandchildren; although I will never share the name of this celebrity with anyone including them. A true gentleman (in which I proudly consider myself) will never kiss and tell even amongst his very own bloodline, so don't ever ask me please.

You wouldn't truly expect a gentleman like me to kiss and tell would you? I am simply just sharing one of my many experiences as chauffeur with you and I do not feel the need at this time to share anyone else's personal experiences with you. I have never shared this wonderful experience with anyone else before the writing of this book maybe because nearly three decades after the fact, I am still in shock.

When I had left I made sure to make sure that she was sound asleep because she had requested my company until she had to take care of her business the very next morning, so I made sure to comply with her request by at least making certain she would not be awake at least until sunrise. I was also more than happy to give her a sweet kiss goodnight as she was sleeping, to say my final goodbye. I had heard her blow out a loud snore as I walked out of the hotel room door. I have never seen or heard from her ever again. That was no problem for me however; that is exactly how I would have wanted it to happen. I am not a celebrity hound and never have been and I have no interest in the celebrity lifestyle not even in being the spouse or the significant other of any type of celebrity. I had truly appreciated the lovely evening that we did have together though for all that it was worth; nice and private and memorable, even though I did not get a cash tip. That was quite OK however; I have never been or wanted to become a gigolo and I would have actually given my entire year's worth of limo checks for that one unique experience that night.

As I left the hotel in that early AM, the beautiful night was somewhat taken away from me because in my haste to get up to my clients hotel room I had forgotten to put money in the parking meter and I had received a parking ticket from the city of Miami Beach. Parking tickets on my car windshield will always ruin my evenings; even if my evening included sleeping with a beautiful and sexy secret celebrity woman.

MRS. CARTER

Another super VIP client that this new company had and that I was assigned to chauffeur, was someone that I had frequently watched on television as a child and had admired and respected her very much. This was simply because she had looked a lot like certain family members in my very own family. This Super VIP client was the Tony award winning Broadway actress as well as the famed actress on the hit television series "Gimme a Break" and of "Hangin' with Mr. Cooper" amongst many other credits, the late and the great Mrs. Nell Carter.

I had been assigned two different assignments for her at the same time, which was to pick her up from the Fort Lauderdale International Airport and take her and her male companion to the Embassy Suites

Hotel not too far away from the airport. The second assignment I received was to take the same couple to Port Everglades, the cruise ship port, the very next morning where they were departing for their weeklong Caribbean cruise adventure.

For this particular Super VIP assignment, I could not do my specialty Super VIP gate meet as I was always able to do at Miami International Airport because I did not have an Fort Lauderdale airport access ID to get back to the arrival gate of the airplane, so I met her as all other chauffeurs do at the baggage claim area for her incoming flight. I had noticed her just as soon as I saw her and her companion coming down the escalator leading to the baggage claim and I held the greeting sign proudly as I directed the sign to her strictly to impress her, it was not like I really needed that greeting sign because most certainly and of course I would definitely recognize her; she also did not require a code named greeting sign because of her very common last name. At the very moment that she had seen me for the first time as she stepped off of the escalator, the very first thing that she would then immediately and very excitedly blurt out to me was, "Hi there sir…would you bare my children please" with a very large grin on her face and she had blurted that statement out even before I had the opportunity to properly introduce myself to her.

I found her to be extremely funny with that one simple statement, but I was also in somewhat of a shock and I was also left a little bit speechless; which is quite unusual for me. I was shocked not only of what she had said to me, but also because her male companion was standing right there in full ear shot of what she was saying to me. This made me ask myself who this male companion that was escorting her actually was; I might have fulfilled her request if Mr. Companion was not with her at that time and I would have definitely turned on the cheetah charm after that statement if she would have been travelling alone. Instead, I basically paid very little attention to her flirtatious comment and I went about the business of chauffeuring this very odd couple to their luxury hotel suite.

I uneventfully loaded the couple along with their luggage into the stretched limousine and I chauffeured them to the Embassy Suites Hotel just as was planned and I wished them a wonderful evening.

The next morning as I arrived back to the Embassy Suites to take the couple to the cruise port, at the first meeting that morning, Mrs. Carter would also then compliment me as to how very handsome I was. No one in my life prior to that had ever actually told me that I was handsome before and she had made me feel exceptionally special that day, even more so than my secret celebrity that I had recently spent time with. Because I still had that sexual cheetah living inside of me, I had always very much considered myself a confident and manly man but I had never actually thought of myself as a handsome man; I had only seen myself as a humble man who had loved women very much and who also knew how to get what I desired from a woman that interested me.

It was however certainly wonderful hearing that from somebody who was actually a famous television star and whom I had regularly watched on television growing up as a child. I thought that there must have some sort of truth to the statement coming from Mrs. Carter and I had truly appreciated the unwarranted and unexpected compliment, although I would never let that wonderful compliment ever affect my ego. I had taken it for what it was, a wonderful and special compliment from a TV celebrity.

You will never ever forget it though, when a famous TV celebrity tells you that you are handsome, and for that reason Ms. Carter I most certainly never will; you have been one in only maybe a few persons in my life who have complimented me as such, and only one other female client that I have had in over two decades of chauffeuring has told me so. Thank you Ms. Carter, may you continue to rest in peace.

As I again uneventfully drove them to the cruise port, Mrs. Carter had requested of me to pick her up from the return cruise one week later, I was honored to get a celebrity request that I had heard so much about, but I had to politely decline because of my prior commitments to aviation and my unfortunate work schedule. This is one of the least desired side effects of not chauffeuring on a full time basis; you cannot fulfill all of your client request' for your services on a regular basis and that will ultimately affect your chauffeur paycheck and client base. I have probably lost out on a lot of special chauffeur requests over the years and this will of course lower your professional reputation as a professional chauffeur.

When I had dropped Mrs. Carter and her male companion off at their cruise ship I would give Mrs. Carter a very warm hug good bye and I also told her how happy I was to have had met her; she very kindly thanked me for my services and we parted ways, never to see her again.

I can recall that later in my career I would share this story with a fellow chauffeur and he informed me that Ms. Carter was known to aggressively flirt with her drivers that she had thought was attractive to her; I do not know how true this statement that he made to me really is, I am just simply sharing the adventures of my chauffeuring career with you. Whether Ms. Carter told those same compliments to all of her drivers or not I probably will never know but I still greatly appreciated hearing them from her.

THE SUPERMODEL

Another Super VIP celebrity that this company had as a client and whom I also had the opportunity to meet and also chauffeur is also someone who I had frequently watched on television, but not as a child as Ms. Carter but rather as a young adult. When I had first seen this young woman on television, I would gawk at her, as she was extremely beautiful and incredibly sexy to me. That show was the Fresh Prince of BelAire and when I had first seen her on television I was instantly infatuated by her intense beauty and allure and have always been ever since that time, up to and including the time of this writing.

This Super VIP client was the beautiful and the then Victoria's Secret supermodel and also then the famous television actress Ms. Tyra Banks of The Fresh Prince of Bel Aire fame. I had instantly fell in love with her amazing natural beauty just as soon as I first seen her perform on that early nineties hit television show. She was also the star of her very own nationally televised talk show the Tyra Banks show and executive producer of America's next top model, a show that I had also admired very much.

When I had first received this very prestigious VIP assignment, I got extremely excited and nervous all at the same time but I knew I had to keep my kool. This was going to be the assignment of all assignments for me in my very young career and I had also had sudden visions of the great adventure that I had experienced some weeks or months earlier with my other famous secret celebrity client. I had to take very deep and long breaths to attempt to slow my fastly beating heart rate and to just try and make an attempt to calm down when I had first received this Super VIP assignment; this nervous type of reaction to clients whether VIP or not, is very unusual for me as a professional chauffeur and I have not ever again felt this kind of way since this day with Ms. Banks or with anyone else.

Ms. Banks was flying in to Miami International Airport, so I of course would give her my very own personal specialty Super VIP gate meet and greet service so as to not miss her or have any other type of screw up during the hectic meet and greet phase of a Super VIP chauffeur/client airport greeting.

I had arrived out to the gate area before the aircraft had arrived to the gate and I just sat there patiently and nervously awaited the eventual early afternoon jet arrival to continue the attempt to calm my jittery nerves. I watched intently as the plane pulled up and parked at the gate and I assumed the attentive chauffeurs position with my meet and greet sign; I cannot recall if the greeting sign was code named for her or not.

Just as soon as I assumed the official chauffeur position, her representative would notice me standing there in position and would then approach me to introduce himself to me as to who he was. I was immediately relieved of any and all of the intense nervous condition I had because I now knew that me and Tyra would not be alone together as I had been with my previous celebrity VIP adventure, but that idea would end up being very short lived.

He had introduced himself to me as Ms. Banks representative and that I would be taking her to her hotel that afternoon and that she was there for a Victoria's Secret video shoot the next morning. He would then look me up and down and say that I was quite a big guy and he asked me if I did not mind doing a little bit of body guarding while we walked through the airport terminal with Ms. Banks. I of course had no problem with that kind of unusual scenario, as I had never been a body guard for anybody before but I told him that I would happily comply with that request and I absolutely looked forward to it.

As Ms. Banks would walk out of the jetbridge she was very easily recognizable although she was very much dressed down; she was very tall and statuesque and of course very beautiful. The representative would first greet her and I would then introduce her as being her chauffeur to her hotel. We would then start the long walk back to sedan parked at my favorite place on the airport; the dolphin parking garage. As we slowly walked through the airport terminal it became obvious to me why I needed to be a body guard; people both men and women of all shapes sizes and colors had more than recognized who she was and were constantly trying to get autographs and take photos, or try to press their way into her personal space; this scenario did not happen at all with the secret celebrity. I found myself constantly keeping people at least an arms distance away from Ms. Banks as was requested from me by her agent representative.

Once we finally got through the secured section of the airport terminal, the fan bombardment really started and Tyra decided to stop and talk to some of her fans and also to sign a few autographs. When the friendly greeting sessions was close to over, her representative would turn to me and inform me that it was time for us to leave and also that he would not be with us for the ride to the hotel and that I should continue to do a good job at taking care of Ms. Banks…by myself.

UhOh!

The nervousness instantly came streaming right back to me and my palms started to sweat profusely as I imagined me and Tyra alone together in that sedan for the ride over to the hotel; I couldn't help but to think about the last celebrity situation that I was in, only some months earlier as well as what had happened between the two of us in that last case when I was left alone with a beautiful female celebrity in almost the very same situation just like the one that I would now be finding myself in all over again; would Tyra be the same as the last celebrity female client that I had driven all alone?

I tried my very hardest to stay Kool and I tried even harder not to let my nervousness show however and I really don't think that the beautiful Ms. Banks would ever know about any or all of the jittery nerves that were running frantically through my body. I believe I had looked on the outside as cool as a frozen cucumber, but certainly not on the inside. I was absolutely terrified and there were several small fast flowing rivers flowing into a large lake forming underneath my dark black suit into my Calvin Klein briefs.

As we continued our walk to the now infamous Dolphin parking garage that I had so much experience with already, I turned the very professional chauffeur charm on and definitely not the cheetah charm as I started the smooth conversations with Ms. Banks; it would now be just Tyra and I on the final walk out to the parked sedan tucked away safely somewhere in that Dolphin garage.

When we finally got into the luxury Lincoln townecar sedan, the good conversations would continue on and would actually start to become enjoyable, and due to that fact, my nervousness would soon seem to somewhat subside a little. I would speak to Ms. Banks in a somewhat of an open fashion with subsequently more difficult and more personal questions and topics arising as Tyra would allow me to go deeper and deeper into our conversations. Tyra would allow me to speak to her in a very open and personal manner and we had discussed topics that would not be acceptable by most other clients who would not be so open to communicate with their chauffeur as Ms. Banks was with me on this particular day. I can still vividly remember the entire conversation that we shared that day; one can never forget a very private adult conversation with a beautiful Victoria's Secret supermodel especially when you're a very single man and an always seeking out woman type of guy, and also have a very excellent memory like I have.

I won't say much about the conversation we shared that day but what I can say though is that the conversation was extremely titillating to say the very least and I cherished every single moment of it; it was of course a very short ride over to her hotel that day but yet it had still seemed as if it was a very long conversation we shared that day.

We spoke for what seemed nonstop for the entire ride over to the hotel from the airport and I had felt as if I had known Ms. Banks very well in just the very short amount of time of the ride over from the Miami airport to her final destination. I was very much enjoying every single minute of the short time that I had spent communicating with her during the ride; so much so that I now had very clear visions of maybe repeating the exact same performance that I had with my secret celebrity client so many weeks or months earlier. Maybe these sexy celebrity women are all very much the same by being sexually open minded and free to be whoever they wanted to be like that, I would try and convince myself. It was truly a wonderful and memorable experience that I had for that very short ride that I had spent with her.

When we arrived to the hotel I let her out of the sedan shook her hand and said my goodbye, I didn't think much of saying goodbye to her for now because I knew that she was going to be in Miami for at least another couple of days and I knew that I would have the opportunity to chauffeur her around again soon, if not the very next day. As she walked into the hotel I had walked in behind her and I stood inside of the hotel by the payphones to phone in the completion of this Super VIP transfer and to also watch the completion of her check in procedure to make sure that all went well with this Super VIP client.

As Ms. Banks made it to the front of the check in line I decided to go outside and to wait at the sedan just to continue to be safe that all had gone well. I do not know why I had decided to stay there as long as I did, but it was a really good idea that I did. I must have known subconsciously somehow that something might have been wrong because of that decision to just hang around the hotel after I had dropped her off, or maybe I was waiting for another invitation upstairs; I truly don't know. While I was waiting there in the sedan at the hotel curbside contemplating exactly what Just happened, it had been a fair amount of time that had passed before I would actually decide to finally leave the hotel. Just at that very moment that I was leaving, I received an emergency 911 code displaying on my pager from the dispatchers at the limo office; I rushed back to the payphone inside the hotel to call the direct 1-800 phone number to the limo office. They would then inform me that I had taken Ms. Banks to the wrong hotel and that I needed to get her to the proper hotel right now and in an absolute flash; I was assigned to take her to the Grand Hotel in Coconut Grove instead of where I had actually taken her, The Sonesta Beach Resort on the island of Key Biscayne about ten miles away from where we currently were.

This was an actual driving difference of about twenty minutes in actual time travelled, but more than that, it was a very unprofessional brain fart on my part to have done this mistake. I was already a very experienced chauffeur with a few years of experience under my belt and more importantly I had a very important super VIP client onboard. This incident with Tyra was the first and also the last time in my long chauffeuring career that I had ever taken someone to an incorrect address.

Thinking about it long and hard over the years, what I think happened that day was that I was so completely nervous on the inside that I completely blacked out on any and all of my brain and of all of its normal and proper functions as a chauffeur. I was concentrating so hard on trying not to visually show any of my jitters on the outside that I lost all other functions, but now on this make up ride over to the Grove it was more than obvious that those jitters were more than there and now finally showing its ugly head by me doing this completely rookie mistake. I had really screwed up big this time and I was now completely embarrassed by what I had nervously done.

I quickly ran to find Ms. Banks and I deeply apologized to her without explaining my excuses of nerves and jitters of having to chauffeur her; this absolutely gorgeous Victoria's Secret supermodel as the reason for the gross error. Instead as she got back into the sedan for the twenty minute ride over to the Grand for whatever reason we did not say not even a single word to each other for the entire ride over to Coconut Grove, because of the devastatingly embarrassing situation for me there was a very deep contrast in my energy levels as compared to the wonderful ride we had coming over from the airport.

I realized right there and then that I was actually a little bit naïve despite my already years of experience as a chauffeur as well as all of the womanizing I had already been doing, simply because I could not overcome my grave mistake that I had just made with this beautiful supermodel on board my sedan like any real gentleman probably could have and as I should have been able to recover from that by brushing it off as some sort of funny joke; but I couldn't. I just remained ashamedly silent for the entire ride over the Rickenbacker causeway to the correct Coconut Grove hotel where we should have originally been.

Well Tyra, just in case I did not apologize before for what happened that day because of my continued complete mental meltdown after that mishap, I must do so now. I am truly sorry Ms. Banks for taking you to the wrong hotel and wasting your precious time. More importantly for me not being the man I was supposed to be by instantly shutting off my, by this time now, world renowned personal charm and completely ignoring you from fear of further embarrassment on that what seemed like a never ending and forever ride over to that Coconut Grove hotel; forgive me please Ms. Banks.

My big male ego that day had been so pumped up and over inflated to such great internal pressures, solely due to a certain secret celebrity client and the situation that arose between us only months earlier that was once again playing over and over in my head, had now been completely and instantly deflated the moment I knew what happened just like that big ole' Hindenburg Airship on a cool New Jersey morn.

Once we had finally arrived at the Grand Hotel in Coconut Grove I let her out of the sedan and we simply parted ways without any words ever being exchanged. I would never have the opportunity to chauffeur Ms. Banks again; this was now an opportunity blown for me and in more ways than one I immediately thought. I had earlier in this assignment very much looked forward to volunteering my services to my limo company to stay and continue to chauffeur Ms. Banks for the remainder of the time that she was going to be in Miami, but I now knew that was not going to happen and for very obvious reasons. After dropping her off, I went about my normal and routine business without ever making that volunteer request; I didn't want to waste my time. However life does go on you know and I looked forward to many more opportunities like this one to come in the future.

My Club Limo official chauffeur badge circa 1995

CHAPTER NINE
The End Of An Era

I had been working this routine of the two careers for many months, if not years and had done so very well at doing both. I had paid off the IRS on time just as scheduled with no harm done; I had originally thought I would have definitely at least gone hungry when the agreement with the IRS had first came about but I never did. I would actually gain weight and I enjoyed myself all the while, while doing so.

I was also able to move out of my little tiny North Miami efficiency apartment and back into my Island Village community where I had a bayfront apartment with full bay and city views from my windows; life again was actually pretty good for me but I wasn't satisfied. I was also able to sell my little 1976 Datsun 260 2+2 Z car and I was able to replace it with a much newer 1995 Jeep Wrangler; it wasn't quite the H1 Hummer that I had been dreaming about earlier, but it was what I could happily afford and I was quite pleased with driving it on and around South Beach especially with the top down in the bright sunshine.

My career dreams of becoming an airline pilot also was not being pursued anymore although I was flying inside the cockpit of a jumbo jetliner. I had only seen that as nothing more than a career tease for me and it did nothing to help fulfill my desire of someday being in control of the same jetliners that I would be flying in on a weekly basis. Being who I am, I could not stop trying to figure out a way to somehow get in that cockpit on a more permanent basis. One day driving through Miami, I would run into an old buddy of mine from back in the day who would help to steer me in that exact direction.

This old friend was somebody who I had worked with on the same work crew at PanAm both in New York where we both started for Pan Am and also here in Miami; we had both transferred to Miami at the same time back in 1989 but had lost track of each other after PanAm's demise, we did however work together for a very short amount of time during my almost two year time at the startup airline.

We soon became drinking buddies and we would cruise the streets of South Beach looking for women to conquer. This buddy of mine had liked my bayfront apartment, where we had invited a harem of woman to come and see, so much so that he would eventually get an apartment in the same complex that I had been living in. We soon also became neighbors and we would enjoy the spoils of a South Beach lifestyle and party with gorgeous women both locals and international tourists on a very regular basis at our beautiful waterfront property; this was a type of lifestyle we were both enjoying very much. I truly think we had practiced and perfected that saying of …"what happens on South beach stays on South Beach" a long time before the city of Las Vegas coined the phrase and we had the many conquests to prove it because everything we done had stayed right there on South Beach never to be heard of again.

Although we were both routinely enjoying this South Beach lifestyle and all that comes with it, we both wanted more for our careers in aviation and we were both already licensed private pilots and we had both wanted to fulfill our dreams of becoming airline pilots. We were both still actively seeking to better our career opportunities and our experiences in aviation. Coincidentally, he was also a flight mechanic for an international cargo airline and he also travelled throughout the entire globe working to maintain the dependability and reliability of the airplanes that we were both paid to do in keeping those jumbo jets flying safely through the friendly skies on a timely scheduled basis.

My buddy and now new neighbor would eventually find a golden opportunity that was a lot more beneficial to his future and he decided that he would go out on an interview with United Airlines which was hiring flightline mechanics in the northern California city of San Francisco.

While he went out West for his interview, he would call me right from the recruiter's office to tell me that the recruiter was actively seeking out experienced flightline aircraft mechanics for their growing fleet of brand new Boeing aircraft and that I should apply for the position with the experience I already had. I didn't disagree with that idea although I had a little reserve about moving all the way across the country to work for another airline; I was enjoying my two current careers in Miami and I truly did not want to give up any one of those careers and leave the general lifestyle of Miami behind. I thought that I would just go through the motions of applying and enjoy the free flight out to San Francisco to see the sights I had never seen before, and for also my now elementary school aged daughter whose extended family had all lived in the San Francisco Bay area. So I decided that I would take that opportunity to meet them all while I was there for the interview. I made the decision right there on the phone to go out there for the interview process and the recruiter sent me a FedEx package the very next day with an airline ticket and all of the necessary paperwork so that I would have all the required paperwork ready when I would arrive at the United Airlines offices for that interview in San Francisco that was now scheduled for some three days later.

I filled out all of the necessary paperwork, got all of my documentation together and I got my interview suit all ready to impress. Three days later I was sitting on an early morning flight in a first class seat bound for the west coast city of San Francisco. I played smart for this trip and although I was extremely tempted to have a bloody Mary, but the first one could have easily led to many more, so I made sure not to start and not to drink any of the free alcohol that was offered in the first class cabin of the brand new Boeing 777 aircraft; I had wanted a stiff drink but I really didn't need any. I was extremely impressed with myself and also very excited just to be sitting here in this almost sudden and completely unexpected position that I would now found myself in.

This may seem purposeless to mention, but I had heard from the interview crew of a certain man that was there at the same time of my interview, also a potentially new employee. I was told that he was turned away from his interview because he had indulged in all of the free alcohol that he was offered on the free flight over from wherever it was that he had come from and he had shown up visibly drunk and clearly intoxicated, wreaking of alcohol for his interview process at United Airlines. Needless to say, but what makes sense to one person may not always make obvious sense to another; or maybe he was like me and really did not want the job and just showed up for the free flight to San Francisco and all the free alcohol that went with the first class cross country flight.

I arrived on time, alert and ready for my scheduled all day interview and took all of the required testing. I had passed all of the exams and interview questions with flying colors and I was offered a position as a flightline mechanic before the end of the day. I had left the interview process with a nice payscale offer that was well above the regular starting payscale for that of a regular starting hangar mechanic with very little or no prior aviation experience; it was nearly an offer that I couldn't refuse, except for the fact that I was living in beautiful Miami and I still did not want to leave even with this handsome offer on the table.

I was very happy about receiving an employment offer from United Airlines, but I was not quite excited about the offer because I had actually still loved Miami and I did not yet know if I was actually willing to leave the city and the jobs that I loved. Although I was still not quite sure if I would actually accept the flightline mechanics position and make the long cross country move, I told them that I would accept their offer and I requested an actual start date that was about two months away from the offer date and they gladly accepted my eight week starting timetable to move on out to California.

After my interview was completed, I contacted my very distant family of my daughter's extended family and they made arrangements to come and pick me up at the airport so that I could finally have a chance to meet them all. I met her aunts, uncles and grandparents. This was the second reason that I had decided to come out to San Francisco for this interview; I did not know if I would ever have the chance or opportunity to ever meet them again, so this would now be the time to meet them if I had decided not to move all the way out to San Francisco. They would come out to meet me and I was able to meet them all, as well as cross the Bay Bridge and of course the World Famous Golden Gate Bridge; I was extremely thrilled to have had the opportunity to have done that. The next morning I would fly back out to Miami, again in first class luxury and aboard another brand new Boeing 777 aircraft. On this particular flight back I would happily indulge in all of the free and unlimited alcohol offered to me in the first class cabin because I had no one on the other end of the flight that would be checking my blood alcohol level.

When I had arrived back to Miami, I continued my regular and routine work schedule just as if I had not told United Airlines that I would start working for them in just a matter of weeks; that was because I actually did not have any real plans to head out to San Francisco. I had still loved my adopted city and really couldn't imagine leaving it yet. I did however start to think about the worldwide travel benefits that I had not seen and experienced since my days at Pan American, so those thoughts could not seal out the deal to take me out west. Although I was always traveling throughout the Caribbean and South America, it was always work and never pleasure and I really could not afford to take a proper vacation.

That would somewhat change during the time inbetween the interview and my actual start date with United Airlines. The cargo airline that I was working with would be undergoing an inspection with the Federal Aviation Administration to make sure that they were running the airline in the proper and safe way. The airline had earlier promoted me to becoming an airline inspector, where I was trained not only to inspect maintenance procedures but also the airlines paperwork and the airlines procedural inspections for its foreign bases. In preparation for that inspection the airline would send me out to all of the Caribbean stations to make sure that the maintenance equipment and facilities there were up to par of the stringent FAA standards.

I had made about three different trips to about four or five different outstations and I did my difficult task making sure that everything was up to par for the inspection. Ultimately for this FAA inspection, the airline also wanted its American based mechanics to man the foreign outstations just in case an incident would happen while the FAA was onboard the aircraft or snooping around all of the facilities including all of the foreign outstations during the approximate two week inspection. I was somehow selected to go to Bogota, Colombia for an entire 2 week period while the FAA were performing their inspections at the airline; I was not fluent in Spanish and I truly did not want to go to Bogota but I was more forced to go there more so than I would actually volunteer to.

Although I did live in Miami, I did not speak the Spanish language fluently although I knew enough of the language to get by, and I had never been out of the country with no other person that I had known, for more than a few days at a time; plus I was supposed to be getting ready for my big move out to San Francisco. I quickly decided that I would go for the two week Bogota trip, but I would have to also contact the San Francisco maintenance base for United Airlines to request of them to grant me a little bit of additional time for my move out to San Francisco; I think they figured that I may be trying to string them along for a start date and although I wasn't, maybe I would have if they would have allowed me to start with a later starting date.

United Airlines would not have anything to do with that and they would not honor my request; I guess they had sensed my little bit of hesitation or they probably had many other people change their minds to head out there at the last minute like I had fully intended to do. I accepted the fact that they would not reschedule a new start date for me and I told them that I would still honor the original start date that they had originally given me, although I still had no true intention of heading all the way out there.

When I had finally arrived in Bogota, I had decided on the flight over from Miami that since I did not want to be here at this particular destination; (I would have much rather been at a much more tropical destination where they preferably spoke English and served strong umbrella rum drinks or maybe even my hometown city of Port of Spain, Trinidad and Tobago) that I would do as very little work as humanly possible and that's exactly what I did, nothing. When I arrived at the luxury hotel suite that they had provided for me I would immediately start to rack up the room charges with gourmet room service meals, pay television and movies, and of course the luxury massages offered by the five star hotel that I was staying with. I did not actually want to be there in Bogota and because I didn't want to be there, I certainly was not going to be paying for all of those luxurious amenities out of my own pocket, so I charged all of those wonderful luxury items to my suite number and when I finally got to leave Colombia all I happily had to do was to give them my well practiced John Hancock.

During my two week stay in Bogota, I never once showed up at airport offices and maintenance facility, rather I would call the dispatch office in Miami every morning to find out if there were any incoming FAA officers onboard the aircraft or if there were any incoming maintenance issues that I should be made aware of or be concerned with. I would also tell the dispatcher every morning to contact the Captain to let him know of my contact info just in case any issues were to come up during his time on the ground in Bogota and I would stay in front of that phone while standing by in my hotel room until the plane had departed and was well past the point of a potential return to Bogota; in those two weeks I never once received a phone call to my hotel room. I would make sure that when the aircraft was inbound from Miami or on the ground in Bogota that I would be fully available and ready to go in my hotel room; I did not see any reason for me to be there at the airport if there were no airplane issues to deal with because I didn't speak Spanish and I couldn't properly communicate with all of the other employees there. I honestly believe the airline specifically sent me to Bogota so that I would not seek out a good time and have fun due to that language barrier; but I also believe that this airline truly did not know who they were actually dealing with in me. Remember, I was born on a carnival night in Port of Spain, Trinidad one of the biggest street parties in the World; I think I just had to make my way out of my mother's womb because I must have known that a party was going on somewhere near me.

I will always find a party, and if I can't find a party I will certainly make one; language barrier or not. When the aircraft leaving Bogota was finally wheels up and headed back due North to Miami with its full cargo loads of flower's, roses, plants and vegetables, and whatever other contraband they could sneak onboard and without the possibility for a return landing at Bogota, it would be now time for me to party like a rock star until the next inbound flight was on its way back to Bogota the next morning. I would jump on a different Bogota city bus every day and just get lost in this big city; I know it was dangerous, I was young and indestructible I never once thought of any danger.

I would be on the hunt for wine, women, and whatever else would allow me to legally enjoy myself in this strange new land that I found myself in. I went to bars, nightclubs, stripclubs, even a private party in someone's house one evening; they invited me in as if I was one of their own even with the very little Spanish that I spoke. Whatever I wanted I found and I had a very good time while searching for it and also when I found what I was looking for; this is what work is supposed to be like, getting paid to party.

During one of those long weekends when they were no inbound flights for the entire two day weekend, was when I would really venture out to see the sights of Bogota and Colombia, I rode the cable car to the highest point of the city on top of the huge Montserrat mountain that is there with incredible scenic views of the entire city as well as the airport where I was supposed to have been working; I will never forget the awesome views that I have seen up there on that huge mountain with what seemed like a view of the entire city of Bogota and all of the surrounding landscapes. I also had a very fancy and wonderful lunch at the fancy restaurant up there just too simply say that I had done so. One of those weekends I also took a bus down to the Amazon River basin for a jungle tour of the Amazon Rainforest and a river ride to maybe see some of the Piranha fish that I had heard so much about in my life. In the jungle I took an Amazonian river tour and I purchased a lovely pet Piranha fish forever sealed and encased in plastic in which I still own to this very day, she has always sat by my side and has kept me company sitting on my writing desk right in front of me ever since I purchased her.

On another weekend, I also followed a very beautiful and very exotic woman whom I had met on one of those city buses. I tried desperately to communicate with her all the way to her neighborhood as I tried to get to know her better with broken communication, but she had gotten extremely frustrated with the difficult time we had desperately trying to communicate with each other. So I left her alone and got back on the bus and I made my back to my hotel room; I had tried desperately to get her back there with me but to no avail...Oh well, there's plenty more where she came from I thought to myself even though I thought of here as extremely beautiful with her very exotic African and Indian ethnic mixture.

Back at the luxury hotel in Bogota, I had been really enjoying myself with my daily New York strip steak and seafood meals, the gym, sauna and the Jacuzzi, and of course the daily full body massages all charged to my hotel room in which the airline was paying for every single penny of it. However, during the second week of all of that luxurious treatment, believe it or not I started to get very homesick and I actually started to miss my home in Miami; it took a week and a half but I was now ready to leave Bogota and finally go back home. With all of the travel I had already done, I had never really been homesick before and I actually didn't believe that homesickness actually existed, but now I certainly knew different. I made my request to come back home to my dispatch office and they told me to just hold out for a few more days, that the inspection was just about over and that we were passing the inspection with flying colors. This response had made me feel optimistic that I would have a job for a while to come and it somewhat settled my unsettling nerves from the inspection even if for just a little while. The second week had finished up with me having my fill of partying and I was more than ready to head back home, the inspection was finally over and the airline was still up and running but I still had to stay one more weekend to get on the next flight back out to Miami which would be leaving Monday afternoon, that last weekend I just stayed at the hotel and had my fill of breakfast in the restaurant, room service was still delivering delicious strip steak meals and the pay per view movies were still rolling right up to the time it was finally time to leave this vacation of work or working vacation; whichever I don't know.

When Monday morning finally rolled around, I showed up at the airport offices for the first time in two weeks. I was greeted with loud applause from my fellow foreign employees because they were all surprised to finally see me; I truly did not realize that they would have recognized that I was actually missing in action because they did not really know me. I shook it off as a funny joke and I ran around the office trying to stay busy until the aircraft finally arrived because I did not want anything to do with the negative attention that I already received when I showed up to Bogota Airport for the first time in two weeks. While I was trying to keep myself busy I also realized to myself that if they had recognized my long absence here in Bogota, someone from management would have certainly informed the Miami Base station and I would more than likely certainly be in big trouble in Miami when I had gotten back to the maintenance base. I would immediately think to myself right there in Bogota that it was probably a very good thing that I did not turn down the offer from

United Airlines out in San Francisco, I thought this thought as a just in case that I was in actual trouble when I had got back to Miami.

It was not until Monday late evening that I would finally arrive back to the Miami base, I was warmly greeted by my fellow coworkers greeting the flight that night. I stayed at the airport late into the night so that I could fraternize with my fellow coworkers who were not there with me and tell them all of the stories that I had accumulated over the past two weeks, it wasn't until very late that morning until I was done putting away all of the tools that I had travelled to Bogota with and finished sharing all of my Bogota war stories from my long Colombia travel and work adventure.

When I got home that late night/ early morning I did not forget about the wonderful attention that I had received from the Bogota office when they finally had a chance to see me after my two long week absence and due to that, I decided right there and then to write up a two week notice letter to my current employer here in Miami. Although there was now actually less than two weeks for my United Airlines start date. The sole reason that I had decided to write this two week resignation notice was because I had to stay one step ahead of the curve and stay in front of the issue of my two week absence just in case there should be some sort of an issue that would arise with my Miami bosses when I went back in to work the very next day.

I went in to start my work shift the next day following my arrival back from Bogota, with the two week notice letter all typed up and signed in hand and ready to be delivered to the powers that be at that maintenance base, but I was not going to actually hand in this resignation notice unless I absolutely felt threatened from my superiors; as I had by now known how to assume that very familiar position of being led into the management office and all of its potential negative results. I also now knew when that familiar position was close at hand and sneaking up on me so I would now be quite armed and ready for any sort of enemy attack.

I had been absent in Bogota for two full weekends and two full weeks straight all while on a salary with overtime and travel pay and I didn't lift a finger except to press the TV remote or the room phone to dial room service for my midnight snack; usually a New York strip steak.

I partied like a rock star while I was down there, but now would be the time for me to pay for it though. Sure enough, just about as soon as I walked in to start my work shift the day after I returned, I was notified that I had been requested to be seen by a certain co-worker of mine in his private office; this was the same Mr. Co-worker that I had driven all around town in the stretch limo for that one crazy night and I also had never been called into his office before. Maybe he was going to speak to me about all the room charges that I had racked up while in Bogota, like the massages, and the late night room service steaks. Or maybe he was going to be referring me to his bosses for my potential firing for being AWOL, I don't know. But whatever the case was, I knew what was potentially ahead. I knew that I would be potentially getting into some sort of punishment for having too much fun at work, but I certainly didn't want to hear it simply because I had a much better job offer with better pay and most importantly unlimited worldwide true flight benefits where I could once again meet women from all over the world and maybe even some lovely California girls.

I walked into his office and before he could even say a word to me, I handed him over my two week notice of resignation that was actually dated for less than two weeks. He accepted my resignation letter and didn't utter a single word in regards to my Bogota AWOL adventure; I never knew if I were to actually be fired or not, but I was already tired of being fired all over the place in aviation and I didn't want to take another chance of being fired once again in aviation and putting my beloved chosen career in jeopardy. It would not have even actually mattered if I did get fired from this job or not, simply because I already had another well paying job already lined up and waiting for me. Regardless of the fact that it was on the other side of the continent; it was simply a matter of not wanting to be fired again for the fourth or fifth time in my young aviation career of only about eight years of already being employed in the aviation industry. I took it as it may and I decided right there and then that I would now make the commitment of going cross country with United Airlines in San Francisco.

Although I did not truly want to go out to San Francisco; it was such a big move and such a long drive to get out there I always thought. I had already left Miami once before and I ran immediately back to my beloved city but the real fear of me being fired once again was my full motivation for finally deciding on taking that position and moving way out there to California. I still could not imagine myself making that move though and I had thoughts of recalling my two week notice letter from the airline; I was truly confused over the matter and I didn't actually know what to do. I was so concerned that if I pulled my notice letter out from the airline they may then turn around and then actually fire me for my disappearing act in Bogota. So I did what I always do when I'm at a crossroads in my life and don't know which direction to turn, I prayed long and hard to God for him to reveal to me a clear answer and a clear direction in which to go in my life and in my career, I had needed an answer from God because I had been clearly lost.

I would wait for a clean and clear answer from God, hopefully like the way God had communicated with me the same way that he did in talking to me in regards to my beautiful daughter; if he spoke to me clearly once before surely he can speak to me clearly once again I thought. But of course that would have been just too easy.

God did not speak to me right away or directly this time around though, but I think he did speak to me in a timely manner through my emotions. I was scheduled to start with United Airlines on Monday April 21, 1997. I was not absolutely certain and confident to make that cross country move until the Thursday prior to that date. God did not actually speak to me like he had for my daughter; rather I felt a very powerful confidence come over me that could not be denied by me. When my mind was made up to make the move I felt as if nothing could stop me and I did not actually pursue the final move until the morning of Thursday April 17, 1997. When I had made that final decision, I put all of my gears in top speed and I was set on the mission to get myself out of Miami for my long haul move out to San Francisco.

My mind would be now clearly made up without any type of doubt and I would now be once again giving up my part time career of chauffeuring in Miami for my love and passion for aviation once again and I did not think anything of it.

After an initially difficult time to rent a U-haul trailer, I had finally been able to rent one to pull behind my Jeep because the very first U-haul dealer that I had went to told me it was not U-haul company policy to rent trailers to convertible vehicles and open top Jeeps due to safety reasons.

I had been completely discouraged by this news because I had a lot of furniture and goods to move. I had nearly called off the entire move out west due to this news but that would soon disappear when I went to the second U-haul dealer and that was no longer an issue because that policy was not at all mentioned to me at the next U-haul dealer that I visited. To me, this I saw as a positive indication From God that I had made the right call on the move out west and that God may be actually helping me get through this difficult move and all would eventually be alright for this, my forever life changing cross country decision.

I spent that entire Thursday cleaning out my beautiful bayfront apartment and I did not get onto I-75 northbound until 5am Friday morning in an attempt to try and get to San Francisco, California by Monday morning 9am; Mountain Dew and Skittles had once again saved the day for me.

I had left my two excellent jobs behind although I truly did not want to, but I was strongly confident that I was making the right choice. I thought about the aviation job that I loved so much, but for whatever reason I did not at all think about my chauffeuring job, they probably even still had a paycheck or two still there waiting for me when I left, I truly have no idea. I really didn't care anymore about that because I was now focused on something else, a brand new adventure in my life to now chase and to discover new things and to meet new people. Even though I truly didn't want to go, I was still very excited.

Looking back, I can say that I had made three near costly mistakes on my decision making process during this grand move out to the west coast. These almost costly mistakes nearly cost me my new job even before I even made it to the new employee orientation starting on that Monday morning at 9am.

The first mistake was that I took way too long to make the final decision to make the move; I had only started driving for the cross country drive the Friday morning prior to my Monday morning start date.

The second near costly mistake I had made was due to the love of my young daughter; instead of taking the direct Interstate route 10 west directly to California, I decided that I could not drive all the way across the country and not pass by to see my beloved daughter, north of the direct route in Tulsa. I decided to get off of I-10 in Louisiana and make a bee line for Tulsa via Texas, this detour probably cost me an added ten hours to my trip especially when I finally made it to her house and I decided to take a three hour nap. I thought that the nap could carry me all the way into California, but by the time the Sun started to rise Sunday morning I found that I had needed to pull over and sleep; the Mountain Dew and Skittles had run their course and were no longer effective. I pulled over at a rest stop to take a nap inside my Jeep, set my alarm clock for an hour.

I went to take that nap right at dusk with the rising sun just breaking over the horizon line behind my back. I did not notice that my headlights were still on when I shut down my engine and quickly closed my eyes.

Regrettably, I did not hear that alarm that I had set for an hour and I actually woke up about eight hours later. I screamed when I finally awoke; it was well past noon on Sunday and I was still in Oklahoma. I really screamed out loud once again and nearly damaged my vocal chords when I realized I had left my headlights on when I dozed off in the early morning sunlight because my engine would now no longer start due to a dead battery. Thank God I had a manual shift vehicle, I would now have to disconnect the trailer and push start my Jeep on a downhill run then reconnect the trailer and continue to make my way out west.

The nearly costly third mistake that I had made, was not knowing what driving across the United States was actually like; maps are usually always flat. I had decided to take Interstate 40 into California but I did not know of the topical geography to actually get me there. I did not know about mountain driving and that extremely high altitude and its effects on an engine while pulling a U-haul trailer, driving under these conditions would actually slow your speed down to around 30MPH. I had driven at that speed in only third gear for hundreds and hundreds of miles. I found myself on the Sunday night prior to my start date only in Flagstaff, Arizona at approximately 11,000 feet above sea level in mountainous elevation. It was cold up there, I was sleepy, and I realized that there was absolutely no way that I was going to make it the rest of the way to San Francisco by the next morning.

After already driving some 2000 miles and by not properly accounting for all of the mountainous terrain driving that I was doing, I now only had enough cash at hand for one more full tank of gas but the fast gas consumption and slow forward progress would not allow me to get all the way out to northern California. I could actually see the gas gauge needle move very rapidly to the left every time I stepped on the gas pedal and I had no more cash to keep filling the tank to continue to go all the way. I did not want to keep on going in that direction with no more cash at hand, run out of gas, and get stuck somewhere out there in the middle of nowhere. I had to think of something to get me all the way to San Francisco the next morning and not jeopardize the opportunity I was given and waste this sacrifice that I was making to get all the way out there.

I did what I always do when I'm lost and don't know what to do; I prayed to God to reveal to me what I should do next as to not blow this opportunity he had laid out in front of me and had now committed to.

God promptly answered-with three little words once again. Start heading south I clearly heard from him, I didn't understand this at all at first because it didn't make any sense to me, but I was desperate and I had to listen and figure out exactly what I had heard from him and sure enough I soon enough would.

I came up with another master plan with that particular direction in mind.

I couldn't stay up at that high altitude only making progress at 30MPH towing a U-haul in only third gear, so I decided that I would find the closest airport that United Airlines flew into, drive there and I would explain to them that I had car problems and therefore beg them for an airline ticket for the rest of the way to San Francisco.

The closest airport with a United Airlines terminal, which sure enough was south of Flagstaff, was Phoenix Arizona and I could be there by the first flight leaving in the morning heading directly to San Francisco. It was also a downhill run from Flagstaff so I didn't have to worry about doing only thirty miles an hour to get there and watch my gasoline evaporate into thin air. I parked my Jeep in the long term parking garage right along with the U-haul trailer. I arrived there just in time to meet all of the United Airlines airport staff just coming in for the start of their shift and I made all the necessary contacts to get my free airline ticket to San Francisco. I got on that flight non-stop to San Francisco; needless to say, I slept the entire way over there.

I finally arrived at the United Airlines San Francisco maintenance training orientation only about one hour late and I was the last person to introduce myself to my class of new co-workers. I considered this to be not bad at all, especially considering the fact that I had literally trekked over three thousand miles from the other literal end of the country and I had left just a few short days ago on the previous Friday morning as well as just some several hours since the time I had prayed about being totally confused and lost up there at that foggy, frozen altitude in Flagstaff. Thank God I had made it entirely on my own with God pushing me all the way. Who would have known that heading away from your final destination would actually get you there quicker, and almost nearly on time; certainly not me. My new adventures would now be beginning in this brand new chapter of my life.

Although I had spent four and a half-years in San Francisco and I did actually want to try and get a California CDL license, I did not ever get that California commercial drivers license due to my hectic schedule with United Airlines and I subsequently never got the opportunity to drive professionally in California.

I truly wanted to chauffeur on a part time basis in San Francisco though, just as I had always done in Miami, but the limousine and chauffeuring industry were just not as popular in Northern California as it is in South Florida and I had never seen help wanted ads for chauffeur positions in newspaper ads. Although I am nearly certain that limousines are actually there in San Francisco, I can hardly even recall ever seeing a limousine in Northern California. I certainly would have truly enjoyed seeing one trying to maneuver world famous Lombard Street in San Francisco; the world's most crooked street.

I had never had the opportunity to drive professionally in San Francisco and for that reason it had only taken me a few months to realize that I had really missed Miami for the work, as well as for the lifestyle and I wanted desperately to go back there as soon as possible. However the near five years that I spent in San Francisco was a very important stop for me in my life and career and a very important part of my ultimate testimony as well as having a very big influence in my personal life as well as my Christian life and walk and thus the telling of this story, so please continue to enjoy the stories that I share with you.

CHAPTER TEN
San Francisco

The first week that I was in San Francisco was a very interesting week for me because I did not have a vehicle to get around in. My buddy who had gotten me the job and who was now also my new roommate had already started in his work crew on his assigned afternoon shift while I was on the dayshift accomplishing my orientation and classroom training. This metropolitan city was not like Tulsa and there were plenty of options for me to cheaply get to work without a vehicle, so I decided to take the city bus to and from the International Airport everyday for that first week. I did not mind taking the city bus at all though; I had actually looked forward to a daily bus ride in a strange city because I've always believed that if you want to get truly intimate with a new city the best way to do that is to get on a city bus, to get to know the different areas and sections of a city and it is also the best and cheapest way to get to meet and greet the people of that city. That's exactly what I did; I spoke to anyone that would speak to me simply because I was very excited to be in this new city that only week's earlier I had absolutely no intention of ever being in. I also wanted to dive in fully to the transition of this new city and its people as quickly as possible to simply have the ability to feel at home in a brand new city.

Although I had enjoyed my first week in San Francisco, I couldn't wait to get back in to my Jeep so that I could drive myself around and truly get familiar with the brand new city that I now found myself in. When my first week was over, I had to take advantage of my free introductory flight pass to go back to Phoenix to pick up my Jeep with the U-haul trailer with all of my furniture inside still attached. When I arrived back to the parking garage at the Phoenix airport, I had been quickly reminded that my battery was still dead, but the garage had been accustomed to that scenario and they had a battery jump start system available for use to its patrons. I started up the Jeep and I made a decision right there as I pulled out of the garage that I would not shutoff my engine until I made it all the way back to San Francisco.

I left Phoenix, Arizona that Friday night and drove all the way back to San Francisco nonstop I-10west and I-5north, only stopping for fuel and food without ever shutting down my engine due to the very dead battery. I finally made it back to the Bay area by early Sunday morning and I had been driving for more than twenty four hours straight. When I had finally gone to bed very early that Sunday morning at about 2am I had slept so well, that it was actually the very first time ever that I had slept for over twenty four hours straight; I had not even waken to go to the bathroom. I had awaken about 27 hours later on that Monday morning about 5am in a panic state because I hadn't known what time it was, or even what day it was and I was completely lost as to where or even who I was. Luckily, I had awakened in time enough to get ready for the start of my second week of work at United. When I had finally gotten my bearings together, I prepared myself for the start of the brand new work week in front of me and I went to disconnect the trailer from my Jeep so that I could push start the engine and go to work, as I still could not afford to replace the drained out battery with a new, at least one hundred dollar car battery.

The second week that I was in San Francisco was quite different from the first simply because I now had a vehicle instead of the bus and I could finally be able to move myself around the city on my own time and terms, but the most significant event of the second week was that my buddy and roommate had seen the new queen size mattress that he had asked me to bring over for him from Miami. I had the mattress strapped to the top of the U-haul trailer wrapped in a sheet of plastic; you can imagine the condition of that plastic and that new mattress after a three thousand mile roadtrip. My buddy did not appreciate the condition that the mattress was in and he made it vocally clear of that fact.

He also made it very clear during the week earlier all of the things that he did not like about me living in his two bedroom apartment. Proudly being who I am and knowing that I refuse to take crap from anyone, I decided that I would move out of his apartment although I had nowhere to go and even after the fact that I had already emptied out the U-haul trailer; I didn't care, I had to go. I packed up all of my things back into the U-haul that I had not yet returned and I left after less than a week of being there.

I took advantage of one of those prominent first month free storage facilities and moved all of my stuff into one. I now had nowhere to go, so I lived out of my Jeep for at least the next two weeks until I received my very first United Airlines paycheck. I thankfully found a backyard apartment that I could afford for rent in Daly City, the southern bordering city of San Francisco. Although we had still worked together at the same airline, it was the very last time that my buddy who had encouraged me to move all the way out to California, would actually be buddies. I would avoid him all the way through our stint at United and I would next hear from him some ten years later when I found out that he had actually become a flight instructor and then eventually a European airline Airbus pilot as we became Facebook friends.

After I had left and I had no place to go, except to sleep in my Jeep. I would actually learn a lot about myself while being officially homeless. Living out of a car for that amount of time really allows you time to self reflect about your life and where you are heading because there are no real distractions away from your thought process. The biggest thing that I could remember reflecting on was what the heck was I doing all the way out here, way out west with no friends, no immediate family and more importantly no real interest in being out there. I had still had thoughts of my beloved city of Miami and I came to the hard drawn conclusion that the only reason that I was actually out there in California was because I was so afraid of getting fired once again due to my heavy partying ways when I should have actually been working hard in Bogota.

I only reflected on that fact for a short time because I realized that my decision had already been made to move out west and there was now absolutely nothing that I could do about that fact now; I knew that regardless of how I felt, I would still have to make the most out of my drastic decision and continue to live my life to the most fullest extent possible because that is who I am and that is who I will always be.

Although I was very happy and excited for this new adventure starting for me out west, I soon realized, and it had only taken me about three months to do so, that I had actually started to miss Miami and I was longing to be back in the tropics with the Caribbean lifestyle, food and weather. Just as soon as I was able to, I put in a transfer request to go back to Miami, but that would take years however. I decided to settle in an attempt to live the best life that I could, as I would now know was a home away from my true home of Miami; an actual good feeling to now know because I had never been so sure about living in Miami before.

One of the things that I had to now do to better my quality of life thus far in this new city was to get a new battery for my Jeep. The battery had been completely dead since that early morning when I had left the lights on in Oklahoma and I also had no money to pay for a new battery until payday, still some two weeks away. I was tired of having to push start the Jeep all the time and I knew getting a new battery would help me to focus on new and better things to come. One night I had slept overnight next to an airport construction site with several construction vehicles parked and waiting for their morning startups. I did not want to do this, but as a desperate man I had to do what I had to do to simply improve my situation. That morning I made sure to wake up around 3am when I knew nobody would be around to see me, I jumped the construction fence and I stole a heavy duty Ford battery from one of those big construction vehicles that were sitting there. The stolen battery fit right into the battery compartment in my Jeep and was fully charged and operable. I put the dead battery from my Jeep which was noticeably smaller than the one that I had just stolen back into the construction vehicle; I was only hoping that maybe the construction crew would only notice that they just had a dead battery in the vehicle and not really realize that the battery had been actually stolen. As well as to also show no hard feelings towards the construction crew by leaving them with no battery sitting in the vehicle. Again, I had to do what I had to do at this very difficult time of my life and I am truly very sorry construction crew.

The battery fit perfectly and also worked perfectly and I didn't need another battery ever again, I had felt like a new man driving a brand new Lexus sedan when that engine once again fired up without me having to push start it. I would end up having that stolen battery so long after this that eventually the same battery was still in it when I sold the jeep some five plus years later. Just like I had thought, life had gotten immediately better for me when I could now simply turn the ignition key and my engine would start right on up. It had been some several weeks unlike this; the good life in California would now finally begin for me was the very first thing that came to my mind at the start of this now brand new chapter in my life.

I would now have the confidence to fully move around San Francisco without the worry of having to only park on a downhill slope and not having to push the Jeep into position for a downhill run. I now felt free, and I truly began to explore the city on my own. I slept in different areas of the city every night just to get familiar with them. I also got familiar with the city government when I woke up early one morning around 6am in a high end area of the city and although I had been clearly sleeping behind the wheel, I received a parking ticket sometime between 2am when I had went to sleep and 6am when I had woke up; parking tickets will always ruin my day. They could have easily awakened me and asked me to move my Jeep.

When I first received my very first paycheck from United Airlines it had gone immediately to my new landlord, I had answered a bulletin board ad in the airlines employee cafeteria. It was exactly what I had been looking for and it was the exact same price that I was paying for my apartment in Miami except that it had no bay or city views. It was an apartment behind a home; the apartment had two small bedrooms and a small living room with no kitchen but a refrigerator and microwave oven, just enough room for everything I had in storage. The only thing that I did not like about this new apartment was that I had to walk through a dark and damp garage to get there. I thought that this was not going to be nice for the ladies to be impressed with, especially after what I had left behind in Miami. But I was a beggar at about this time and I couldn't be choosy, I was happy that I would now have a roof over my head. I moved in on a Saturday morning and the first thing I had done was to take a one hour shower, I had not done that the whole time I was living out of my Jeep. I now had a place to live and a fully working Jeep; I moved all of my stuff in from the storage unit and my new life would now truly begin in this big new city of San Francisco.

The very next thing that I had to do was to get a haircut, I had not received one since I had left Miami and arrived in San Francisco because I was waiting to have a small excess amount of cash funds and it was now going to be time to try and attract these California women. After my first paycheck, I had that small amount of excess cash and I went to my nearest barber shop; I was quite surprised to find out that in San Francisco you cannot get a haircut without a scheduled appointment, this has never been the case in Miami. I made my appointment at the shop closest to my new home and I went to get my long needed haircut.

While I was waiting for my turn at the shears and watching the news airing on the shops television, I couldn't believe what had just come over the airwaves and what I was watching on the national news. An airplane had just departed Miami International airport and had crashed just outside the airport killing all four crewmembers on board and one innocent man on the ground. That airplane was from the same airline that I had just walked away from, I immediately went to a payphone and made an immediate long distance phone call to my longtime high school friend AL, who had gotten me the job at that airline and who was still a flight engineer there. I just had to make sure that my buddy Al was not one of the flightcrew members on board that doomed DC-8 airliner. I did get in contact with Al and he was not one of the flightcrew members on board that flight, I would now be relieved although I had felt for those flight crew members that I more than likely had already flown with or maybe even knew professionally.

I had had serious doubts about my move out to California, one of the reasons I had had doubts about coming out west was because I truly did not want to leave this airline that I was with, especially when I had known about the fact that the airline was going to go public with an Initial Public Offering on the New York Stock Exchange for public funds to run the airline. I thought that would have bought a definite and immediate success to this airline and I truly did not want to miss out on that success that it may have brought, but the crash did just the opposite. The airplane crash had occurred on the exact same day of the initial public offering of this airline and all of my doubts about moving out here had immediately and clearly dissipated and I would never have doubts about the move again; what a coincidence I thought.

Due to my doubts and confusion about making a move that I truly did not want to do, I had sincerely and humbly prayed to God about what direction I should go. I already wrote about the confidence that I had soon after received after praying about finally deciding on making the move out west and that bold confidence did not allow me to look back on any of the hard decision making that I had already made.

With the breaking news that I was receiving on the TV news station I had no other choice except to take it in as some sort of confirmation from God that I had made the right decisions on my long hard move.

I know that must be hard to hear for the family members that have lost their loved ones on this tragic flight, but I still have to share my story and this is what this plane crash did for me, this crash truly helped me to move forward and to also look forward. I could have very easily also been part this tragic life ending flight if I would have decided to stay onboard with this airline and not walk away from the flying job that I truly did not want to leave. But rather I had felt forced to leave due to the circumstances that I had found myself in due to my hard partying ways even while I was working in Bogota, Colombia.

I was very surprised and hurt by the news of this tragic plane crash and I felt for all of the families of the crewmembers involved and the innocent man on the ground, but this plane crash did give me closure on that chapter of my life and could now move on and not look back at what could have been and what may have been. To me it was now the absolutely right decision that I had made, whether it was actually the right decision or not and this closure would make my life going on out forward from this point a whole lot simpler and better for me, by not having to look back anymore, especially knowing that this now defunct cargo airline could not withstand the pressures from that awful plane crash that day.

Me and Raynece near the Golden Gate Bridge.

NO LONGER NAÏVE

This next story that I will share with you is about my starting career at United Airlines, my love of aviation and people and how the men of aviation had still continued to be hateful and potentially harmful to my career, at this point in my aviation career I had not yet realized or accepted this negativity towards me.

One afternoon while I was training on my assigned work crew at the San Francisco maintenance base on the afternoon training shift during my probationary period, I was waiting on the arriving flights to arrive so as to begin accomplishing the assigned routine maintenance. As was routine procedure for mechanics waiting for their arriving flights, we would all gather at an airplane where the scheduled maintenance was already accomplished and lounge in the first class and business cabins while waiting for our work to come in from their revenue flights. This is a somewhat routine procedure throughout the aviation maintenance industry and had been my experience for the length of my now ten year aviation career. I had also been introduced to this common practice at this new job.

On one particular probationary training day I was doing just this with at least a dozen or so other mechanics all waiting for our assignments to arrive at the maintenance base to begin assigned work. We were all there together on board of a parked Boeing 747. Some mechanics were watching first run movies on the airplanes entertainment system, some were reading books or onboard magazines, and some of them were actually dozing off all while we waited for our later aircraft assignments to finally arrive back to the maintenance base. The cabin entry door was closed and shut so that we would not be easily disturbed by anyone who attempted to come onboard the aircraft and who maybe did not like or agree to this very routine scenario.

I was in the first class cabin simply lounging with the rest of my peers on board, immediately adjacent to the only accessible entry door of the aircraft. I chose this seating location because I had the intention to simply make my way to the rear of the aircraft and not be seen by someone who did not like this scenario. Sometime later, this is exactly what eventually happened, I jetted off to the rear of the aircraft as I saw that my lead technician was coming onboard the aircraft as he wrestled with the entry door to gain entry. He had not immediately seen me sitting there as I darted to the rear of the aircraft just as soon as I noticed him, but for whatever reason he came on board looking and asking especially for me. He would make his way to the back of the aircraft specifically looking for me. As I met him further back in the aircraft cabin, I was no doubtedly chewed out by this lead technician for being on board the aircraft with the rest of the mechanics; of course no one else would get chewed out except for one and only me.

Not only did I get chewed out for being onboard of the aircraft by this lead, but this lead technician would also report me to the supervising manager on duty at the time and I would be called into the supervisor's office for a verbal reprimand for my…"Whatever it was that I was doing wrong at that time" office chat. This meeting between the three of us would last about thirty minutes and all we did was talk, but I was still quite concerned about being there because I was still in my probationary period; I didn't want or need any unnecessary attention towards my very new and short employment file at United Airlines, but this man had only bought me into the supervisor's office for a reprimand, what about the other dozen or so technicians who were also onboard the aircraft with me!? I had to ask why.

I took my beating like the man that I am and nothing would actually happen to me or my brand new employee file during this brief meeting, but I still did not like what had been done to me by my lead technician as he was also a fellow trade union member in a leadership position.

This lead technician did not know who I was, or what I was about, or what I had done previously in my life, such as being introduced to union leadership during my days at PanAm. He also didn't know that I knew that with him being a fellow union member, he was dead wrong for him to be turning in a fellow union member into management for reprimand, especially while I was still on probation. Just as soon as my meeting with my manager was over I would find my way to my local union representative's office; I had already had knowledge of union rules and regulations because I had dealt with my union a little bit as a former union member at PanAm and I knew what was tolerated inside the union and I knew what was not. Some ten years after I was told that I smile too much, I was no longer naïve to the ongoings in aviation or specifically aviation maintenance; no more "too much" smiling for me or happy disposition especially when it came to trade union rules. I would explain to my union rep all that happened leading up to me being called into the supervisor's office for my reprimand and of course my union representative did not like what he was hearing at all.

Once I was done explaining all that had happened to my union representative, he was quite upset with what he had heard from me and immediately made his way over to my assigned work area and crew to have a long discussion with my lead technician. When we had both arrived back to my lead's office, the entire crew was there to witness the conversation to come in the office area. The union representative would walk into that office with his big ole' intimidating union jacket proudly displayed and then have a closed door meeting in the lead's office with the lead technician; but the door did not have to be closed to hear what was going on inside because the voice volumes were quite elevated and the extreme tension streamed out of that office door even though the door was fully closed. We all knew exactly what was going on behind that closed door. Everyone in my crew that had been there to witness this, had all looked over to me. They were all laughing at me because of what I had obviously caused. We had all heard the yelling going on inside, behind those closed doors and I had felt somewhat vindicated. When all was said and done in that office, the union representative would finally come out, shake my hand and promise me that all would be fine from here on out. I had believed what he was telling me and I actually felt quite relieved and that was the end of that issue, for now that is, because someone would now be very mad at me.

My now very upset lead technician had felt quite differently however and was quite upset with me with what had just happened. Now I would be paying for his vengeance with my future job assignments for the next few months to come. I would now be routinely assigned to maintenance on chapter 38 discrepancy items for the next several months while working with this lead technician, who was obviously really upset with me and what I had bought to his crew in my attempt to correct the wrong that I had felt was done to me. Aircraft maintenance items are broken down into numerical sections to categorize all of the aircraft's systems; on this particular subdivision, chapter 38 is the category for water and waste in the aircraft, in other words, everything that has to do with the onboard toilets, water and bathroom waste systems. I did not mind this at all because my very first year at PanAm I was assigned to a crew that removed, rebuilt and installed the entire bathroom systems on the Boeing 747, so I was very good at troubleshooting and fixing any type of toilet or water problems that arose in those areas of the aircraft; I would continue to do my job proudly because I knew exactly what I was doing in the toilet's and waste systems of this particular aircraft and I proudly let it be shown to all who were watching by doing an excellent job regardless.

It was certainly not the first time and it was certainly not going to be the last time that I would be retributed against by someone. This retribution would not last very long however, soon after when my leads had almost immediately seen that this chapter 38 punishment was not going to actually be a problem for me, as I had handled every single chapter 38 assignment and issue given me in that timespan in a timely and professional manner. Over a little bit of time the retribution had soon disappeared when my lead had finally realized that I was strictly a professional and that I was only there to perform my duties as assigned to me to the best of my abilities. We would also eventually become good working partners; so much so that I would eventually also become a fill in lead mechanic when the regular lead technician was not there. I was also allowed to become a certified technical maintenance representative for Japan Airlines at San Francisco, responsible for the maintenance release of all of their cargo outbound flights. I also would eventually become a run-up and taxi mechanic on the Boeing 747, all from my leads recommendations. I even joined in a roofing party that he had at his house to help to replace the worn out roof in his Pacific Ocean seaside home. I never did have any hard feelings towards him; I just wanted to have a professional career at my time spent there at United Airlines San Francisco maintenance base.

One good positive thing that did come out of this event was that because my entire work crew had witnessed my quick and reactive response as well as the instant response from the union representative that had come about from my sole actions to try and correct a wrong that I felt had been done to me, they all had liked what they saw from me in my quick and decisive response and they had truly appreciated the confidence that I had shown to do something in such a response without worsening my situation as a probationary mechanic.

So soon shortly after this event on the airplane with the lead mechanic, when my crew was looking for a union representative for our specific work area, I was the only one nominated for the position. I gladly and humbly accepted the nomination and I became the union representative for my crew and my entire work area that included three other work crews of about a dozen technicians each. I would be the only union representative for that work area for the entire four year period that I was employed at United Airlines San Francisco. I also would think that what happened with my lead may have been actually a true blessing for me because it had directly led to my nominations for the union position and all of the subsequent management labor relations in our work area, the legal training that I had received from the local labor union organization, and the many experiences in general, which ultimately came in very beneficial for me, especially a little bit later on in my life when I had needed legal assistance on several occasions but I couldn't afford an attorney, which you will soon be reading about in upcoming chapters.

During my time as a union representative I would take any and every training class that the union would offer me, to learn all about the union rules and regulations, bylaws, constitutions, conflict resolution and even contract negotiations. I also wrote very official arguments and contract grievances used for fellow union members in their conflicts against the management at United. I was very much like a high priced defense attorney and I had always felt like a supporting cast member as a naval defense attorney in a role in the Caine Mutiny movie. I would truly enjoy hunting down and snooping out overly aggressive maintenance supervisors and managers that were only motivated to make a union member's day as miserable as possible. I would legally and contractually fight for many of my fellow co workers in intense sit down meetings and disciplinary hearings with top and middle management and I am proud to say that I was beneficial to all of the dozens and dozens of fellow employees whom I have ever fought for. I won nearly every single case, all except for one sole technician whose case could not be helped because he had clearly falsified a time document that was negated by an official computer time stamped document that could not be denied. I could not help him in this case, but I gave him all of the best encouragement that I possibly could as I escorted him off of the property for the very last time.

To this very day I still have all of my individual case files that I have accumulated and fought for over the years there. I also tried my hardest to attend all of the monthly union meetings and training sessions that were made available to me and I have earned several personalized union jackets including a beautiful leather jacket that I truly cherish for all of the hard work that I achieved for fellow union members as a United Airlines union representative. I will always honor the time that I had spent helping my fellow employees when and where I could at United Airlines, and I was certainly always pleased when I was able to get them off of any harsh attacks and disciplinary action from the management personnel at United Airlines.

One of my most prized possessions.

THE BUS RIDE

When I had first moved into my very own San Francisco apartment with a new roof over my head and a new working battery in my Jeep, that was when it was the time I had decided to go back to work and when I say back to work I am not necessarily talking about work at United Airlines. While I was actually working hard and fighting for others and building up my career at United; all of that hard work wasn't enough to keep me distracted from my first true love... of women. I still could not forget my true roots of being a natural born partier and once I finally had my own roof over my head and a dependable vehicle I would soon come back to what I had learned as a chauffeur and more specifically what I had learned when I was a personal driver for the not so good doctor. The only difference now was that I did not need any fancy car to attract the opposite sex, my Jeep was all that I had needed; my hard learned and hard practiced confidence was all that I needed to meet and attract all of the beautiful California beauties that I had heard so much about before I had even imagined of living there. I would just try and show all of that confidence that I had been showing in that Lexus, right there in my Jeep. It worked well.

That's exactly what I did when I wasn't working at the airport and it all came quite easily for me ; it did not take me long before I started meeting gorgeous women and was doing all the same things that I had been doing in that brand new Lexus four or five years earlier. It wasn't even before the end of the very first week in my new apartment before I had a beautiful woman spending the night with me there, I didn't even have a bed to sleep on rather just a mattress on the floor; she did not mind at all. We spent the entire night on the mattress on the floor just talking and doing what consenting adults do together late at night.

When the evening was finally over very early in the morning, I took her back to her home in San Francisco while the sun was still down because I had an early morning training class to attend at the United maintenance base. Unfortunately, again I never made any type of attempt in contacting her ever again once I had dropped her off at her place although she was very beautiful, smart and sexy black woman; I was just so excited with the opportunity to meet and possibly conquer as many beautiful California women that I possibly could in this brand new adventure for me, this was my only motivation outside of my growing aviation career.

At that particular time in my life, I didn't have or even want any typical type of lady friends. Especially the ones that I could call on at anytime to do whatever I was in the mood for at that particular time, just as I had done for such a long time while living in Miami. I was much more interested in having a quantity of women at this time in my life and not necessarily that of quality; this certain woman that I had just recently been with, could have very easily been considered a quality woman but I wasn't at all interested in her in a permanent way or even temporarily being committed to her. I had fully wanted to get to know and experience what I had previously heard so much about prior to moving out to San Francisco and that was California girls; I would certainly amass my share of them in the very little amount of time that I was there and I wasn't in any way shape or form was getting tired of them, I always needed more, but this would soon all change.

This flirtatious behavior by me went on for the first several months that I was living in San Francisco and I had amassed and amounted many happy conquests in the very short time that I was there, and I was quite happy with what I was doing until...the bus ride; this would be when my crazy bachelor lifestyle would suddenly and abruptly change and change forever.

Anybody who lives in San Francisco knows that you do not want to drive your vehicle into the city to park your car and then go about your business, parking is very limited and very expensive as well as time limited; it was much more economical for me, if I had the time to spare, to take the city bus into the city.

I was now living in Daly City, the southerly bordering suburb city of San Francisco and I had off street parking right inside of the garage of the house that I was living in. I would always park my convertible Jeep inside the garage and I would walk half of a block away to take the city bus into the city to do all of my business and my familiarization within the city of San Francisco; this was quite a frequent routine for me on my days off from work or whenever I was bored, I considered these simple bus trip as a great and big adventure for me to venture out into the city and see sights and of course people that I have never seen before.

On one particular day as I was riding the city bus back from a jaunt in the city, I noticed a very beautiful young lady sitting alone in the bus. I wanted the opportunity to get to speak to her and to also maybe get to know her so I decided that I would sit as close as possible to where she was so that I could possibly strike up a conversation with her; I did just that and the conversation that we struck up went absolutely wonderful.

In the very short time that I had spoken to her I had known almost everything about her life, like where she was born and the fact that one of her parents was black and that the other was white and that she lived all alone in the city of San Francisco; a very expensive endeavor for even way back then I had thought to myself; she must be well to do as well as I continued to think, of course a definite bonus.

When the conversation was finally over and it was time for her to get off of the bus she handed me her phone number as I watched her get off the bus with her tall, beautiful voluptuous body and long flowing hair, she smiled a broad smile at me as the bus that I was still in drove off into the sunset with me still sitting there wondering what and how such a great thing that just happened, happened; I was now once again extremely excited and I couldn't wait to call her later on that very same night.

Once I was done with all that I had to do that evening I would wind up calling her at about 10pm, I had wanted so bad to just simply continue the wonderful conversation we had shared on the bus and that's exactly what had happened when I had called her that late in the evening. We would speak on the telephone for about an hour when she had decided to invite me over to her house that very same first night, I couldn't refuse and I jumped into my Jeep and I quickly made my way over to her house that very same late evening.

She lived in one of those picturesque and very expensive multi level San Francisco homes on a steep San Francisco hill that you see on one of those popular San Francisco post card pictures, it was a beautiful home and I had immediate thoughts of as to how this young lady could afford to be living here all on her own. That all changed when I came to her front door, which was cut out of the actual larger garage door. She had led me through the garage to her own living area, this was where and when I had realized that she only lived in the garage apartment that was set up for her inside the back of the garage; somewhat similar to myself and how I lived except for the fact that I actually was in a seperate apartment just outside of the garage at the back of the house where I was living. I had thought of this as some sort of really weird coincidence that we both accessed our living areas through a dark damp garage and that would mean she would be more than open to visit me where I had lived and that she wouldn't actually mind the idea of visiting me at my apartment because we both lived nearly exactly the same way.

She had walked me to the back of the garage where she had a very lovely living arrangement setup all to herself in a lovely pink and girly décor. This apartment, which was completely cordoned off from the rest of the garage, was very well lit up and setup so that you now could not know that you were actually in a dusky garage of a home. We talked for a little while until the tension was too much and we soon quickly attacked each other with an intense ferocity as if we needed each other's bodies for our very own human survival we made a sweet and intense love to each other as if we were on a long anticipated virgin honeymoon.

When I left some several hours later well into the early morning I kissed her goodbye and I told her to have a good night and that I would certainly call her later on that day, I was so excited about this new woman in my life because I had truly loved everything that I had learned about her so far and she was absolutely gorgeous. I think I had truly fallen in love with her, even in that very short amount of time that we had known each other. Not only for her natural beauty but also her mannerisms as she was so well-spoken, her calm tone of voice and basically her general positive attitude towards life in general; I can remember thinking and feeling to myself that I would be more than willing to give up my playboyish type of lifestyle for her because she was simply... just that beautiful to me.

When I had left her early that morning I was feeling more wonderful and positive about a relationship with her more so than I had ever felt with any other woman that I had ever spent time with. When it came to leaving this woman that I had just spent an evening with, I was still very excited about that fact of my new found feelings towards her, even more so than the time I had spent with that secret celebrity affair years earlier, as I had never felt that excited with this celebrity beauty when I had left her and the Ocean Drive hotel room that we had just shared together also leaving her on a very early morning.

The next day I made sure to call her back just like I had said I would, this was very unusual for me to call back a conquest the very next day because it was usually and routinely not at all, but this affair was obviously and completely different. It was all about the positive vibes that I was feeling towards her and I wanted to try and pursue a real and true relationship with her as quickly as possible because I was now in love.

When I had placed that very much anticipated phone call to her the next evening, she answered very pleasantly as I now knew what must have been the routine for her and she kindly said hello to me.

Right along with that very kind hello, she would immediately state to me that she had something very important to tell me; I would immediately become nervous because I had no clue as to what she wanted to tell me about and all sorts of negative thoughts were now racing through my much confused head. Especially about certain types of sexual bugs out there that she may have passed on to me, or maybe for her being a resident of San Francisco that she may have once been a man or something to that effect. It had seemed like forever as I waited for her to get out what it was that she had to all of a sudden tell me and why it was so important for her to tell me right now at this exact moment and not the night before when we were actually speaking together or when I had first met her on the city bus the previous day before when she had nearly told me all of her entire life, but why not this thing that she deemed so important to tell me right now, I would reluctantly ask myself.

She had finally got out what she wanted so intently wanted to tell me; she had told me that although we had a very enjoyable adult experience together the night before, she told me that she was in fact not an actual adult but rather the fact that she was just - -teen years old, I had just recently celebrated my twenty eighth birthday somewhere around that time prior to our meeting.

Don't judge me as if you sit on high on a high bench and hold a gavel in your hand; we all make mistakes and confession is good for the soul and this is my confessional.

Rather, all of you should be sincerely and graciously praying for me. When last have you confessed your sins to God or maybe even simply one to another as God himself suggests in his very own words?

How could this possibly be? She absolutely tricked me! I guess with her being born in the city of Los Angeles like she had earlier told me, she was a naturally born actress. She could have easily told me from the second I approached her that she was not of an adult age. Instead she greeted me with a warm and friendly smile and a very welcoming attitude and went on to continue to give me her contact information for a potential future reunion between us.

This is not an excuse on my part, maybe I should have known better and have been able to judge a very young age, but I have never been very good at distinguishing the ages of people especially when people are purposely trying to act outside of their particular age range which was exactly what she had been doing by acting, speaking and dressing so maturely and also by so quickly inviting me over to her very own home where she portrayed to me the simple fact that she had indeed lived alone.

I had never had any problems getting woman, as you all may now already know by now, and I certainly did not want to mess up that blessing by going to jail or getting some sort of a sex crime charge from someone that was not of legal age. I would have done all I could to avoid this scenario if I truly knew her age, but what happened, happened and I must live with my life without regret just as long as I can continue to move forward.

I was very much surprised at what she had told me because that was actually the farthest thought from my mind, I really could not believe her, she had been so womanly, so mature, so voluptuous, so well spoken, so grown, in fact, I actually refused to believe her and I asked her to somehow prove to me that she was just a - -teen year old kid; she happily obliged and immediately did just that.

She went into at least a two minute continuous speal as to how her day had went for her and what she had done in school that day, her homework assignments and projects due, her school life in general and all of her teachers, she spoke of all of that with an intense precision that just could not be denied.

Her voice also went up a couple octaves as well with a little quicker snap to it and the proper speaking turned a little bit ghetto with a much younger mind frame than what she had originally portrayed to me. I now completely believed everything that she saying, including the confession of her very young age. She also told me that she did not get along very well with her mother whom had lived right upstairs in the main section of the house that I had visited her at the previous night, and that they had both agreed that to prevent the daily arguments and fights that they both frequently had, that she would live in the garage area as to stay away from each other so that they did not have to see each other and so that a certain amount of peace could also be kept in their house and not affect a younger sister that she had. Moms of combative teen daughters living separately in the same house, please be on notice of your daughter's potential activities that may be being done literally right under your very nose.

Even though I now truly believed her, I still felt like some sort of a shady character in the lyrics of a Benny Mardones one hit wonder song, where I just wanted to sweep her off her feet and fly her away into the night forever and ever; but I knew that of course that this was not at all possible and I could not do this, California don't play that game. I had a good thing with grown woman so I had never wanted to mess that good thing up playing around with jailbait. I had felt extremely lucky that she was as nice to me as she was and that she did not attempt to blackmail me or simply report me to the local authorities. Since the day of that shocking phone conversation, I had now always felt somewhat nervous and extremely cautious of my immediate surroundings after she had told me what she had told me, simply because I had a landline phone in that apartment that could have easily been traced to my address at the time so I was extremely suspicious of law enforcement pulling up on me one day as I pulled into my garage to park my Jeep.

I took this experience for all that it was worth and I decided that I would have nothing more to do with this beautiful young lady, but that did not mean that this adventure was not still very heavy on my heart and I felt extremely guilty for what had taken place. I had come to the long and hard conclusion that with all of my wicked behavior towards women that this was bound to have eventually happened at some point in my wild sexual life and that if I did not stop my wild and crazy ways with women that it would more than likely happen once again and probably soon; I had to do something about my very bad behavior when it came to my treatment of women and I meant right now at this exact moment.

In my shock and disgrace to what I had allowed to have happened with this young lady, I prayed and cried out loudly to God himself and I begged him for his forgiveness for what I had done to her and I also promised God that I would change my wicked ways towards women. I was sincere in what I was praying about and I believe God knew that as well, so for that no one can judge me. I knew what I did was wrong and I now also knew that if I kept on going about what I had been doing so much before with women, that things may become worst than just the news that this young lady had just broke to me. These wild and irresponsible actions by me would have to stop and stop now. I would then think to myself; women were my kryptonite and my weakness and I didn't know how I was actually going to stop the lifestyle that I had grown so accustomed to over all of the years and almost a decade of wildly misbehaving with the opposite sex, but of course God knows exactly that about me and he also knows exactly how to get that accomplishment done for me, if I really and truly wanted to. At this point in my life and after this very memorable bus ride, yes; I really and truly wanted to change my life around concerning my addiction to women and of course not for the worst of the matter, but rather for the better.

MS. LOVELY

Some weeks and maybe months had passed by and I had honored my promise to God in the sense that I seriously made an attempt to try and curb my raunchy behavior when it came to my treatment of the many women that crossed my path; I had made a concerted effort to always remember what had happened with my very young lady friend on the bus. I was no longer consciously looking for women to conquer on a reg-ular and routine basis and I had been on my relatively speaking... best behavior. God was closely there in the back of my mind and my thoughts and the sincere promise that I had recently made to him regarding my love and treatment of women.

That would somewhat change on a day when I had pulled into a local gas station to fill the gas tank on my Jeep. While I was there pumping the gasoline into my tank, this absolutely most beautiful woman that I had ever seen even to this date, had also pulled into the same gas station where I was at, to also fill the gas tank in her vehicle. I did not want to, nor could I stop staring at this gorgeous looking woman and it was more than obvious that my lower jaw was sitting on top of my shoes all the while that my googly eyes were intensely staring at this beautiful woman right in front of me.

I more than usually would have said something to her by this time that had seemed to be so slowly passing by. Especially from the fact that she was also staring right back at me with the same type of intense stare that I normally would have stared at beautiful woman except for the fact that I was now thinking about the promise I had made to God. With that beau-tiful smile on her face, I couldn't stare back and I kept looking away from her simply because I still had God in the back of mind and the promise that I had made to him just some weeks or months earlier. I had felt as if I was caught between a rock and a hard place because I felt that I would be potentially breaking my promise to God if I had only attempted to simply strike up a conversation with this beautiful woman that was staring right back at me; even though I truly had no intention of speaking to this woman strictly based on that promise. In that very brief time, I still had thoughts however of what I could be doing with her if I could have actually spoken to her and gotten to know her as I had with so many other previous women who had strolled into and out of my life prior to me seeing her. I honestly felt like a recovering crack addict being handed a free bag of white powdery stuff and experiencing withdrawal symptoms all at the same time.

I had absolutely no intention of ever saying anything to this natural beauty and I actually didn't have to say anything at all, because she kept right on staring at me right on up to the point where she would confidently walk right up to me at my Jeep while I was still pumping gas into my Jeep and she would then very proudly introduce herself to me. I was completely shocked and for the first time ever, I couldn't speak to this very beautiful woman. I was still googly eyed and my heart was now beating intensely; I was extremely nervous solely because I was clearly thinking of God at that very moment still and I knew what this may eventually lead to. I couldn't be rude to this beautiful woman though, smiling brightly and directly at me. I finally said hello right back to her and I also politely introduced myself to her, we had a very small conversation. She then handed me over one of those small religious cartoon gospel tracts that Christian pilgrims hand over to people to try and introduce them to the basic principles of Christianity with a Bible story and chapter verses. I had seen and been accustomed to this type of Christian missionary people before as I am sure we all somehow are exposed to them at one point or another in our lives, but this one was completely different; she handed this tract over to me with her full name and personal phone number hand written on the back of the tract. What had I done to deserve this I would ask myself as I left the gas station and when it was all said and done that afternoon?

To this very day I still have this exact same tract that was given to me from this gorgeous woman still in my possession with her full name and phone number in her own handwriting still clearly legible on the back of the Christian tract.

I couldn't believe what was happening to me here; this tall, slim, beautiful café au lait complected sexy black woman with the friendliest personality that you could imagine was giving me all of her contact information in the mere moments that we had seen each other and without me even having to ask for it or even attempting to get it. I immediately thought that I must be truly somehow be blessed when it came to attracting beautiful woman; I had never thought that before, but now it was somehow very clear to me and I had literally felt as if I was in heaven on Earth. I just simply felt wonderfully privileged to just make her acquaintance and my previous experience with the last young lady would now be instantly and completely dissipated with no regrets as to what had happened with her at all. A bit of clarity had finally came for me to be able to move forward without having to ever look back at that very bad and unusual experience that I had with the young lady on the bus; I had since that experience been always looking over my shoulder for the authorities to be right there behind me because this young woman had had my landline phone number and I could not but help to believe that the police would soon come knocking on my door at any moment that I was at home. This beautiful woman, whom I just met, had magically changed all of that for me and those scary memories and thoughts would soon dissipate into thin air.

She asked me to call her that very same night and that was exactly what I excitedly rushed home to do; I thought that it would be quite OK to communicate with her because this potential relationship would have been founded on a Christian tract right at the same time that I had God firmly and primarily in my thoughts and mind. I remember thinking that if a Christian based relationship were going to start, which is what I had now been wisely thinking of, this is obviously the best way that a Godly relationship could start. With God being the primary focus on both of the involved parties thoughts and minds; what could possibly be better for me than this wonderful Godly situation that I had found myself in right here!? I was now once again very excited at my future outlook for my life and relationships in San Francisco.

I was so looking forward to once again being able to call and speak to a beautiful woman on the phone as I had not had that kind of opportunity again since the fiasco on the bus, and I called her just as soon as I was able to when I arrived back at home. We spoke on the phone that evening for a very long time on the very first conversation we shared and the beauty shock and my shyness towards her was slowly dissipating away from the way I had first felt in the gas station; my confidence was growing because of the obvious intelligence that she openly revealing to me during our long conversation on that very first evening.

She told me everything about herself on the very first phone conversation that we shared, like the fact that she was a devout and dedicated Christian who had always gone to church on Sunday Mornings.

Ms. Lovely would also tell me that she had been working professionally as a figure and fashion model and she had been doing music videos, television commercials, print and magazine ads and she did that type of work on a part time basis, only as frequently as she got accepted for jobs at casting calls and model casting shoots. Even at the time of this writing, decades after our first meeting, I have also just recently seen her on national television ads on my local television stations here in Miami although we still currently live three thousand miles apart. I am still in touch with her even today via social media and I messaged her the exact moment that I had seen her most recent commercial and she was quite surprised to know that fact. I knew that she was genuinely beautiful when I had first laid eyes on her but I didn't know that she was actually that beautiful to actually be on a lifelong professional modeling level and I truly felt like I had really hit the jackpot with this beautiful woman. I had never actually envisioned myself seriously dating any type of professional model type like her before, although I would never have any problem courting any of this type of woman for a quick one evening adventure or two if they had ever pleased as I chauffeured them around town such as I had done with the secret celebrity.

Ms. Lovely would further also go on to tell me that she was no longer married due to a recent divorce and that she had two small children at home and that she was a single mother fully taking care of her two girls. I did not think anything of this as she was extremely beautiful in my eyes and I felt that nothing could come between me getting to know this woman better. She would also go onto tell me the very same first night that she had full intentions of not having sex with anyone until she was once again married; I also did not think much of this because of the solemn promise that I had made to God. I had actually seen this statement to me as a bonus, as I was actually quite relieved in that this statement to me immediately took off all of the pressure off of me at attempting to return to my old macho ways with women that I was so truly tempted to do with her. I truly respected her for saying that to me because I had never ever heard that from any other woman before in all of my many experiences with the women that I had dealt with prior to her.

For once in my life, I was truly looking forward to getting to know her for who she actually was and not for someone to be conquered with an abundance of mutual pleasure.

Over the next few months that' s exactly what happened, we had become very good friends, but not the kind of friends that stay in a sort of friends zone. It was as if we knew that we were both working up to something good between us. Ms. Lovely had taken me to her casting calls and model shoots, we would frequent the gym and work out together, sharing conversations in the sauna's and steam rooms. I had also routinely brought her lunch at her regular full time job, we had watched the beautiful California sunsets from various different locations throughout the city of San Francisco. Ms. Lovely was genuinely my very first good female friend of a woman where we were not actually sharing sexual encounters and yet I was most certainly loving every single minute of it. She would also put me on the official pickup list from her children's elementary school for her two small daughters. I had thought this as some sort of a wonderful responsibility that she had kindly extended to me to be responsible for her two beautiful little girls who I would pick up from school and take them home on the afternoons that I was available to; I had felt blessed, honored and undeserving all at the same time to be doing this for her. At that time I felt like I truly did not deserve this beautiful responsibility because of my previous wild behavior with women but she must have definitely seen something in me that allowed her to give me responsibility for her most precious belongings. I most certainly appreciated that fact however and I did my absolute best to try and impress Ms. Lovely by doing an excellent job for her even while those two sweet little angels of little girls were actually a tough handful for me to control, but I certainly did not ever let her know that and I truly did my best with those two little girls.

Even though Ms. Lovely had done all of these beautiful things for our friendly non committal type of relationship, it was not at all the best thing that she had done for me; that would be the fact that right at the beginning she invited me to her church. I couldn't refuse her invitation; I truly think it was a sort of an unofficial first date type of invitation thing and I gladly escorted her to church the very next Sunday. When she had initially invited me to her church I didn't have to think twice about it and I had went that first Sunday just to be with her and to also be seen with her although I knew that I had not visited a church routinely since I had left my parents home some now ten years earlier.

I had started to routinely visit this lovely cityside church with Ms. Lovely and I would soon after actually start enjoying the Church services more so than actually just wanting to be seen with her as was originally the case for me.

Not too long after I had started coming to the Church services with her, there was always the routine altar call at the end of each Church service by the Pastor calling anyone to the front of the church for anyone who was willing to publicly give their life to Christ in a more significant and visual way and for all there to see.

On one particular Sunday for whatever reason I felt called to go up there. I felt as if I were being pulled to the front of the Church like a piece of steel to an electro-magnet; I had not been prompted by Ms. Lovely or anyone else for that matter to make my way up to the front. I made my way up to front of the Church on my own and the Pastor would then ask me if I was willing to repent of my sinful ways and to also hand my life over to Christ; I confidently said yes and that I was ready to do so. The Pastor would then place his hands on my forehead and begin to loudly pray over me. As he was praying for me in front of the congregation, I remember falling to my knees and the next thing that I could clearly remember after that was me being fanned by several women of the Church as I was laid out cold right there on the floor of that Church. I do not know what actually happened to me in that moment but I think I fainted to the floor. I had thought that it was amazing that nobody in the Church body had not thought anything of my fainting by not calling any sort of medical attention for me.

I had seen this sort of things on late night television Church shows and in movies where people had been incapacitated by being prayed over but now I was experiencing this sort of thing first hand; it was very much real and I have never been known to be any type of actor or faker or false fainter.

I was not a person to be known to ever have been a fainter and I really had no reason to faint, it wasn't like I was hungry or malnourished; I hadn't been hungry since my early days of Pan Am when I would jump on an airplane just to be fed. This fact lends perfect credibility to my favorite Bible verse which is John chapter 6 verses 35 and I have vowed to always have a plaque of this Bible verse in any and all of my kitchens where I will permanently reside. I was picked up by an older gentleman from the church congregation and escorted back to my seat. I sat there next to Ms. Lovely dumbfounded as to what had just happened, I was confused and I couldn't explain to myself what had just happened all I knew was that it was real. I also knew that this must have been some major life altering event that I had just experienced, this was powerful and I knew my life would certainly not ever be the same for here on out. I had always heard about people coming to their knees and changing their lives over drugs, alcohol, or due to sickness or illness, but I was changing my life over an abundance of sex; it was actually the guilt of me having sex with that very young lady that had finally brought me to my knees to God, for his forgiveness and to not receive his ultimate judgment and eventual punishment for my guilty sins.

God had of course known exactly who I was and exactly what I had needed to bring my life to him; this beautiful woman who I call Ms. Lovely. For no other object in this World could have ever brought me to faith in Jesus Christ except for a very beautiful woman and who would also have the brains, the beauty, and the power to lead me to where I had needed to be when it came to the almighty GOD.

I now knew that my promise and commitment to God was going to have to be real and that I probably needed to do a little bit more, so I started to do more in the church and I started to attend Bible studies both in the Church and also at the Bible studies that Ms. Lovely hosted at her home. I was now excited to get to know more about the Lord and more about what I had just experienced in the front of that Church. Who would have ever thought that a beautiful woman and a religious tract could actually lead me to want to make a change my life?

Ms. Lovely and I had remained good platonic friends who would accompany each other to Church functions and family outings, the Beach, the Gym, the mall and we also enjoyed long phone conversations.

This was the ideal male female relationship that did not involve sex; we had truly become good friends. I would change all of that though at a Thanksgiving dinner at her house that she had so kindly invited me to.

The Thanksgiving dinner at her house in 1997 was a big affair with all of her extended family being there and me meeting family faces that I had not met before in the six months or so that I had known her.

Although my heart had truly felt strongly for Ms. Lovely, she would end up doing something that Thanksgiving afternoon that I truly did not like and it sort of turned me sour towards her almost instantly. Ms. Lovely on a few occasions would introduce me to her family and friends as her future husband; this truly upset me because we had never spoken on this subject matter before and I felt as if she had known about something that I didn't know. From this point on in our friendship, I would now undeservedly think of Ms. Lovely as maybe somewhat a little bit crazy although I had already known her for some months as completely sane, and this was just for simply introducing me to her family as her future husband.

Most men would have been honored to have such a beautiful woman who was hard working, sexy, smart and a professional figure model all at once. Who just so happened to also be your best friend and who would also introduce you to her extended family as her future husband, but not me; I was just not smart and maybe just plain old stupid. Ms. Lovely had both aesthetic beauty as well as a spiritual inner beauty unlike any woman that I had ever seen before. I honestly believe that she was a true gift from God for me but I just simply couldn't see past my judgment on her for telling her family that I was her future husband without any prior agreement between us and maybe also for being a divorced mother of two children, although I may not have been thinking that thought directly at that time; I know I'm bad but this is still my confessional folks.

Looking back now on that time back then, with all that had happened to me in that moment. I can clearly see that God himself had probably provided this beautiful woman for me, but I was blind and could not see at that time; in my opinion, being the devout Christian that Ms. Lovely had shown herself to be, Ms. Lovely must have been told or shown by God that I was the man that he would be providing for her, but I did not do my part by keeping an open mind so as to listen to God speaking to me this time, just as I had done so many other times previously. God was probably more than likely speaking to me in the only language that I truly appreciated; beautiful women, but I was not open to listen at this particular time in my life as I had genuinely listened before such as the time that I was told to stay in bed back in the days of Tulsa.

Ms. Lovely had welcomingly taken me into her close family network as if I were already a member of her family, not only by inviting me to a very personal and family orientated celebration such as Thanksgiving dinner with all of her family and friends over but also by allowing me to take care of her very own children. Ms. Lovely had also singlehandedly lead me to forever change my life and for that I will be forever grateful to her.

I honestly feel that Ms. Lovely had very responsibly answered her own personal call from God at least when it came to me by simply offering me that personalized tract, but I did not follow through with the call that she was probably relaying over to me.

After I left the Thanksgiving dinner with a very nice take home package of food goodies, unfortunately I would now start to reject Ms. Lovely for the stupidest of all reasons. I was in such a state of shock about her introductions of me that I would now start to have made up excuses as to why I should not do the things that we used to do so happily together. I even began to now pass judgment on her in my mind saying to myself that she was divorced and she had already had two children that were not mine although I had already grown to love those two little girls and I myself had a daughter out of wedlock. I had passed unfair judgment on Ms. Lovely even though I wasn't at all perfect and I had already done what I done with all of those women prior to her and I myself was also unwed and already had a daughter of my own about the same age as her two young daughters.

I'm really sorry Ms. Lovely you did not deserve all that negative judgment that I had secretly and unjustly placed on you and you most truly deserved much better; looking back now all of these years later, I truly wish that I had not been so secretly judgmental towards you. God's timing is always perfect and for whatever reason known only by God, you were probably absolutely correct in your thoughts, and your actions regarding your introduction of me to your family. I have always regretted nothing in my life, but if I were to ever one day regret anything at all this situation would most certainly be it.

I am certainly happy that you were not a shy person for that is a true sign that you were actually more than likely called by God, I had no intention to ever speak to you in that gas station for fear of where it might of lead and my promise to God, yet you did approach me and it changed my life from there on. Shyness is a true form of human fear, and fear is certainly not of God. You are truly an example of a lovingly caring Christian missionary and I now truly feel that maybe I should have really been your future husband as you so boldly and confidently stated to your family at that Thanksgiving dinner; I was very young and I was also very dumb. Even though I did not marry this woman who maybe I should have; I still must continue on with living my life with absolutely no regret, as what I have done in my life.

Although I had no intention to ever approach this woman that day solely due to the promise I had made to God, I am certainly happy that she confidently approached me. This woman I can honestly say is the one person solely 100 percent responsible for the change in my life that I desperately needed at that time and leading me to Jesus Christ. I truly do not know where my life would be if she hadn't done so.

Even with this fact, I had now still purposely chosen to slowly separate myself from Ms. Lovely due to the very surprising family introductions at her Thanksgiving dinner, but we still remained close friends and we would still contact each other from time to time just to keep in touch and I was still content with doing all of the things that we were doing previous to Thanksgiving like going to parks, the beaches and lunches. Ms. Lovely never actually knew what my thought process actually was towards her at that time and when it came to me slowly separating myself. I also continued to go to Church services either way, with or without her, and I no longer depended on her to make sure that I went to Church on Sundays; I actually chose to go to Church on my own and I was now somewhat dependent on going to Sunday Church services on a regular basis. I kept my promise to God that I would no longer wildly chase women and I did not have any other lady friends up until the time that I met an "Afropean"; a beautiful European woman of African descent.

THE AFROPEAN

Some time had passed and I was still honoring my promise to God by no longer being out on the streets of San Francisco trolling for beautiful women. I guess that I was happy with the casual relationship that I had with Ms. Lovely and Ms. Lovely and I had still remained good friends but our friendly relationship could not advance because of the twisted thoughts that I had about her since Thanksgiving dinner, our casual relationship was getting old and I was also getting bored. I would soon enough figure out that I now needed a full time woman that would actually help to make my life feel complete. That wish would soon be realized during the Spring Break of 1998; this would be when my elementary school aged daughter would spend her spring break from school in Tulsa, out in California. She would be visiting with her maternal grandparents and to also for the very first time, actually get to spend some time alone with her real father.

My sister and her new husband would also come out to visit me in San Francisco during the same time of this spring break vacation; this was a complete coincidence and it was never actually planned like this. This get together was like a great big unofficial family reunion that was not actually planned but somehow actually came together as such.

On the evening of April25[th], 1998; I think it was a Saturday night, there was a small get together of a sort of welcoming party thrown to get all of the unfamiliar faces familiarized with one another as we were all relatively, a family. This get together for adults was thrown together at a close relative's house and was quite an informal gathering with the only intention as to get everyone to get to better know each other. My sister and her husband were there, I was there, and she was there...the Afropean. She was the sister of my daughter's aunt's overseas correspondent or just simply her old school Pen pal.

She was a very sexy, slim, beautiful woman with the most intensely shocking eyes of sparkling green that I had ever seen in a woman of pure African descent; she was a Western European born woman of West African parentage, the image of her in my eyes at that time was extremely unique and purely exotic.

She had a bald head with the likes of that of Kojak and I instantly fell in love with the cool and confident smile that this woman had shown me for the very first time when she was finally introduced to me; if there was such a thing as love at first sight, this was it. I had not believed in love at first sight before this chance meeting although I had believed in MAKING love at first sight. It wasn't like a shock of beauty type of instant love like it was for Ms. Lovely this was completely different; it was like a kool and confident feeling of love somehow knowing that this was going to be the future woman for me with absolutely no shock value attached to the very first meeting.

Even though we were partying at a relative's house in Richmond, California a suburb city of Oakland. She was actually staying with my daughter at her grandmother's house not too far away in San Pablo, also a suburb city of Oakland and I knew of this fact even before I was introduced to her. Now that I had finally met this woman I had heard so much about, I was now extremely excited about the fact that I could very easily get to know her better by simply visiting my daughter at her grandmother's house at any time at all after that initial introduction and meeting.

I tried to spend as much time as possible with her at the party that evening as I could, but that proved to be extremely difficult because she spoke absolutely no English and I spoke absolutely no French as she was visiting from France; it was difficult trying the language barrier hand signs and game of charades form of communication at a party with a bunch of loud, wild and drunken revelers, so I made the decision that I would have to have that happen on a more personal basis sometime in the near future.

By the time that my sister and I left that party in the city of Richmond, I would tell her and her husband that the woman that we had all just met together, who did not speak any English at all, was soon going to be my wife; I told my sister and her husband she was going to be my wife after our very meeting with this Afropean exotic beauty. Of course they laughed at me and seriously doubted me because although I already had a child and you the reader all know who I am when it comes to women. No one in my family had known this about me or my habitual flirtaseousness and they had never actually seen any of my sexy antics when it came to women.

My sister and brother in law probably just could not see me with such a beautiful woman by my side. I had known this was real and I felt this feeling of instant love and connection deep down in my heart of hearts at that very first introduction to her.

When the partying was all over and it was now time for return to normalcy in the next week to come, I made sure to visit my daughter during the week that she was visiting her grandmother and during those visits I really got to know this European beauty better by asking her out on a date before she would be heading back to France; she had agreed and we went out on a date that same week. I took her out on a date to a movie and lunch on Fisherman's wharf where we shared a wonderful seafood dinner together, although the conversation was quite lacking due to the very obvious language barrier. At the end of the evening when I returned her to Grandma's house in San Pablo, we shared an enticing good night kiss that left my mind and the door wide open to future sexual engagement with this beautiful woman.

When the date was over, I was very happy as to how it had went and I truly looked forward to seeing her again, but I played the very childish waiting game with her and I did not call her or go to see her again for another week or so because my daughter had already left to go back to her home in Tulsa. I did not do so to just simply stay away from her, I just did not want to come across as a desperate individual looking for a woman to devour. After about a week had passed, I had finally got up the nerve and called her at my daughters Grandmother's house and she had asked me to come and pay her a visit; I thought it was going to be a friendly visit. When I arrived to see her, she asked me if I could take her somewhere so that we could speak, I took her to the shores of the San Francisco Bay at a lovely Bayside Park.

We went to a park bench to speak; I thought it was going to be a friendly I missed you conversation and maybe a makeout session continuing where we had left off a week earlier. Rather, she would end up chewing me out a new rear end because I had not gotten in touch with her for the one weeks time since we had last seen each other and she was demanding to know why.

Are you serious young lady!? Are you my spouse!?

She had led me right into an argument over this and I fought right back with her, I had not even known this woman for more than the accumulative time of 24hours, and here we were, already fighting. Who did she think she was I thought to myself. At that very first argument, I can clearly remember telling her that God had always come before every-body and anybody in my life and that I hadn't owed anybody anything, including her. I should have learned from this very first experience with her though, but I didn't; that love at first sight thing was blinding me in both my eyes.

I think that was now understood between God, me and her and I would now go back about the business of getting to know her better. I would think to myself that only after knowing her for only a couple of weeks that the argument was some sort of confirmation to me that she actually was going to be my future wife because she had cared enough about me not calling her for a week to actually raise an argument over it; I had thought about this early fighting as her pure passion for me and I took it in as such. I now continued to pursue her based on the passion that she had now stirred up in me and also the feeling that she also had this same passion for me. So much so, that in just a matter of the next few days I would finally break the promise I had made to God and I would eventually end up making deep and passionate love with her in my tiny apartment in the back of that garage when she came to pay me a visit on her own. Three weeks after that we would be living together in the tiny apartment that was meant for one; the passion between us was that intense. I also especially thought it as passion that she had for me when later on in the relationship when Ms. Lovely would still frequently be calling me at my home and she would always have to speak her mind to Ms. Lovely whenever she answered the phone. Ms. Lovely would never pay her any mind at her telephone rants though and Ms. Lovely never once ever gave me any type of 'Blackittude' about it, or even when I turned all of my attention to this new woman and suddenly stopped doing all I had been previously doing for her and her two daughters. Ms. Lovely had always had a very strong passion for Christ and that is where she would always proudly showed her passion and now this is where she actually proved it to me by not hassling me over the decisions I had made about who I would now be spending all of my time with even though we already had a very good thing going on between us. Looking back at this so many years later, I can say that not only did Ms. Lovely always show her beauty on the outside, but this was also her way of showing me her beauty on the inside as well; a truly humble spirit if you ask me.

I was now fully aware that the promise I had made to God was now broken; yes I am a full fledged sinner. However, I also now knew the power that God had offered to me in the power of repentance and forgiveness and I moved on with my life with no guilt involved. I also continued on my mission of getting to know this woman better, whom I now had deep passionate feelings and continued to grow love for.

I had so much passion for her that I now wanted her to stay here with me in my tiny apartment. So, me not knowing about the US Visa system and more specifically about her French tourist Visa, I would then convince her to try and find a job in the American modeling industry because she had earlier told me that right along with her European Bachelors of Arts degree from a European Ivy league school, she just like Ms. Lovely, also had done professional modeling on the European fashion runway circuits and she also had the photos to prove it; what a dream come true for me I would think of her resume. I would then research the modeling industry in the San Francisco area all without the help of Ms. Lovely and I arranged a couple of model photo shoots and casting appointments for her that I would more than gladly take her to; I was so looking forward to having her becoming a professional model once again and strutting her sexy stuff down the American runway circuit for all to awe at my very beautiful girlfriend.

One of those modeling agencies had appreciated her look and wanted her to represent their agency and that they would keep her loaded with all kinds of paying modeling work, but they needed all of fifteen hundred dollars to make all of the tourists Visa change over arrangements and processing fees to make this dream come true, she did not have the money to give to them, so I gladly fronted the cash. I didn't mind doing that as I was so looking forward to having a sexy, beautiful working French figure model as a live in girlfriend; nothing then could have possibly made me happier than the bright visions that I had for me and her and our future together.

The only problem with that story from the agency was that US tourist visas can never be changed once they are issued and used by an individual; I of course did not know this, the agency blatantly lied and I was now going to be out fifteen hundred bucks.

I don't think so!

By this time I had already started training in the union and I now knew about laws and where to find them and how to go about taking action to resolve issues such as this. I would spend many hours in the San Francisco public law Library trying to figure out what actions to take next against this modeling agency and how I would go about of getting back my hard earned fifteen hundred dollars.

It had taken nearly the entire ninety day period of her tourist visa before I had found out about the misinformation given to us by the modeling agency and their "visa change over" scam. So by the time it was time for her to head back home to France, I was still fighting in the legal system to try and attempt to get the cash back from the agency. Her tourist visa had now been expired and she was still here in the USA helping me to get the funds back. Once I had finally figured out exactly how to get the cash back, I did just that and managed to get every cent back from the agency outside of a San Francisco court-room. I was very happy with myself in what I had accomplished and it would be my very first successful legal fight outside of the labor union and the first of many more legal fights to soon come for me. We were happy to have gotten all of the cash back in full but it was now time to figure out what was going to be next for me and my very own Ms. Afropean.

We had decided to visit the US immigration office in San Francisco to find out what rights that she might have had for being an overstayed foreign Visa holder who was a victim of financial fraud and what her status of being allowed to re-enter the United States would be once she finally had left the country. The immigration officer told her that she had no rights at all when it came to overstaying a tourist visa and that there was nothing that could be done for her at that time except to actually leave the country and hopefully let time dissipate the fact that she overstayed her tourist visa by some months. Then maybe one day once again be allowed to re-enter the United States some years or decades later. This was totally unacceptable for us to imagine as a young couple, but there was nothing else that could be done. So that's exactly what we had decided to do and I prayed to God for the best outcome for us. I would use my excellent flight benefits with United Airlines to finally fly us both back to her hometown city of...

...PARIS. FRANCE

I had taken my very first two week vacation with United Airlines to go over to Paris with her and before we made that jump over the pond to Paris, we made an overnight stop in Atlanta to reintroduce her to my sister and my sister's immediate family; it was a type of presentation to my family to let them all meet this woman and to also know of my good intentions with her. It was also to show my sister and her husband that I knew exactly what I was talking about so many months earlier after we had all first met at the party in Richmond. We spent a few days in Atlanta to see all of the sights around town before we boarded the transatlantic flight. We sat in our first class seats bound for Paris, in which we boarded in Washington DC; she had arrived in San Francisco flying on a coach class seat but was now returning to her hometown on an International first class flight with top notch first class service. Not too bad for her I would think to myself; she MUST now see me as THEE... Mr. Right.

When we were sitting in our first class seats sipping on the Mimosas and enjoying our Filet Mignon somewhere halfway across the Atlantic Ocean, I was curious to see what sort of documentation the US immigration authorities would have placed on her French passport to keep her from having the ability of coming back into the USA due to her unintentional overstayed tourists Visa. I had asked to see her passport to find out what they did and she handed it over to me. When she had given her passport to me I was very surprised, shocked and also very happy to see that they had not removed the exit portion of her tourists' visa documentation and the exit card was still attached to her passport!

I removed that exit document out of her passport and quickly discarded it by flushing it into the first class toilet. This mistake by the wonderful gate agent simply translated to the fact that the United States immigration service now would never have an actual exit date out of the country for her; in other simple words she now would officially never have overstayed her tourist visa!

Sorry USofA but a future husband has got to do what a future husband has got to do with this future bride of mine with absolutely no regrets, in which I now would have absolutely none. I now happily knew that the plans that I had had for with this woman would now go unimpeded by the United States immigration service and their limitations on some stupid overstayed tourist visa rules. I most definitely took this grand coincidence as an answered prayer and a definite sign from God that he was Ok with my intentions with this woman and we could now continue to go on about the business of planning how and when we would be having her to come back to the United States so that we could quickly resume our life and our future life together.

Although I had absolutely no reservations about taking her home to Paris to meet her family, she did have a little bit of reservation because her family was somewhat large and they had only lived in a very humble three bedroom apartment in a suburban town of Paris. She had been quite concerned as to where I might be able to stay for the week or so that I was going to be staying there, as I was not rich enough to stay in a Parisian hotel for more than a night or two. When we arrived to her family after the taxi ride from the airport, that would all change and her reservation would be gone when she found out that her family was in the process of moving from one three bedroom apartment into another three bedroom apartment only about half a mile away and they had not yet moved everything into the new apartment.

Her family had warmly invited us to stay in the not as yet occupied apartment while I was there and we were extremely happy to have a place to stay for free in Paris, while still having our very own privacy amongst ourselves; I was also glad that we were happily able to "christen" the apartment with true love for the family before they officially were able to move in.

Sorry Mami and Pappi; we christened that new apartment based on our true love that we shared for each other at that time and I saw this invitation into your personal space as a confirmation of your families blessing to receive your daughter in a potential for future matrimony between us. This very odd coincidence, happening so far from home and with no prior knowledge of the move happening at the exact same time that we were visiting made me believe that I must be with the right woman and in the right place.

Because I truly had love for her and I would now have love for her generous, inviting and warm family, is why I would see this as another coincidence and probably some sort of positive sign from God that all would be OK between us because although I was taking a trip a quarter way around the world to a place that I had never been before, we had never actually spoken on the subject of where we would be actually staying and I had never made any type of plans as to where I would actually be staying when I got to Paris; what if they weren't so inviting? I had never actually thought about that because I simply just assumed that all would be alright between us and her family and obviously all was now good all the way over in Paris, France.

Now that we were settled in with a warm roof over our heads in the French fall season, it would now be time for us to see the sights of France that I had heard and seen so much about throughout my life. We visited the Louvre museum, sat streetside at many French Café's sipping lovely espresso, had lunch on the famous rue de Champs Elysees, and of course toured the world famous Eiffel Tower where I came to find out that the tower is not just some rusty old landmark of a monument but rather an entire large entertainment complex where we would see a movie, had a nice lunch on the main level and rode the elevator to the top of the tower to take in such wonderful views of the beautiful city below. I also rode the Chunnel train over to England to visit my physician cousin who was practicing in London. Most of these things I had only been dreaming of ever doing in my life and they were only made to be possible just months earlier by meeting this beautiful woman and I was quite surprised to actually see myself here in France as if it were as if I were in some sort of a wonderful and vivid dream.

The best thing that we had done while we were there however was a river boat cruise around the city of Paris, it was not necessarily the cruise that was so memorable, but rather what happened right after the cruise. After all the other passengers had left the river boat, for some odd and unexplained reason, something hit us both and we both had to excuse ourselves to the ships head (bathroom)before we actually left the boat right along with everyone else; it was in no way planned by either one of us. We were there together enjoying each other's company in that head of the ship for about twenty minutes, happily answering natures call between us. When we finally left that ship's head, the Captain of the ship was standing right there in front of us as we exited the head and watched us as we guiltily made our way out of the head; he was extremely surprised that we were only now getting off of the boat but he was also very pleasantly pleased at what he must have thought was going on for all those minutes of us being alone as he beamed us the biggest, widest grin of enthusiastic acknowledgement that I had ever seen from anybody else before him. He spoke only in French and I couldn't understand him but it was as if he was congratulating us on a beautiful job well done.

I now knew exactly why Paris is called the city of Love. The Captain had seemed very pleased and happy to have been part of this blossoming of Love that he had just partially witnessed; Love was truly in the air and we both simultaneously got bit by that lovebug right there and then on that riverboat cruise. This slight detour of our plans had not at all been planned by myself or by her but it made a definite difference in our relationship; on my part any way.

I had always loved this woman ever since I had first seen her at that party. However I had always thought of her as somewhat routine and a little bit boring when it came to our private time together and this had made me extremely hesitant about taking our relationship to the next level, but this boat cruise would change all of that for me and I finally saw a side of her that was anxious and exciting and passionate and that did not fall into some type of normal and boring routine. With the experience of this river boat cruise being in more ways than one, one heck of a very romantic boat ride, I was now convinced that this Afropean was actually going to be my wife for now and forever more and I wanted her to be mine more than ever after this very beautiful day.

Although I was in no way shape or form actually ready to get married right away I did however let her know of my future intentions of marrying her and she would respond by telling me to honor her West African tradition of honoring her father by asking him for her hand in marriage in the traditional West African way and that was exactly what I did before I would leave France alone to head back to San Francisco.

Her father would then acknowledge and accept my rather informal request for her hand in marriage in the typical West African tradition; he would give me his blessing for his daughter's hand in marriage. Her father also thanked me for taking care of his daughter during her lengthy extended stay in San Francisco; he would also continue to thank me for bringing his daughter back home to Paris safely. We would then go ahead and plan for her eventual return to the United States and the eventual typical American proposal and eventual wedding. We had informally planned together that she would go back to work in Paris, save all of her income so that she could then have the tuition and fees for a technical education and degree from a technical college in San Francisco. I promised her that I would sponsor her for the education visa back over to the United States and that she would reside with me for the length of the technical training that she would receive; it was another fine plan for the ages even despite the fact that she had previously overstayed her visa and technically should not have been able to revisit the USA.

It was a very sad day in Paris when it was time for me to leave her behind because although we had made all of these wonderful plans there was no way of actually knowing if these plans would really come to fruition. We had already spent close to a year together and had shared all sorts of emotions, adventures and excitement between us and it was now difficult for me to envision any sort of life back in San Francisco without her; I had never in my life missed anyone else before like I was certainly going to be missing this wonderful woman who had been such a part of my life for such a little amount of time.

An afternoon in Paris.

A Parisian subway ride

GOING BACK TO CALI

But that is exactly what I did for a year and half, I missed her dearly. We had our weekly overseas phone conversations, and we shared our love in more ways than one over the long distance international phone lines. We kept our master plans alive and well and she did manage to save up all of the necessary funds to pay for her technical education with her now decided upon career as a dental hygienist. She applied at the technical school and also for an educational visa from the US immigration service where her overstayed tourist visa had absolutely no affect on the application process and she would soon achieve a positive result on both of her application processes as well as a US temporary work permit.

That year and a half seemed like forever to finally come, but the day did finally arrive and it was a happy day once again for me in San Francisco. She would eventually finish up her degree in dentistry and go on to a successful internship and eventual career all within the eighteen month time span of the visa.

When her visa was soon about to expire, it would have to be decision time for me. This woman had fulfilled all the plans that we had made together, she had accomplished her dental degree and had an excellent paying position in a very nice dental office right along with her European Bachelor's degree. How could I not decide to marry this woman that had spent the last few years with me and had more than accomplished all that we together had set out to do as a non married but committed couple.

Since the time that I had become a committed Christian, I had since found out about being equally yoked and its importance in a Christian marriage when it came to potentially having a long and loving marriage. Because of this knowledge that I now had, I had also informed her that I could not marry a woman that had not been fully committed to the Lord in her life and that she should do just that if we were to move forward to the next phase in our relationship. Don't judge me; I was a brand new Christian who absolutely knew it all.

This was also based on the fact of what Ms. Lovely had shown me in the life of a committed Christian woman and she had set such a high and wonderful standard for me to set of what a beautiful Christian woman would look like in a Christian marriage. Ms. Lovely had portrayed herself to me as a wonderful example of a Proverbs 31 type of woman and I didn't want anything less than what she had shown me for a future marriage. My soon to be fiancé would agree with me by honoring my request for honoring the Lord and she would do just that when we both were publicly baptized together at our local Oceanside church that she herself had gone out and found for us because I had long ago since left the Church of Ms. Lovely for more than obvious reasons. With both of our baptisms now accomplished, I thought all of my I's were dotted and all of my T's properly crossed when it came to our future together. I then decided that it was now time for us to move on to the next level in our already long relationship.

I had honestly thought that making this request of her would actually mean something better for the both of us and I had made this request with the honest intention of potentially having a better life for me and my future wife and our hopefully long and beautiful marriage together; however, I would soon enough learn the actual truth of doing such a supposedly noble thing and I would be learning that very expensive lesson the hard way.

I had already lived a very long, memorable bachelor life and there would be no way that I couldn't decide NOT to marry this beautiful woman who had set her sights so high and reached every goal; I surprised her by proposing to her at our Church services in front of our entire Church congregation with a one carat diamond marquise cut engagement ring, she undoubtedly said yes right there and then.

We were happily married on August 25th, 2001 in a Las Vegas wedding chapel with the presence of all of my immediate family; especially my sister and brother in law who had so doubted me so many years earlier. Her brother was also there, who was at the time a very popular French rap artist and music producer to represent her side of the family, right along with his then French trophy type of girlfriend; her parents were not present at our Las Vegas wedding.

We had still been married that hot summer day in Vegas despite the fact she had bought up to me some serious reservations, doubts and fears that she had about us tying the knot that same day, as well as despite the fact that it had been clearly revealed to me that she should not be my wife. I have never given into fear during the course of my life and I ignored all those feelings and I brushed them all aside, both hers and mine. I didn't care though; I was blinded by love or maybe by lust, thinking about it now after more than a decade later, I really don't know which. I truly didn't want to see the truth of our argumentative ways of arguing and fighting somewhat like that of a pair of professional gamecocks to stop us from walking down the aisle that day. Soon to be newlyweds please pay close attention. This would be quite OK with me though…this is where I would eventually learn that God is truly bigger than any of the mistakes that we could ever make in our lives.

My marriage day was a day that I will never forget not only due to the fact that it was the day that I had first been married, but also because it was the day that one of my then favorite singers had been tragically killed in an awful plane crash; Ms. Aaliyah Haughton, the beautiful singer and actress had been killed in a plane crash in the Bahamas. I had been getting ready to be married in our Mandalay

Bay hotel suite when the news had come over the television news station that Aaliyah had been tragically killed in the Islands of the Bahamas earlier in the day.

This news had now severely affected me because I had known of these types of South Florida air charter operations. I had quite a lot of familiarality with them for the type of aircraft they operated and for the types of operations that had been responsible for killing her because that was the type of aircraft and operation that I had worked with so much in my already long South Florida aviation career. This had especially hurt when I would months later find out the exact cause of the crash and the fact that it was solely due to pilot and operational errors. Life must go on however and I was just shortly after the tragic news broke more than happily united with my new wife just only few hours after being notified of this horrible tragedy. I would also feel a whole lot better some many months later because I was happy to know that several laws that had surrounded the events leading up to the plane crash were changed to better prevent what had happened in the events leading up to that horrific plane crash that tragic day.

It had now been several years since I had made that solemn promise to God that I would no longer use women in an over aggressively sexual way as I had been doing so much earlier in my younger days. Although I had made this certain promise to God and I did break that promise with this woman, I could now "officially" say that I actually DID break the promise with my now WIFE and I would now feel somewhat vindicated and victorious towards God and that broken promise to him. I had remained faithful to her since the day I had met her and we would go on with our married life together and I actually would enjoy being committed and faithful to only one woman for that entire amount of time. We would go on to have three beautiful children together, and we remained in marital bliss for the next eleven years until our eventual separation, very bitter divorce and very ugly child custody sharing battle within the Miami Dade county court system; but that will be another long chapter of discussion in this book; but again I must say that I will always proudly live my life without any sort of regrets; rather I will always see life as an open book where there is always a lesson to learn.

I would also like to make the fact; if you haven't already noticed, that me and my now wife's meeting and eventual marriage was solely due to my wonderful, at this time, pre-teen daughter whom without her I would have never met my new wife as well as also to the fact that I was specifically spoken to by God to remain in bed the day that me and my daughter's mother were scheduled to have that very specific procedure done on that morning in Tulsa, Oklahoma almost one decade earlier. This very unusual circumstance was now a confirmation from God for me and I could only see it as a reward of a true blessing from God himself for my listening back in 1987. My eldest daughter, whom without me listening to God that early morning, and who should not have technically been here, had now blessed me with my new wife; God and my daughter had now somehow paid it forward directly back to me.

My Baptism

THE PATENTS

Not only was this marriage a blessing but there would also be more blessings to come when it came to my pre-teen aged daughter as you will soon enough find out about.

While I had been employed by the cargo airline in Miami, I had always enjoyed what I called ..."skating" throughout the cargo cabin of the all cargo aircraft, which was consisted of me running through the empty cargo cabin and then sliding or skating on the roller ball floor track system to an eventual stop. This had given me an idea to literally re-invent the wheel by thinking about replacing the flat disc like wheels on an inline skate with a golf ball sized round wheel acting as an omnidirectional roller ball type of wheel with ball bearings supporting the main golf ball sized roller "wheel" so as to allow a skater a more universal directional control of the skate boot and therefore more precisely controlled roller skating; it was just an idea that I had and I held that idea in for years until this particular time of my life.

I held this idea in until I had a few extra bucks sitting in the bank while living in California, where I then went to one of those patent help agencies that you so prominently see advertised on television and radio and such. The agency had loved the idea and also wanted and agreed to pursue the patent process to bring this idea to life. They wanted cold hard cash though to, no… pun intended … get the ball rolling; I named them Rollersoles. I put up the majority of the cash they asked for from some money that I had already saved up, I also borrowed some cash from my younger brother, and I would also borrow some cash from my parents; they had all loved the concept I sold them on and were more than willing to put up some investment cash to help and get this idea off the ground. The total that I had handed over to the patent agency was well over twelve thousand dollars in an attempt to secure and get a patent pending on the idea while doing a patent search and to also market the idea to potential manufacturers during the time while the patent was pending in the US patent office. I was very excited about this process and was definitely looking forward to a better life that this patent would bring for me and my family. The entire patent process would end up taking well over a year to be concluded.

This bright idea would become dim and soon fall flat on its face and become a complete dud because the idea had already been thought of on multiple occasions with multiple similar patents already issued therefore I could not secure a patent for my idea. I would later find out that a simple quick and easy patent search prior to all of the marketing and all of the other hoopla that was accomplished was not at all necessary because a quick and simple patent search all by itself would have eliminated all of the other cost that were involved totaling up the more than twelve thousand dollars. I did not like hearing that and I felt that I needed to do something to try and attempt to get some of the hard earned funds back from the agency for my myself and much more importantly for my family. My father had liked the idea so much so that he had once said to me that if the idea did not work for a shoe that they could also be used on the bottom of luggage such as the popular spinning wheel suitcases that are so very popular today. While the idea was not exactly the same, the concept was the same along the lines of precise maneuverability that my father had originally thought of for suitcases. I didn't agree with him on that and I tossed out the idea but somebody did see the same vision that he originally had and that person is very rich for it today. I didn't want to and I certainly wasn't looking forward to letting my father down by telling him about this busted up deal, and I wanted to do my best to attempt to get some of the cash back from this patent development agency who had sold us on a dream and a dance.

I would eventually decide that I would put my limited legal training into effect and I took the patent agency to small claims court in their small hometown city, this would be my second attempt to retrieve a wrong being done to me in a completely legal manner. I of course represented myself in the municipal court, I filed all of the necessary paperwork and I presented a good case in front of the judge with all of my proper documentation and proof for the case; I won the case easily. The judge however did not award me any money and I did not retrieve any funds from the lawsuit because as the judge had simply said, I simply forgot to enter a specific dollar amount for recovery on the proper court documentation. So although I was congratulated by the judge for winning a somewhat complicated case, I would not be retrieving any funds due to the simple paperwork mistake and I haven't received any funds at all since, even thought the judge did award me court cost recovery.

During the course of the year or so that I was patiently waiting for my patent application to come through, I was very excited about this potential patent and I found it necessary to tell my young daughter Raynece and her family of that fact; I had wanted my daughter to be proud of me and to also look forward to a potentially much better life for her ahead. When I did have that conversation with her, it was much to my surprise that Raynece too also had a patent pending application with the US patent office. I could not believe this, what Raynece was telling me, and I was completely surprised by this fact; we both had patent applications pending at the exact same time without even knowing this weird fact between us. It was only because I had decided to fill Raynece in on what was going on with my life that we would actually find out what each other were doing. I was certainly glad that I did decide to let her in on it, I may have never known of this unusual coincidence otherwise.

Unlike my failed patent application, my daughter's patent application was successfully approved by the US governments patent office; I was extremely happy for her and I again would feel extremely blessed by God to have this lovely young lady as part of my life and I was of course more than happy that I had made the right decision about her now more than a decade ago; I took this as another confirmation directly from God himself.

My daughter's patent application was for a table game that Raynece had thought up for her middle school project for their annual math and science exposition. As Raynece once told me, her idea for the game was originally based on the popular table game of UNO but upgraded to a much deeper level as to actually teach participants all aspect of multiplication, addition, subtraction and division; it is a game that actually teaches the player math without the player even knowing it. I had obviously already known how difficult it was to secure a patent, but she had secured a patent with something that had long been already established in that of numbers and math; her newly patented boardgame would be named" Math-a-mania" and was sold and marketed on her very own website setup by her mother named Mathworkz.com.

Soon after her US patent approval, Raynece would then start her very own successful online business selling this game that she had patented via her very own website. This was accomplished only after all of her school faculty and her very own teachers had enthusiastically encouraged her and her mother to do so due to their love of this project. This game has been sold all over the world and has been translated into several different languages.

Not only was this game a success for Raynece at her middle school math and science exposition, it was also a success for her in her already very short and young life. Raynece and Math-a-mania has been featured in many local and national publications and television news programs such as being featured on CNN's news Lou Dobbs tonight program, Tulsa's Fox 23 news, Ebony Magazine, The Tulsa World newspaper amongst various other news publications. Raynece has also been nominated for the Black Entrepreneur's magazine "Entrepreneur of the year" award and Raynece has also been the recipient of the National Alliance of Black School Educators "NABSE" excellence award in Washington DC and Raynece has received countless college academic scholarships, including Ivy league, based solely on her early achievements in school as well as in her young life; I could not be a prouder father of such a beautiful young woman.

Raynece has been featured and has proudly been an invited key note speaker at countless education conferences and gaming conventions throughout the country since her middle school science and math fair exposition just a few short years earlier. I was more than thrilled when Raynece and her mother had informed me that the retail giant Wal Mart had wanted to license, market and sell her game on their store shelves, but for whatever reason the deal did not fall through; I had never asked them the reason why the deal fell through but it did not matter to me because I was still very proud of them.

Raynece has also been the featured and invited guests of many important dignitaries' including that of her very own state Governor of Oklahoma. This was all accomplished by this very young lady that technically should not have been here; if these accomplishments were not a true blessing from God, I have no idea what a true blessing would be then. I could not have been a prouder or happier father to this very wonderful and beautiful young lady who God had now more than obviously blessed me with by simply following those three little words that I kept hearing and repeating in my head that early morning back in my days of Tulsa.

Math-a-mania was a commercial success for the short time that it had been popular and Raynece was soon able to purchase her very own home and her very own brand new vehicle right after her high school graduation and all before she could legally buy an alcoholic beverage. This game was not only a commercial success for Raynece, it was also an educational success for her in the fact that because of Math-a-mania's commercial success, the game also bought her numerous Ivy league full academic scholarships to many and various Ivy League schools throughout the country; Raynece would have the pick of the litter of where she could attend college and all for free. This is when I as her father had become very emotional because ever since the day I had found out she was actually going to be with us on this Earth so many years ago, I had always worried about how I would actually pay for her to go to college; I couldn't even pay for myself to go to college. This had always been my one and only concern as to having this child and now I would no longer have to worry about affording a quality university education for her; another blessing from God that truly did not have to be. Thank you Lord.

I can still clearly remember the exact day that I found out that Raynece had received her very first full academic scholarship offer from an Ivy League school. I was deadheading an empty stretch limousine back to the base one early evening when she had called me on my cell phone while I was driving, to announce to me that she had just received a full scholarship after receiving her NABSE award in Washington DC. I had to pull over that limousine onto the shoulder lane on I-95 northbound to let out all of the pure joy and emotions that had just instantly rushed into me; I was jumping around and screaming right on that emergency shoulder of I-95 like a true mad man. I truly couldn't contain myself because I was just so happy not only for Raynece but also for my final relief in no longer having to worry about somehow paying the very high cost for her higher education; I could not have done much better than this for her no matter how hard I could've tried to save up the large amounts of cash required for a college education completely on my own and without the recognition and acknowledgement of God.

All of these positive emotions and good vibes would be short lived however because after all of the scholarships offers had come through, Raynece would inform me that she would not be accepting any of them and that she would also be taking a break from school. I could not believe what Raynece was telling me; how can it possibly be for anybody to actually turn down full academic scholarships to their choice of Ivy league American universities!? I was devastated and I just had to ask her why, Raynece simply told me that she did not want to leave her family and more importantly she did not want to leave the steady high school sweetheart of a boyfriend that she had for well over a year now. I refused to accept this nonsensical response from her, but there was absolutely nothing that I could do about her decisions, for I had never been an "active in her life events type of father" and I had never been in any parts of her decision making before. I however, still needed to do and to say something to now show my disapproval of her decision making, so I did what I do best; I pulled out my pen and note pad and I started pouring out my heart to her on paper so that I could of course show my complete dismay and disappointment in her decision making in regards to her not going to college and turning down full university scholarships, and I did the smart thing by leaving the rest of the worries to God.

My entire family had attended her high school graduation in Tulsa, and a very big party was thrown for her at her childhood house to celebrate the occasion, but we could not celebrate what was next for her because nobody had known what that was actually going to be; it was out of anybody's control.

I was very glad that I had written her that very long and emotional letter to Raynece while she was still in high school because it had seemed to me as though she had listened intently to what I was writing and Raynece paid attention to my tough but heartfelt words. After Raynece had taken her year off from school to do what she wanted and needed to do, she did manage to secure a full college scholarship to locally attend Oklahoma State University where she did eventually graduate as an OSU cowgirl with a Bachelor of art in business management degree with a minor in marketing. I was of course once again very proud of this very major accomplishment for her in her life and my entire family once again was more than happy to again make the trek all the way to Tulsa so as to be certain to attend her college graduation and to watch her make the walk up to the podium to receive her university degree and to also be there for her to help her celebrate this very special milestone in her young life and career.

Not long after her college graduation everyone in my family had to once again make the long trek out to Tulsa for her wedding to her same high school sweetheart that she so did not want to leave behind for college so many years earlier. I walked her down the aisle of her very own Christian Church in front of her Church family and right along with her stepfather; we both were holding on tightly to her as we both walked her down the aisle to give her away. Her stepfather was who she had known as an actual father figure all of her life since she was about one year old; I was surely proud to have been able to share the aisle with the man that had done such a wonderful job so extremely well, the job that I was actually supposed to have done for Raynece as a present father.

Shortly after her wedding, she would soon be giving birth to her very first daughter Moriya and my very first granddaughter. Prior to her getting married, Raynece would also purchase her first home, all on her own without the help of anyone else. As well as eventually becoming a successful realtor in her Tulsa community and would also start an over the road trucking company that she helped to start with her new husband, right along with the purchasing of the brand new Volvo big rig that goes with it, all of this done before her twenty fifth birthday. At that age I could never have imagined accomplishing anything like this, my concentration and focus was squarely focused on you know what! Young men and women please learn from this.

Good job baby girl, keep up the focus on doing nothing but the best, I couldn't be a prouder dad.

The blessings from God would now continue on and Godwilling the blessings will continue to continue on...unimpeded; thank you Lord for the wonderful blessings both past, present and future.

My Brilliant Daughter...

...the inventress.

COUSIN ROM

Just shortly before I had been married, we were finally able to move out of the small backyard garage apartment that I had been living in for a couple of years already in Daly City and were able to move to the more upscale suburban city of Pacifica, California just a few short miles away. This new apartment would now be a regular one bedroom apartment with wonderful views of the Pacific Ocean, the fishing pier there and of course the California beach with all of the beautiful nightly sunsets that that view had provided to us right along with the nightly fog that always rolled in right around sunset.

With this move I would now have lived in different apartments on both American coasts having stunning views of both the Atlantic and Pacific coasts within my lifetime; I have always thought of this as special to me. I also now with the new Pacifica apartment and the accommodations that it had provided, I was now able to proudly invite friends, family and guests over to visit us unlike the garage apartment.

Not only did I invite over friends and co-workers, I also invited over immediate family like siblings and my parents. I was now also able to invite and reconnect with my long lost cousin Romany Malco. Although I had followed Romany on television through his various appearances, I had not seen cousin Rom or even spoken to him since I had last seen him for an aviation training session that I had attended while Rom was in Texas. Rom had still been living there and I was sent there to work and train for about a week; that last time I had seen him was approximately in the year 1989 about ten years earlier from my Pacifica move-in date.

Romany had already been featured on many television programs including some MTV commercials and the character Bulldog on the nationally syndicated CBS series Touched by an Angel, and the character Jerry Hooten on the cable series Level 9 which was one of the only TV police series that I ever followed after the fall of Miami Vice. Rom had already had a few movie credits to his name and was now an up and coming screen actor in Hollywood. Rom also had his Washington DC based rap group The College Boyz but had not been part of that group for a while and was now seriously pursuing his acting career.

Romany would now start to take weekend trips up to San Francisco to visit me and my new wife so that we could reconnect from all of the time that we had let slide on by without us communicating and I had felt very privileged to have someone whom I had seen frequently on television staying with me in our new apartment home. We would have all night long conversations to catch up on the life events that we had missed together and speak of life in general and we would also talk philosophy, religion and such. I learned a great deal from and about him from all of those long late night conversations we had while he visited the San Francisco Bay area all the way up from Southern California.

At this point when cousin Rom would visit, he was already quite wealthy; as wealthy as anyone I had previously known and he did not mind showing it. He would wine and dine me and my wife at fancy restaurants with expensive bottles of wines and gourmet meals. Rom also enjoyed antique shopping which me and my wife had also always enjoyed, Rom would spend a lot of money on us and I didn't mind that at all except for the fact that I had never seen my wife in such a happy state before; this made me realize my inadequacies as a husband in my ability to put a smile on my wife's face. I had never seen her happier with an over abundance of laughter than when we were with Rom and when he would come to visit us and we would show him around the town that we were living in.

I could in no way at all afford at what cousin Rom was doing for us, yes I could take my wife out for a fancy dinner with expensive wine maybe once a month if that much and even then I would closely watch the bill. With Rom it was different, he didn't watch the bill; he wanted to have a good time primarily. So did my wife, she would laugh at all of his quirky jokes, listen intently to what he was saying and open up with him like she had never opened up with me before. They frequently spoke of how Rom had previously lived in France for such a long time and how well he had known of the French culture and lifestyle but barely knew the language; he was proud to say that France was his favorite destination in the entire World. Rom knew exactly how to put a wide smile on my wife's face; I would look at my wife and watch her with that very happy look on her face, gazing right at him as if they were the ones who were actually in love; they both did not know of my inner feelings of our get togethers and the fact that this was not something nice for me to be witnessing.

I was never really jealous, only seriously concerned that my new wife was getting swept off her feet; although it seemed like I had done that at one point or another in our young relationship, I couldn't actually do that like Romany professionally could. All that it ever seemed that I could ever to do with her was to just constantly, consistently and continuously argue and fight with her ever since shortly after our very first date; I would now witness and know the powerful force that is celebrity and its effect on women.

I never mentioned these feelings I had to Romany or even to my wife, I just decided that I would have to increase the distance between the three of us without them even knowing it, or what I was thinking or feeling about what I had personally witnessed. So I decided to once again keep my distance from my cousin Rom as it had previously had been before moving in to this beautiful new apartment in Pacifica.

I'm sorry Rom; I had to do what I felt I had to do to try and attempt to protect my very young marriage. Now that I am finally divorced with no fault of your own; I prayerfully hope that I can once again make up all of the lost time and that I can return the favor by wining and dining you and your significant other.

When I had come to that hard drawn out conclusion, I would not see Romany again until I had moved back to South Florida where his mother still lives to this day and Rom would then also already be a huge movie star with the release of the hit movie "The Forty Year Old Virgin" and he would again pay me and my wife a visit at our Miami Beach apartment shortly after that movie release.

It would not be too long after these visits in San Francisco from Romany and also my marriage that the horrible events of September 11, 2001 would take place in New York City. I was at work on the overnight shift at the United Airlines maintenance base when the attacks had occurred; it would be an especially very sad day when my crew found out that the second airliner was actually one of our airplanes that had been hijacked and destroyed into the twin towers of the World Trade center. Before I left work that morning an entire team of federal officers and agents would be staged at my hangar while the agents and airline sorted out what to do next on that awful day.

It was very hard for me to leave the hangar that early morning after my shift with all of the activities that were frantically going on there, but my new wife was at home all alone and she had not known anything about what was happening three thousand miles away because she was still sound asleep. I decided that I could not let her sleep through all that was tragically going on after seeing the destruction of the Pentagon and I called home to wake her up while I was still at the hangar. I asked her to put the national news on the television set. Shortly after I hung up the phone with her, I would then decide to leave the hangar and finally head home a couple of hours after my regular scheduled departure time.

By the time I would make it up the mountain pass that I had to cross every day to make it home, the first tower had fallen into the ground and I heard the coverage of the tower falling over the radio. I had to pull my Jeep over as I balled out loud right there in public view; I was now way too emotional to drive and I stood by the side of the road crying for about twenty minutes while I allowed my nerves to somewhat calm. When I did finally make it home, my wife would be there crying and we both watched together as the second tower also fell to the ground; it would now be an entirely new day for me at United Airlines in San Francisco. I had visited those twin towers as a child on a few occasions both at school and at home, I even had lunch at Windows on the World during a school field trip as well as my mother who had once worked there; I can still remember the views vividly.

United had just hired a large amount of mechanics to work at the maintenance base and they were all going through indoctrination and training at the San Francisco and Oakland maintenance bases. They were all immediately laid off from duty due to the tragic events of September 11th. I was not part of that initial lay off because I had already been there for close to four years; my seniority had me safe, for now. I would be safe from lay off for about another year, but being part of the union leadership and having privy to company information that other mechanics did not, I knew that the second and third rounds of layoffs were fastly approaching and not too far away. I did not want to get stuck in California without my chosen fields of work because the aviation industry had not been as abundant in Northern California as it had been in South Florida and during the whole time that I was in San Francisco I had always been looking for Limo driving jobs in the newspaper classifieds, but I hardly ever even seen limousines driving through that city not to mention classified ads for chauffeurs for them.

Since I had first moved to San Francisco, it had only taken me about three months to know that I had actually wanted to move back to Miami as soon as I could because I had so missed the tropical lifestyle of South Florida and the beautiful warm blue green waters of the Atlantic Ocean that was so missing in California as well as the delicious Caribbean cuisine that was so few and far between on the west coast of America. So I had always looked for any potentially beneficial job openings in Miami that I could easily transfer to with United Airlines when and if I ever finally had enough of living in California.

Knowing that these layoffs were more than eventual and with me now intensely looking for any open positions in Miami that I could possibly do just to get me back there, I had found an open position for a start out customer service clerk in Miami and I went down there for the job interview and once again passed an interview with flying colors.

This position was different from that of a customer service representative in that a representative was paid a whole lot more than a clerk and also in the sense that I would be responsible for customer service interactions minus the computer reservation system knowledge and the ticket sales portion of the customer service transactions, but because I had already maxed out my payscale at my last position as an aircraft technician I would also remain maxed out at the much lower paying clerk position. Even with the maxed out pay offer for that position, the pay would still amount to be more than a fifty percent paycut from what I had been receiving as a technician. However, I knew that my career in aviation as an aircraft technician would not stop in Miami because of all of the technical job offers that would always be available to me back in South Florida; I thought that I had to and I could easily work two jobs as was going to be required to feed my growing family because my wife was now expecting our very first child together. I also knew that the limousine industry would also always be readily available to me in South Florida, unlike in San Francisco where I had never really even seen an advertising classified ads for chauffeurs in the newspapers and also not that many limousines for that matter driving around San Francisco and the Bay area as a whole.

Although I hadn't actually wanted to move out to San Francisco in the beginning, this big city stop would end up being a true blessing for me despite my very big mistake on the bus and the sinful ways that I had come over here with, with my eventual baptism, my brand new wife, and the first Godly blessing of our new marriage, my second child conceived and on the way into the world; our first son together. Thinking about this after all these years, from being lost and confused up in Flagstaff, to the plane crash, and to meeting Ms. Lovely which ultimately lead me to my faith, I can honestly say that God had indeed showed me the way in my life as well as career path simply because I had asked him for that guidance.

Most people would say that with all the sins I had committed up to this point in my life, especially with the very jailable teenaged fling that I was involved in, that I could not receive any blessings from God. Obviously though, those that would say that don't know any better because God himself saw things differently; a sincere prayer for forgiveness is always a very powerful thing in God's eyes.

However, it would now be time for us to go back to the very sexy city that I loved so much, but now as a happily married man. Going back to Miami with all of the beautiful bikini laden woman all around and the sexy nightlife on South Beach would be a real test to my marriage and to the person I had used to be before California. I knew it wouldn't be a challenge for me however; I had just seriously committed my life to a new Godly faith.

The drive back to Miami was quite different from my drive to San Francisco, in that this was now a job transfer as compared to a brand new job and I used my two weeks of vacation on my technicians pay to slowly drive back to Miami. My wife was now very much visibly pregnant and my Jeep was being towed by the big box truck that we had rented. We stopped every single night and slept in a comfortable hotel bed; we made it to Miami in about ten days mainly because I had wanted my new foreign wife to have the opportunity to see her new adopted country while she had the chance on this cross country trip.

Coincidentally, while we were driving through Los Angeles on the very first night of our cross country travels to Miami was actually the night for the Hollywood movie premiere for Le Chateau, which was an independent film that Rom had a starring role in; this film is actually one of my most favorite movies in which Rom had a starring role in. We missed its Hollywood premiere. Rom had invited us to the red carpet premiere showing of this film but all of our proper clothes were packed away in boxes inside of the box truck that we were driving in. We had a great big box truck and a trailer that my Jeep was being towed on; I could not imagine myself driving through the streets of Los Angeles with this box truck and trailer and attempting to park at a Hollywood movie red carpet premiere. Besides the fact, I was still actually working on the plans that I had made with myself earlier in the year in regards to keeping Rom and my so happy to be around him wife happily separated.

CHAPTER ELEVEN
Miami – The Final Return

When we finally made it to Miami after almost two straight weeks of driving, we had previously secured an apartment in Miami before we even left San Francisco so it was very easy for us to get started with our new life right away. We had moved into the new apartment almost one year to the date after the tragic events of September 11, 2001 and about four and a half years after I had left Miami for my San Francisco adventure.

The first thing that I had to do when I returned to Miami was to reinstate my Florida driver's license and also pay the additional fees to reinstate my Florida commercial driver's license and my county chauffeur registration. I needed to do this because I always knew the benefit and potential income for having a CDL with a passenger endorsement, my experience from the years past had already taught me that I could always make a quick buck for my family if need be as a professional chauffeur and luxury bus driver once again.

The second thing that I found it necessary to do was to secure an additional job in aviation to be able to supplement my now relatively low paycheck as a customer service clerk with United Airlines. I had absolutely no problem accomplishing that fete with the aircraft maintenance experience I had already. My shift at United was from four am to noon and I would get a part time job repairing those tow banner aircraft that you see towing advertising signs over the beach and public events. I would work there part time from one pm to six pm on the weekdays and then all day on Saturday's from 8am to 4pm; this new opportunity was exactly the reason why I had decided to move back to South Florida.

Although I had already had my private pilot's license, I had not forgotten about my dreams of becoming an airline pilot and I was still very much interested in completing my professional pilot training. So for that reason I worked for a whole lot less money as an aircraft repair technician than I normally would have because I had secured an agreement with the banner company that would allow me to get specific flight training in their type of aircraft that is called a taildragger and I would soon get a very valuable certification in a taildragger type aircraft. I was then also allowed to fly their aircraft at anytime that I had wanted to on my own free time as well as after maintenance flight checks, which I had always taken full advantage of. The lower pay from the aerial banner company really did not matter to me because the two incomes combined was sufficient enough for me and my wife to make a decent living in South Florida all the while I was still building very expensive flight time towards my commercial pilot's license certification as well as also working for a paycheck and gaining additional maintenance experience.

I was also able to make an additional income, when I think because of my large size, the Miami base station management at United Airlines had asked me if I were interested in becoming an airline ground security coordinator for the Miami Base station operations; I couldn't say no to them and I would soon also become a certified airline ground security coordinator. I had never been in the security industry, or any type of security business before and I also hadn't ever coordinated anything in my life. So for this reason I would once again feel that people would put a certain trust in me that I truly felt that I didn't deserve and that obviously they must have seen something in me other than my big size; I would once again feel blessed and honored to have been asked to go above and beyond by my bosses to go above and beyond my normal call of duty.

That job entailed all what is seems and sounds, I would now be responsible for coordination of security between flight crews and ground crews, Miami-Dade county airport management, plain clothed US federal air marshal's, and of course flying passengers at the boarding security gate. This new found responsibility did not pay all that much, but I certainly loved the newly found power that I had and all of the attention and adventure that it bought to me; I would have actually paid to do this wonderful job.

Another responsibility that I had as a security coordinator which also bought in a little bit of overtime cash and also some flying adventure for me was having the opportunity of being the charter flight ground security coordinator over on the ground in the city of Havana on the Island nation of Cuba.

My job for that sometimes weekly or twice weekly roundtrip Miami to Havana charter flights was to ascertain the smooth flow of the passengers to the boarding gate on the early morning charter flight going on to Havana, make sure that all of their visa documents for the trip over to Havana were proper and to also make sure that they had paid their cash only visa fees which were going directly to the Castro brothers so that the passengers could pay visit to the Island nation; there was always a lot of cold hard cash on board that flight. If you can imagine a Boeing 767 full of over two hundred passengers who were all paying hundred of dollars in cash each so as to satisfy the communist's countries tourist visa requirements. The very regular looking rolling suitcase which was used to carry all of the cash was always extremely heavy with nothing but American greenbacks in it and our aircraft was not given permission to leave the gate in Havana for the return trip to Miami until every penny was accounted for by the Cuban authorities and found to be exactly correct per the passenger head count for that particular day and flight.

In Havana, the other part of my new job was to actually fly to Havana and do the exact same thing for the Miami bound return flight except my job was even more critical because my responsibility was to ensure that United Airlines did not receive a large fine from the American government by having stowaways on board or having an improper head count or even having passengers with false or improper documentation. It was also my job to search each and every compartment of that 767 to make sure there were no stowaways on board. When I was completely satisfied that there weren't any, I would then give the OK to start boarding the passengers onto the Boeing jet and also coordinate with the heavily armed Cuban Para-military to guard each and every area that I had just searched and to keep the areas I just searched sterile from any potential stowaway rider.

I would next start the actual boarding of the aircraft; I would have to get and know my exact head count beforehand from the flight manifest and count each and every passenger coming on board the aircraft. As well as to also check each and every travel document and look at each and every face to make sure the face absolutely matched that travel document. This part was extremely time consuming yet critical because if there were any mistakes in the head count as compared to the passenger flight manifest or mistakes in passenger documentation, we could not close the door of the aircraft. This was the most time consuming part of the very long day whenever I accomplished this charter flight, I always took my sweet ole' time without regard to the scheduled flight departure time, potential delays, or pressure from rushing flight officers in the flight deck who always wanted to get home quickly to their families; I knew what the consequences could and would be if I screwed things up down there in Havana.

I was the only one authorized to say when that cabin door could finally be closed for final departure and that was only when the cash handed over to the Cuban authorities was all fully accounted for and only when I was completely satisfied that the head count and flight manifest all matched together perfectly. What an awesome responsibility I always thought to myself when we taxied away from the boarding gate; I still would never stop making sure that my headcounts and documents were all correct, the only time I would stop counting and checking was when I handed over all of the flight documents to the American customs and immigration service officer's in Miami.

In the dozen or so times that I had done this Havana charter flight, I am very proud to say that the airline never received any type of fine and I never received a single complaint from my airline superiors.

Another wonderful benefit that I received during this incredible experience at work was that once all of the seats were occupied in the cabin of the 767, I would then be allowed to fly right in the flight deck of the Boeing 767 or 757 taking us to Havana, this was such a thrill for me already being an amateur pilot and future airline pilot. It was exhilarating and pure motivation for me to decide to go out and finish up my professional pilot training, getting all of that positive experience from a high paying, high flying job to me was just purely unbelievable and must have been a true blessing from God. I also felt more than blessed than ever to be actually doing this job and riding way up front with the experienced pilots especially after September 11th, when this type of activity was frowned upon because of the events that had actually lead up to that tragedy; but then again I was a certified airline security coordinator I thought.

I had worked all three jobs simultaneously with absolutely no problems at all for about a year when I had received the news from management at United Airlines that they would be conceding to American Airlines and swapping gate positions with American Airlines between the Miami and Chicago airports; United said that they would give American airlines their gate space in Miami, if American Airlines would give United their gate space in Chicago. American Airline s would now once again get in the way of my professional career; I had the opportunity to transfer to Chicago to continue the work that I had been doing in Miami, but I had earlier promised myself that I would not ever leave Miami again.

Due to labor union rules, I still had the ability to transfer back to the maintenance base in San Francisco because I was in a transfer position that was less than a year old and which was also no longer required at the base that I was transferred to. So I was technically allowed to transfer back to my previous position in San Francisco. The only problem was that my previous position in San Francisco was no longer available, almost a year had already passed and the layoffs did eventually hit my seniority date and my old position out west was now gone. This was actually a good thing, with the union rules in place I then applied for a transfer back to my old position in San Francisco and I received a layoff notice from the maintenance base. My entire layoff package came with all of my old maintenance pay, vacation, benefits and severance package; it was a financial windfall for me and my family but it was of course not enough to retire with, so I would have to find another good paying job because my part time banner sign job could not cut the cake for me and my quickly growing family; it was now time to go back and drive professionally as a chauffeur. Even though I hadn't yet used my CDL since my return to Florida, I was certainly glad that I had thought and had acted proactively by reinstating my CDL and chauffeur registration almost one year earlier.

I would now once again go out and seek out another limousine company in an attempt to seek out another round in my chauffeuring career. This was primarily to help make ends meet for me and my growing family but to also seek out bold new adventures, where I had yet to venture in this field where no chauffeur had ever gone before, in which I have certainly done with the many more stories that I have to come. But this time with a brand new Christian outlook on my now very different life as compared to the very beginning of my chauffeuring career, where the dependence on Christianity in my life was actually nowhere yet to be found at that particular time in my life and career nearly a decade earlier; I would now be a completely changed man certified by God himself.

You the readers have now been perfectly setup and prepared to fully understand how God continues to work in my life and you will continue to read what's still to come in my continued adventures as a career chauffeur, some more stories as a professional aviator, and how I would eventually utilize my very limited legal training to benefit my life and the life of my children in the upcoming volume two of my complete life story. If you think that you have read about some miracles in this volume one of my book, just wait until you read about some of the additional miracles to come, as well as some of the many mistakes that I have made even after I had actually given my life to Christ in the stories of volume two. You will then also be able to clearly see some of the contrast of me both before and after I gave my life to Christ and how God has worked in my favor only after I put my complete trust in him even despite my many more mistakes to come.

So Please be sure to go out and get your hands on a copy of the second volume of Miami Stretch to find out so much more about what is to come as you continue to ride with me through my life, times and even more close interactions with celebrities in my continued confessions as a South Beach Chauffeur.

I truly hope that you have enjoyed this ride through volume one with me because you have finally come to...

...THE END OF VOLUME ONE.

ABOUT THE AUTHOR

NIGEL ANTHONY CONRAD LEADER was born on Trinidad and raised in New York City. After spending his early years dreaming of Miami and the South Florida lifestyle, Nigel eventually moved there to work in the aviation field. After the collapse of Pan American World Airways, he became a professional chauffeur. This is his first book.

Printed in the United States
By Bookmasters